Researching Teaching

RESEARCHING TEACHING

Exploring Teacher Development
through Reflexive Inquiry

Ardra L. Cole

*Ontario Institute for Studies in Education
of the University of Toronto*

J. Gary Knowles

*Ontario Institute for Studies in Education
of the University of Toronto*

Allyn and Bacon

Boston • London • Toronto • Sydney • Tokyo • Singapore

Vice President, Editor in Chief, Education: Paul A. Smith
Executive Editor: Stephen D. Dragin
Editorial Assistant: Bridget McSweeney
Director of Education Programs: Ellen Mann Dolberg
Marketing Manager: Brad Parkins
Editorial-Production Administrator: Annette Joseph
Editorial-Production Service and Electronic Composition: Omegatype Typography, Inc.
Composition Buyer: Linda Cox
Manufacturing Buyer: Dave Repetto
Cover Administrator: Jenny Hart
Cover Designer: Brian Gogolin

Copyright © 2000 by Allyn & Bacon
A Pearson Education Company
160 Gould Street
Needham Heights, MA 02494
Internet: www.abacon.com

Library of Congress Cataloging-in-Publication Data

Cole, Ardra L.
   Researching teaching : exploring teacher development through
reflexive inquiry / Ardra L. Cole, J. Gary Knowles.
     p.   cm.
   Includes bibliographical references (p.) and indexes.
   ISBN 0-205-18076-0 (alk. paper)
   1. Action research in education.   2. Teachers—In-service
training. I. Knowles, J. Gary. II. Title.
LB1028.24.C65 2000
370'.7'2—dc21   99-17833
                                      CIP

Printed in the United States of America

10 9 8 7 6 5 4 3 2 1   04 03 02 01 00 99

Dedicated to our mothers, whose words

"Stop asking so bloody many questions!"
we thankfully chose to ignore. Through our
disobedience, we found inspiration.

And to the many teachers who, through acts of
disobedience of another kind, continue to ask
"so bloody many questions," all for the purposes
of transforming themselves, their teaching,
and their students' learning.

CONTENTS

PREFACE

This is a book for teachers and other educators who are interested in exploring their practice through independent and/or collaborative inquiry. Explorations of practice and the improvement of practice (that is, both teaching and research practice) are together the primary impetus for writing and using this book. We believe that teacher learning and professional development are facilitated by opportunities for ongoing critical reflection on and inquiry into the broad spectrum of experiences that influence professional lives and careers. We therefore place emphasis on the importance of engaging in ongoing exploration of practice, with attention to the multiple roles and contexts that comprise it.

When we characterize our work as university professors and educational researchers we place teaching *at the center* of what we do. Prior to our entry to the academy as faculty members we were teachers of children and adolescents. Our work in schools as classroom and resource teachers totals nearly twenty years and spans several national and local systems of education. In public and private schools we were teachers of students ranging in age from preschool through adolescence and young adulthood; students from diverse racial, ethnic, and class backgrounds; and those with identified special needs. Collectively we have worked in preschools, elementary, junior high, and high schools, and in a variety of other "special" contexts, including residential schools, reform schools, classrooms and schools for deaf students, resource settings for learning-disabled students, and home education settings, including parent education and counseling programs.

Since joining the academy we have committed ourselves to the field of teaching as teacher-educators and educational researchers. All of our major professional roles are variously defined within the context of teaching. We conduct research on teaching, we write about teaching and ways of studying teaching practice, we engage in professional development work aimed at facilitating the understanding and ongoing improvement of teaching, and we carry out our roles as teachers in a variety of ways and contexts. In our various teaching roles associated with preservice, inservice, and graduate education we advocate a self- or reflexive inquiry approach to teaching and teacher development. And because of our commitment to our own professional development as teachers and teacher educators, we endeavor to practice what we preach.

This book is informed by our own experiences and insights as teachers, teacher educators, and researchers, and by our work with other teachers in preservice, inservice, and graduate education contexts. It builds on an earlier book we wrote for and with preservice and beginning teachers. In 1994 we published *Through Preservice Teachers' Eyes: Exploring Field Experiences through Narrative and Inquiry* (Knowles & Cole with Presswood). That book was intended to provide preservice and beginning teachers realistic views of the prospects and problems associated with working in schools and a framework for critical reflection on and inquiry into the practice of teaching. Throughout the book we drew heavily on experiences of preservice and beginning teachers, articulated in narrative form because we believe that meaningful and relevant learning begins with experience (or articulated re-creations of experience) and because we think that teachers are themselves teacher educators and have much to offer other teachers. In this book we carry those notions forward to the inservice and graduate education contexts, especially those contexts in which practicing teachers engage in formal study and learning in the academy. We offer a framework for reflexive inquiry into teaching that is grounded in principles of experiential learning and self-directed professional development and in the belief that the perspectives and experiences of teacher-researchers offer important insights into researching and practicing professional development. As in *Through Preservice Teachers' Eyes,* in this book we draw heavily on accounts written by teachers about their experiences of researching their practice.

PURPOSES AND PERSPECTIVES OF THE BOOK

Our overall purpose is to provide readers opportunities for insights into the value and process of reflexive inquiry for facilitating and exploring teacher learning and development, broadly defined. There are several specific purposes:

- to facilitate understanding of the interrelationship between theory and practice in teaching and research through a "teaching as inquiry" model
- to illustrate the notion of teaching as an autobiographical project that fosters a recognition of the place of the "personal" within the "professional"
- to promote, by both design and example, forms of reflexive (autobiographical) inquiry variously focused on self, contexts, and relationships in educational situations
- to foster reflexivity and professional development through both independent and collaborative inquiry
- to explore issues associated with researching teaching

Our perspectives on teaching reflect who we are and what we value as teachers, teacher educators, and researchers, and what we know and believe about the essence of "good" teaching, which for us is a commitment to *ongoing inquiry*. When we talk and write about teaching we reflect both an experiential and analytical or theoretical understanding of what teaching is. Hence we view teaching as a complex and personal expression of multiple and varied forms of knowledge and knowing, influenced by an array of intellectual, physical, psychological, spiritual, political, relational, and societal factors, conditions, and events.

Autobiographical or reflexive inquiry forms the overarching framework of the book. We believe that teaching is rooted in the "personal" and powerfully influenced by prior experiences within and outside professional contexts. We view the process of professional development as essentially an autobiographical project—a process of search and discovery that uncovers the relationship of self to situation, of personal to professional. Following Pinar (1981) we believe that understanding of one's self (through autobiographical inquiry) is a "precondition and a concomitant condition to the understanding of others" (p. 186). We therefore highlight the role of ongoing inquiry into self, contexts, and relationships in educational situations, and both implicitly and explicitly advocate autobiographical or reflexive inquiry as a form of professional development.

Our reflexive inquiry framework is constructed around notions of personal empowerment and self-directed learning, the primacy of practice, and personal history. We validate self-directed growth and honor individuals' past and present experience-based understandings. From the perspectives of practitioners and outside researchers we explore methods, practices, phenomena, problems, and issues associated with researching teaching. We believe that the perspectives and experiences of teachers and other researchers offer important insights into researching teaching. The book contains numerous stories of practitioners and researchers exploring their own experiences within the context of professional development inquiry. These are essentially stories of researching.

THE TEACHER-RESEARCHER CONTRIBUTORS

The teacher-researchers who contributed reflections on their experiences of researching teaching are a diverse group. They range widely in age, teaching and researching experience, and personal and professional background. For example, at the time of writing, Danila and Catherine are beginning teachers and Jerry is a retired superintendent of schools. Some, like Todd and Michelle, are new to researching their own practice; others, like Jane and Vicki, are experienced teacher-researchers. With a few exceptions, none previously has written for publication. The authors hail from different parts of Canada and the United States and from public and private elementary and secondary schools, community colleges, and university settings.

We came to know most of the teachers when they were students (preservice teachers or graduate students) in our courses; others we met in different professional development and research contexts. Although they do not all know one another, these coauthors share a strong commitment to teaching and ongoing professional development, and all place value on understanding themselves and their teaching through reflexive inquiry.

We invited the teacher-researchers to write accounts of their experiences of researching teaching. Because we wanted the book to speak to teacher-researchers and others about the behind-the-scenes issues associated with engaging in various forms of research on practice, we asked that the accounts be focused more on the *process* of researching than the outcome of inquiry. The result is, we think, a rich and diverse array of reflections and perspectives on experiences of researching teaching. We trust that others will learn a great deal from listening to what these teacher-researchers have to say about researching teaching through reflexive inquiry.

ORGANIZATION AND OVERVIEW OF THE BOOK

The book is divided into four parts. In Part I, Researching Teaching through Reflexive Inquiry, we lay out the conceptual framework and foundational principles of the book. We challenge traditional perspectives that separate the practical elements of teaching from their theoretical groundings (and vice versa), the personal from the professional, and teaching from the numerous contextual factors that influence it. We explain what we mean by teaching as reflexive or autobiographical inquiry, offer some examples from our own reflexive inquiries, and present some ideas about how to begin the research process.

In Part II, Researching Teaching through Researching the Self, we move from general notions of autobiographical inquiry to particular ways of researching teaching through autobiographical exploration. We focus on autobiographical expression and present ideas for and reflections on researching teaching through writing personal history accounts, journal keeping, and forms of artistic expression. The strength in this and the remaining parts of the book lies in the accounts contributed by practitioners of their experiences researching their practice. You will notice that the text of the book appears in two different fonts. Our writing is in one font and the writing of the teacher-researchers is in another. We did this to distinguish the narrative accounts from our text and to highlight the narratives as writings that can stand alone.

In Part III, Researching Teaching through Inquiry into the Elements of Practice, Relationships, and Contexts, we move from a focus on the self to ways of understanding teaching through researching elements of classroom practice, student experiences, and school contexts. As before, stories of researching are central as practitioners reflect on issues associated with their researching experiences.

In Part IV, Researching Teaching through Collaborative Inquiry, we shift from researching alone to researching with others and provide suggestions for and reflections on researching with peers and colleagues, involving students as research partners, and working with outside researchers.

To conclude the book we offer a postscript in which we extend the notions of reflexive inquiry we advocate for teachers to the university classroom. Our rationale for doing so is rooted in our endeavors to articulate through theory and practice an ethic of authenticity.

USES OF THE BOOK

We expect that the book will fill several gaps in the available literature and texts associated with teacher development. Though close in intent and focus to Connelly and Clandinin's (1988) *Teachers as Curriculum Planners,* it differs in the more substantial focus on issues associated with researching teaching and teacher development and on the role of contexts and relationships in personal and professional inquiry. Texts such as Holly's (1989) *Writing to Grow* and Newman's (1989) *Finding Our Own Way* serve as useful complementary resources for particular methodological aspects of this book, particularly the emphases on journal writing and self-directed professional development. It is a worthy companion to books such as *Inside/Outside* (Cochran-Smith & Lytle, 1993) in that it challenges traditional notions of what counts as educational knowledge. It is, however, focused on a particular approach to researching teaching and explores the connection between reflexive inquiry and teacher development.

There are two groups of books on "action research" that explore the notion of teacher as researcher, and we draw on these for support: one group contains, for example, Kincheloe's (1991) *Teachers as Researchers* and Elliott's (1991) *Action Research for Educational Change* and is primarily theoretical in nature; the other group represents research accounts written by and for teachers. For example, Goswami and Stillman's (1987) *Reclaiming the Classroom,* Daiker and Morenberg's (1990) *The Writing Teacher as Researcher,* Bissex and Bullock's (1987) *Seeing for Ourselves,* Burnaford, Fischer, and Hobson's (1996) *Teachers Doing Research,* and Dadds's (1995) *Passionate Enquiry and School Development* offer examples and accounts of research on teaching primarily focused on exploring elements of classroom practice. *Researching Teaching: Exploring Teacher Development through Reflexive Inquiry,* with its attention to personal history influences and the broader contexts of teaching, extends the notion of teacher research beyond a curriculum focus. We look at the people teachers are, the understandings they bring to and express in practice, and the classroom, school, and community contexts of teaching.

Researching Teaching: Exploring Teacher Development through Reflexive Inquiry can serve as centerpoints for work in a number of areas. The book has several applications at the graduate level. First, it can serve courses on teacher development. As such it is invaluable to inservice teachers participating in graduate degree work. The focus on exploring one's personal history and the contexts and substance of one's practice makes for a powerful link between theory and practice, a central notion of the text. Also, exploring the links between professional development, personal histories, and the contexts and conditions of the work of teaching are likely to have an empowering influence on teachers. Second, it can serve as a foundational text for coursework and workshops that explore research on teaching and teacher development. Again, this is most suitable for inservice teachers. Focused attention on real experiences, problems, and issues associated with researching teaching from the perspectives of other experienced teachers is likely to have a particularly strong appeal to teachers. The text also can be one of several used to facilitate the development of reflexive practices in the early years in the profession because some of the contributors are new and relatively new teachers. As such it can be used by teacher educators who work in teacher education programs (at both the undergraduate and graduate levels) where extensions are made into the first year of teaching. Finally, the text has a direct application as a guide and resource for those using qualitative approaches in teaching and teacher development research, including action research.

There are at least two applications of the book at the undergraduate level. First, it is applicable to courses perhaps variously called Teacher as Researcher, Teaching as Reflexive Inquiry, or Inquiry into Our Teaching, in which the practices of teacher-directed research are brought to the fore and given relevance for preservice teacher education. For prospective and beginning teachers, the text offers a vision for crafting a trajectory of career-long teacher learning through inquiry. Second, it is also relevant to courses that explore, more generally, research in education, especially that relevant to teachers. This book could also serve as a central text in courses focused on teacher development.

In the context of school reform initiatives, in which, for example, teachers are being asked to take a greater role in the governance of schools as well as in their own professional development, the text provides a useful guide for teachers exploring the contexts in which they work and for designing their own inquiry-based professional development plans. The text could well be used as a guide for teachers involved in university-school restructuring efforts. In our wildest dreams we see groups of teachers using the book as a guide and incentive for inquiries into their own practices and contexts. (Indeed, teachers who have been in classes in which we have used drafts of the book indicated their intention to do so.)

Other interested readers—teachers, teacher educators, and those engaged in formal research—will find the book potentially useful, particularly because of its presentation of stories of experience and their relationship to informed positions relative to teacher development.

ACKNOWLEDGMENTS

Some things we do in our professional and personal lives are solitary and other endeavors are not. In our personal lives we strive for some degree of balance but, as professors of education in contemporary North America, we know that our lives are seldom balanced as we might like. The pressures of schools and universities are great! Here in the text of this book we have found another kind of balance, a balance of perspective that was only possible by working in relation with peers firmly located in schools and classrooms.

Although parts of the text for *Researching Teaching: Exploring Teacher Development through Reflexive Inquiry* were written in isolation in the sense that we wrote them behind the closed doors of our offices and home writing spaces, the "whole" was written "in community" and within a powerful circle of experience. Our coauthors are from both Canada and the United States and represent a range of interests and experiences in schools. The teachers and researchers whose accounts of inquiry processes are found between these covers enriched the book and made the process of writing more expansive. Our interactions with their vast array of experiences beckoned us out of the confines of our writing closets, brought us face to face with dynamics and contexts that we now do not typically experience on a day-to-day basis, and gave us a hefty measure of understanding and insight beyond those of our own construction. Their accounts and reflections on processes of inquiry lend a credibility and authenticity to the book that we on our own would not have been able to engender.

Without the willingness of our twenty-two coauthors to share elements of their personal professional experiences, we would not have been able to write this book. We are grateful that they saw this as a worthy endeavor and we are appreciative of their patience as we modified, several times, the structure of the text and the integration of their written narrative accounts.

We also would not have been able to bring the initial drafts of the book to completion without the help of a large number of readers. In the summer of 1997, Ardra used several chapters as text in a graduate course entitled Researching Teacher Development through Reflexive Inquiry at the University of British Columbia, Vancouver, British Columbia. There the graduate students enthusiastically delved into and applied elements of the text to their own investigations of practice. There also they provided helpful critique of the substance and form of the work. Their comments provided much needed impetus to bring the text to completion.

In the 1998 winter session we both used various elements of the manuscript in our courses at the University of Toronto. For example: Master's and doctoral degree students in Ardra's course, Teacher Learning in School Contexts, provided useful feedback on relevant chapters; likewise, the graduate students in Gary's Practitioner/Ecological Identity and Reflexive Inquiry course made subtle suggestions for improvement to the opening chapters. A small group of experienced teachers initially led by Lynnette Surrette and Fran Halliday at Bishops University, Lennoxville, Quebec, did the same. Later in the spring Gary used portions of the book to teach a spring/summer course, Inquiry as Art/Art as Inquiry, through Mount Saint Vincent University's extension program in St. John's, Newfoundland, and Labrador. Together we developed and taught another summer course with the same name as the book in St. John's. Gary also used the book in two summer courses at Bishop's University in Lennoxville, Quebec. One course was with experienced and novice teacher-researchers and the other was directed toward school administrators. The participants in all these courses were extremely helpful with their comments and encouragement. Opportunities to field test the manuscript with so many experienced teachers and new and emerging researchers were invaluable. We were especially encouraged by teachers' responses to the stories of inquiry written by the coauthor-teachers and the foundational principles about teacher learning on which the book is based.

We also urged our coauthors to share their respective chapters with others, and those new readers, too, provided extra guidance. Their and our perseverance has paid off.

We extend special appreciation to Margie Buttignol for her careful and thoughtful comments on drafts of Chapter 1 and index preparation; to Jacquie Aston for her assistance with the review of literature that informed Chapter 1; and to Fran Halliday for her encouraging and helpful response to sections of the manuscript. Jeanie Stewart, with her patience and technological wizardry, provided much needed assistance and support at the final stages of manuscript production.

We are clearly indebted to a large number of teachers and inquirers who worked alongside us in the development of this book and the ideas presented within it. With this in mind we dedicate the book to all those practitioners who, at whatever level of education, are constantly searching for ways to deepen their understandings of their practice through inquiry. We hope that through this book we are able to provide some guidance and support to those who are committed to understanding the "self," those with whom they are "in relation," and the complex educative contexts in which they work and live.

A. L. C.
J. G. K.

Researching Teaching

P A R T I

RESEARCHING TEACHING THROUGH REFLEXIVE INQUIRY

The title of this section and of the book needs some explanation because it reflects the book's central underpinnings. In this introduction to the first two chapters we explain the meaning of our title and provide a brief overview of our conceptual framework.

First and foremost, we see teaching *as* inquiry. In other words, teaching *is* researching. This view is counter to traditional notions of research on teaching, which typically conjure up images of professional researchers (perhaps white-coated, clinical, and usually university-based)—"outsiders" with little experience or context-based understanding of classroom and teaching life, at least from a teacher's perspective—conducting scientifically controlled investigations primarily for academic or pseudopractical purposes. Our perspective on researching teaching challenges traditional conceptions of a dichotomous theory-practice relationship and traditional views of how knowledge is defined, by whom, and where. When we say, "our perspective," we do not mean to imply that it is ours alone or that we are alone in our efforts to challenge traditional viewpoints. Indeed, we are in the strong and good company of a whole movement of educational researchers who share this view.

We see teaching as a complex and personal expression of knowing and knowledge, not an application of a set of disembodied, acontextual principles or theories. In other words, we see theory as embedded in, not applied to, practice, and we see teachers as knowledge holders and developers, not just knowledge users. Likewise, our perspective on teacher development rests in both personal and professional ways of knowing set amid a complex array of historical, political, societal, local community, school, and personal contexts and circumstances. We view teacher development along a continuum beginning well before entry into formal programs of teacher education and continuing through formal preparation, into the early years of teaching, and through experienced practice to retirement. In this view teacher development is emerging and ongoing, individual and collective, personal and professional. It encompasses the span of life and professional commitment.

Extending this line of thinking, we see the researching of teaching, especially for purposes of professional development, as a purview and responsibility of teachers. For us, researching teaching involves teachers making the focus of study their day-to-day interactions with students; their curricular decisions and the relationship between those curricula and social, historical, and political influences; their instructional techniques; or the contexts that facilitate or hinder their ongoing professional development. Studying one's professional practice, therefore, promotes ongoing improvement of both those practices and associated contexts for learning and teaching. Through systematic reflection on and analysis of practice, teachers take charge of their own professional development, and they have the potential to substantially contribute to the resolution of institutional problems and issues. They continue to learn to teach and teach to learn.

We call the process of researching teaching that we advocate and illustrate in this book *reflexive inquiry*. Although the term *reflexive* is similar in meaning to the general notion of reflection that is widely used in the professional literature on teacher education and development, our use of and preference for *reflexive* is purposeful. It is fundamentally connected to another of our assumptions: that teaching and teacher development are rooted in the "personal." By this we mean that teaching is an expression of who teachers are as people, that it is imbued with the beliefs, values, perspectives, and experiences developed over the course of a teacher's lifetime. We believe that in order for teachers to understand their professional lives and work and therefore continue to develop professionally, they need to understand the formative as well as the continuing experiences and influences that have shaped and continue to shape their perspectives and practices.

To further clarify the distinction between reflective inquiry and reflexive inquiry: *Reflective inquiry* is an ongoing process of examining and refining practice, variously focused on the personal, pedagogical, curricular, intellectual, societal, and/or ethical contexts associated with professional work, perhaps, but not necessarily, from a critical perspective. Underpinning all such reflective inquiry is the idea that assumptions behind all practice are subject to questioning. *Reflexive inquiry*, on the other hand, is reflective inquiry situated within the context of personal histories in order to make connections between personal lives and professional careers, and to understand personal (including early) influences on professional practice. In other words, reflexive inquiry takes into account the personal history–based elements of contextual understanding, emphasizing the foundational place of experience in the formulations of practice in a way that reflective inquiry does not. Reflexive inquiry, unlike some forms and interpretations of reflective inquiry, is rooted in a critical perspective. Such a critical perspective is characterized by interrogation of status quo norms and practices, especially with respect to issues of power and control.

Another way to think of the meaning of *reflexive* is in terms of the properties of prisms and mirrors. Mirrors and transparent prisms reflect and refract light. They change the direction in which light rays travel, sometimes even bending them back on themselves, causing them to move in directions opposite from their original path. Reflexive practices associated with teaching and teacher development have somewhat similar qualities and may induce somewhat similar responses. Being reflexive is like having a mirror and transparent prism with which to view practice. Examinations of practice, with an eye to understanding and/or improving it, sometimes lead to complete turnabouts in thinking. Mirrors and prisms also separate light rays into component wavelengths, making visible the color of the spectrum. Similarly, reflexive inquiry affords opportunities for the analysis of various components or elements of teaching practice. The ideas and thoughts bent back through reflexive inquiry may derive from a whole range of experiences and interactions throughout one's life inside and outside classrooms and schools, as students and as teachers. In a reflexive stance, making sense of both prior and current educational experiences within the context of present practice may shed new, perhaps brighter, light on understandings of teaching.

In the remainder of this part of the book (Chapters 1 and 2) we elaborate the ideas just mentioned. In Chapter 1 we further discuss traditional/conservative and contemporary perspectives on researching, teaching, and teacher knowledge; various characterizations of teacher development; and the relationship between theory and practice all as they relate to the underpinnings of the book. In Chapter 2 we focus on the idea of teaching as an ongoing autobiographical inquiry and further explore the notion of reflexivity and the reflexive inquiry process. In a sense, Chapters 1 and 2 provide the theoretical framework that we describe, illustrate, and reflect on throughout the remainder of the book.

1

TEACHER KNOWLEDGE AND MODES OF TEACHER KNOWING

WHAT DO TEACHERS KNOW? WHAT DO TEACHERS NEED TO KNOW?

What do teachers know? What do teachers need to know? These two basic questions (and elaborations and extensions of them) have formed and continue to form the basis of teacher educators', educational researchers,' and theorists' work. Efforts to answer these questions have taken numerous and varied forms and have resulted in wide-ranging responses. The various approaches to the questions and subsequent attempts to answer them reflect a set of underlying assumptions about what knowledge is, how it is developed, defined, and by whom, and how it is understood. Each of these various approaches to knowledge also reflects fundamental assumptions about what it means to teach and be a teacher. Answers to these questions, however inadequate, have informed the curriculum, design, structure, administration, presentation, delivery, and resource base of initial and ongoing teacher education and development programs since their formal beginnings.

EVOLUTION OF RESEARCH IN TEACHER KNOWLEDGE

Although we do not intend to provide a comprehensive overview of the different perspectives on teacher knowledge advanced over the last century, it is useful to have a sense of how the study and characterization of teacher knowledge have evolved over the past several decades. The study and characterization of teacher knowledge that extend beyond behavioristic notions are only a few decades old. Prior to the mid-1960s investigations of teaching and teachers focused on teacher behaviors and teaching skills; the implication was that what teachers knew and all that informed teaching practice was observable, measurable, and could be replicated and applied with a degree of certainty. Teaching was viewed by researchers, or at least represented by their research designs, as a superficial and simplistic activity. It was viewed as a skill performance that could be learned: a set of competencies to master and apply, sets of goals or outcomes to establish and achieve, and a set of prescribed procedures to learn and follow. The setting and accomplishment of sequential objectives reigned supreme in the preparation of teachers and in classrooms.

In the mid-1960s the research agenda shifted from behaviorism to cognitivism. Studies of teacher knowledge and practice focused on teachers' decision making and the cognitive structures and processes contributing to "expert" performance. The goal of these studies was the articulation and application of "expert thinking" rather than "expert behavior." The intent was to identify qualities, characteristics, and cognitive processes and capabilities associated with expert performance suitable to use as bases for the preparation of novice teachers and others not considered to be "expert." Despite attempts to reduce the complexity of teaching to a set of cognitive skills or particular personality traits, there was an eventual acknowledgment by researchers that much of what teachers know and express in their practice is tacit—personally held and not easily explained—and not immediately observable and replicable. Reflecting on a decade of research on teacher thinking from the mid-1970s to the mid-1980s, Clark (1986) observed

> *All this has led to a constructive turning away from the goal of "making good teaching easier" to that of portraying and understanding good teaching in all its irreducible complexity and difficulty. Quality portraiture may be of more practical value and inspirational value than reductionistic analysis and technical prescriptiveness. (p. 14)*

A subsequent shift away from the information processing or process-product model of teacher knowledge reflected the inadequacies of such a perspective for capturing the spontaneity and complexity of teaching and teacher knowledge. The mid-1980s marked another significant turning point in the conceptualization and characterization of teacher knowledge. Since then, research in the area of teaching and teacher knowledge has variously taken into account the personal and complex nature of teaching. Current research also considers the influences of personal, contextual, historical, political, societal, and experiential dimensions on the characterization and articulation of teaching practice. New explanations and depictions of teachers and teaching emerged, reflecting diverse views on teacher knowledge and modes of teacher knowing. For example, studies of *personal practical knowledge* and narrative inquiry were initiated by Clandinin and Connelly (e.g., Connelly & Clandinin, 1985, 1990). This work emphasizes the inextricable link between the personal (who a teacher is) and the professional (what a teacher does), highlighting the individualistic nature of teaching. Teachers' biographies are identified as an essential component of teacher knowledge.

The *pedagogical content knowledge* group originating with Shulman (e.g., Grossman, 1987, 1990; Gudmundsdóttir, 1990, 1993; Richert, 1990, 1992; Shulman, 1987) developed views on teacher knowledge that challenge claims that subject matter knowledge directly translates into good pedagogy. The focus of this work is on understanding both what teachers know about content in various academic or subject areas and how they effectively communicate that knowledge to learners.

The concept of situational or *classroom knowledge* (e.g., Carter & Doyle, 1987; Doyle, 1986; Pinnegar, 1988, 1989) extended conceptions of teacher knowledge to include ways in which teachers organize and manage classroom spaces and routines and how they understand and respond to situational cues and exigencies.

Research that places teachers, teaching, and teacher knowledge within the broader context of *personal and social histories* also became prevalent (e.g., Ball & Goodson, 1985; Bullough & Gitlin, 1995; Bullough, Knowles, & Crow, 1991; Goodson, 1992; Knowles & Cole with Presswood, 1994; Knowles & Holt-Reynolds, 1994; Zeichner, 1987, 1993). In this work the domain of teacher knowledge includes but extends beyond the individual or personal, subject matter, and situation to include social, political, historical, and cultural dimensions. Viewed this way, teacher knowledge is clearly personal but always contextualized.

Further, Munby and Russell's distinctive program of inquiry into the role of *practical experience* as a significant form and source of knowledge in the learning to teach process began in 1984 inspired by Schön's (1983) concept of practical epistemology (e.g., Munby & Russell, 1994; Russell & Munby, 1991; Russell, Munby, Spafford, & Johnston, 1986). Central to this work is the inclusion of practical experience as an authoritative component of teacher knowledge.

Researchers also advanced alternative explanations and frameworks for characterizing modes of teacher knowing through, for example, the representational forms of *role-related image, metaphor, and story* (e.g., Bullough, Knowles, & Crow, 1991; Bullough & Gitlin, 1995; Clandinin, 1986; Cole, 1988, 1990; Hunt, 1987, 1991; Jalongo & Isenberg, 1995; Knowles, 1993; Munby, 1986, 1987; Russell, Munby, Spafford, & Johnston, 1988). Of particular importance in these characterizations is the honoring of the personal and complex nature of teaching and the recognition that practice is an expression of "mindedness" (Ryle, 1949) or, as Schön (1983) would put it, an expression of "knowing in action."

In this book we make the assumption that the act of teaching is informed by multiple forms of knowledge and is representative of a variety of ways of personal, professional, and contextual knowing. In the run of a normal day teachers draw on knowledge about subject matter of various kinds, as well as general and subject-specific pedagogical knowledge. They also look to research and relevant professional literature; rely on the wisdom of experience and practice; make use of personal learnings and intuitions; are mindful of how to operate within the bureaucratic structures of state or provincial departments of education, school boards and districts, individual schools and other educational institutions, and even local community and government bodies; negotiate complex personal interactions with students, parents, peers, and others;

and situate themselves and their work within the larger historical, political, and so-cial forces within local, regional, and national communities.

We also operate on the premise that teachers come to understand and communi-cate what they know in a variety of ways: through examining elements of their per-sonal histories, journal writing, various forms of creative expression; through empirical inquiries into elements of practice, contexts, and relationships; through various forms of relational discourse and collaborative work; and, simply, through living full family-, community-, and society-situated lives. These are the modes of teacher knowing we describe and illustrate throughout this text. In stating and supporting these views we are also making the claim that much of what teachers know can be accessed and communicated only by those who own that knowledge—teachers. We elevate the notions of teacher-as-inquirer and teacher-as-researcher. This is inher-ently a political statement related to the politics of knowledge. Because the political dimension of knowledge is a central underpinning of this book, it is important to elaborate.

THE POLITICAL DIMENSION OF TEACHER KNOWLEDGE

If you take the time to browse literature in the area of teacher knowledge you will notice that for the most part theories and analyses about what and how teachers know and how they express that knowledge in practice are conducted by "outsiders," usu-ally university-based researchers. (To be fair, however, it is also important to ac-knowledge that many university-based researchers inquiring into teacher development were themselves at one time elementary and secondary school teachers. Their prior locations in elementary and secondary schools are often the driving forces of their research actions.) You will also note that there is an intention, which may or may not be stated by educational researchers, that teachers should take the knowledge advanced and apply it to their situations. In other words, teachers are understood to be practitioners and receivers of knowledge but *not* developers or generators of knowledge. This is inherently a political issue wherein privileges associated with knowledge—how it is defined and developed and by whom, who holds it, and where it resides—are assigned to those with sanctioned authority to "know." Histor-ically, teachers have been excluded, perhaps for reasons as much related to the gen-dered and classed composition of the teaching profession as to the labor force conceptions and hierarchical governance of teachers' work and the pervading funda-mental goals of schooling. Those without such authority—teachers, for example—"are knowledgeable…, but they do not participate in the generation of Knowledge (capital K) or official, 'principled,' 'discipline'-based knowledge" (Cochran-Smith & Lytle, 1993, p. 42).

We further elucidate the politics of knowledge with another example. In a chap-ter in *The Teacher Educators' Handbook: Building a Knowledge Base for the Prep-aration of Teachers,* edited by Murray (1996), Virginia Richardson distinguishes between two kinds of research that should inform teacher education: *formal research,* which "can contribute to knowledge and understanding...for the larger community of scholars and educators"; and *practical inquiry,* which "can lead to the improvement of one's own teaching" (Richardson, 1996, p. 715). The author goes on to suggest that while "practical inquiry may lead to its consideration as formal research and to publication [it] should not necessarily be undertaken to contribute to the general knowledge base of teacher education" (p. 727).

In direct opposition to the viewpoint expressed by Richardson, Marilyn Cochran-Smith and Susan Lytle (1993, p. 62) articulate a need to "redefine the notion of knowledge for teaching and alter the focus of the knowledge base and the practitioner's stance in relation to knowledge generation in the field." They assert that school-based research or teacher-research (what Richardson calls practical inquiry) "is well positioned to produce precisely the kind of knowledge currently needed in the field" (p. 59). We concur. Such research practices acknowledge teachers as Knowers and Knowledge producers and identify practice and practical contexts as starting, not ending, points of theory and knowledge generation. We believe that the view represented in Richardson's statement does little to honor the profession of teaching and advance the generation of knowledge, insights, and improved teaching contexts.

Although it is important not to undervalue the significance of formal research and the knowledge and understandings gained from it, it is also important to question what is *not* known when teachers do not have a central role in theory building and knowledge-related inquiries. How much can be known when knowledge is defined apart from the knower? The autobiographical nature of teaching means it is impossible to understand teaching without understanding the teacher; that it is impossible to understand the practice apart from the practitioner; that it is impossible to understand the knowledge apart from the knower. We challenge any positions that support the objectification, disembodiment, and decontextualization of teacher knowledge. Put another way, we counter traditional views of theory and practice that continue to separate the creation of theory from the practice of teaching and teachers.

PERSPECTIVES ON THE RELATIONSHIP BETWEEN THEORY AND PRACTICE

The existence of a theory-practice gap that separates the real world of practice from the ivory tower of the university or laboratory is a prevalent notion long-held by school- and university-based practitioners alike. This traditional dichotomous conceptualization of theory and practice locates theory generation and the study of educational theories (and, by extension, knowledge) within the context of the university and recognizes the field as the site of practice and practical action that is neither informed nor guided by theory.

The position that theory and practice are distinct entities that bear little relationship to one another reflects problematic assumptions about the two dimensions of knowledge, and these need to be examined and challenged. Such an either/or view sets up misguided and inappropriate frameworks for understanding teaching and guiding ongoing career-long teacher development. As Carr and Kemmis (1986, p. 11) note,

> *The twin assumptions that all "theory" is non-practical and all "practice" is non-theoretical are...entirely misguided.... "Theories" are not bodies of knowledge that can be generated out of a practical vacuum and teaching is not some kind of robot-like mechanical performance that is devoid of any theoretical reflection. Both are practical undertakings whose guiding theory consists of the reflective consciousness of their respective practitioners.*

To challenge traditional notions of the theory versus practice dichotomy is also to reconsider traditional notions of knowledge. When practice and practical action are recognized as an embodiment and expression of theory, teachers are, by extension, recognized as theory builders. Theory, then, becomes redefined to reflect the multidimensional, personal, and complex nature of teaching and teacher knowledge. As such, theory and practice become inextricably linked and mutually dependent.

One way to redefine theory and its relationship to practice is to think about two kinds of theory: that which might be termed global, macro, general, or abstracted theory; and that which could be called local, micro, particular, or idiosyncratic theory. In the former category are those theories typically, though not exclusively, generated by academic researchers and studied in teacher education programs and which are intended to have more generalizable applications. In the latter category are those theories that emerge from focused inquiry into individuals' beliefs, values, perspectives, attitudes, ideas, and practices, and which are more particularistic or personal in nature. Abstracted theory generated by researchers studying classroom practices, contexts, and phenomena and idiosyncratic theory developed mainly by teachers (or other practitioners) through the examination of their own experiences of and ideas about practice offer different but complementary knowledge bases. Macro theories are developed at a distance through the use of systems of externally derived constructs or frameworks for understanding and may be derived from formal observations of collective contexts and phenomena. Micro theory is an explication of individuals' implicit understandings. Macro theory and micro theory can influence one another in important ways.

REFLEXIVE INQUIRY AND THE THEORY-PRACTICE GAP

Reflexive practice comes about by melding the two kinds of theory and processes of theory generation, that is, by considering elements of general theories in the context of one's own particular theories. As such, teachers are both theory generators and theory users. The integration of elements or principles of both kinds of theories is the essence of reflexive or inquiring practice. (This orientation is appropriate as well in the academy, and so we also direct these comments to academic researchers. In the realm of the university, reflexive research practice also would involve the melding of both kinds of theory and processes of theory generation.)

When theory is redefined in this way the gap between theory and practice is also redefined. There is no longer the concern about the relationship between formal educational theory and nontheoretical professional practice. Instead the theory-practice gap describes incongruities between teachers' own theories (which are likely to also be informed by general theories) and their practical actions. Inquiring teachers are intent on revealing theory-practice dichotomies for purposes of self-awareness and improvement. Understanding and closing this kind of theory-practice gap is the focus and intention of reflexive inquiry. And, by attending to teachers' reflexive inquiry explorations and articulations, outside researchers can enhance their understanding of teaching practice and, by extension, the abstracted theories they develop.

PERSPECTIVES ON TEACHER LEARNING AND DEVELOPMENT

So far we have pointed out some of the ways in which the views we hold and advocate about knowledge, theory, and research might be considered nonconventional. It is also important to elaborate on the assumptions about teacher learning and development reflected in the reflexive inquiry framework we promote in this book. This framework or approach is built on notions of personal empowerment and self-directed learning, the primacy of practice, and the significance of personal history. It also represents a challenge or alternative to traditional perspectives on and approaches to teacher development.

Like the study and characterization of teacher knowledge, research and analyses of how teachers learn and develop as professionals have been guided primarily by a preoccupation with categorization and typologies, measurement and performance, and diagnosis and prescription. Numerous researchers, drawing on different developmental theories—cognitive, moral, conceptual, psychosocial, lifespan, and career development—have offered stage models to describe how teachers develop in various domains and at different points in their careers. At a practical level these models or theories have been used to design diagnostic strategies to assess teacher characteristics and determine appropriate programs of intervention or remediation to facilitate teachers' development. Although the motivation for this work is well intended—that is, to make teacher education more meaningful and relevant to teachers—the assumptions about teachers, learning, and teaching upon which the research and the programs that follow it are based are highly problematic. Labeling, pigeonholing, or categorizing teachers based on either how they perform on, say, an attitude inventory or anxiety scale or on their seniority as teachers, or on their knowledge of particular programmatic processes or mandated curriculum does little to take into account teachers' individuality or the complex and contextual nature of teaching. And, designing and delivering professional development programs with the expectation that teachers receive the prescribed knowledge and dutifully incorporate it into their practices does little to honor the complexity of teachers as learners or teaching as a professional practice.

The "deficit," standardized, or "training" model of teacher development that historically has defined how formal professional development programs are designed and delivered to teachers is gradually being replaced by more substantive, long-range initiatives that reflect different, more progressive assumptions about teachers and teacher learning and different goals for teacher development. For example, Eraut (1987) identifies four characterizations of teacher development initiatives that in essence trace the historical changes in orientation:

- a defect model oriented to the improvement of skills or competencies in response to changing priorities or educational goals
- a change model oriented to broader restructuring of programs or institutions to meet changing societal or institutional needs and demands
- a problem-solving model oriented to ongoing identification and resolution of practical and situational problems
- a growth model oriented to facilitating a continuous process of professional growth through inquiry, interaction, and reflection

The last characterization is clearly the direction and spirit of professional development we support.

Despite the increased diversity of perspectives and practices, however, most formally recognized teacher-development initiatives are still, for the most part, conceptualized and designed *for,* and delivered *to* teachers, not *by* teachers. Although we recognize that teachers continue to learn and develop through a variety of self-defined and self-guided activities such as professional reading, writing, individual or group work, work with colleagues, community volunteerism, and personal or social creative expression, these activities are not typically acknowledged or sanctioned by a professional body or institution as bona fide professional development efforts. Individually and collectively, teachers still are not given or have not taken authority over their own learning and development. This does not mean that teachers cannot learn from or be informed by the wisdom of others—university-based teacher-educators, researchers, or other professionals—but it does mean that teachers have little opportunity to take hold of their own professional development. They have little opportunity to shape their institutionally sanctioned learning through control over either the process or focus of their own professional development. (It is worth noting here that, at the time of this writing, in the province of Ontario, Canada, efforts are under way by teacher-centered organizations to determine ways of accrediting teacher research and other forms of individually guided professional development. We watch with interest to see the outcomes of this struggle for control over how teacher knowledge and learning are defined and by whom.)

The teacher-research movement, which continues to gain acceptance in professional and academic education communities, has made a significant challenge to long-held perspectives on teacher-development processes and programs. Proponents of teacher research operate on the assumptions that teaching is a form of inquiry and teachers learn from and through the process of teaching. In other words, a teacher's practice is the site of both inquiry and professional development. Such an approach involves teachers making the focus of study their day-to-day interactions with children, their curricular decisions and the relationship between that curriculum and social and political influences, their instructional techniques, or the contexts that facilitate or hinder their ongoing professional development. Studying one's professional practice, therefore, promotes ongoing improvement of those practices and associated contexts for learning and teaching. Ultimately, it improves and promises to improve student learning. Studying one's practice is a way to further the individual and collective contribution of teachers in schools and other educative communities, and it is a means to re-create the way schools are. Through systematic reflection and analysis of practice, teachers can take charge of their professional development. They have the potential to substantially contribute to the resolution of institutional problems and issues. Processes that promote the exploration of and response to these notions that challenge conventional perspectives on teacher Knowledge and modes of teacher Knowing are what this book is about.

RECOMMENDED READINGS

Ben-Peretz, M., Bromme, R., & Halkes, R. (Eds.). (1986). *Advances of research on teacher thinking.* Lisse: Swets & Zeitlinger.

Carlgren, I., Handal, G., & Vaage, S. (Eds.). (1994). *Teachers' minds and actions: Research on teachers' thinking and practice.* London: Falmer Press.

Cochran-Smith, M., & Lytle, S. L. (1993). *Inside/outside: teacher research and knowledge.* New York: Teachers College Press.

Murray, F. B. (Ed.). (1996). *The teacher educator's handbook: Building a knowledge base for the preparation of teachers.* San Francisco, CA: Jossey-Bass.

Olson, J. (1992). *Understanding teaching.* Buckingham, England: Open University Press.

Ross, E. W., Cornett, J. W., & McCutcheon, G. (Eds.). (1992). *Teacher personal theorizing: Connecting curriculum practice, theory, and research.* Albany, NY: State University of New York Press.

2

TEACHING AS AUTOBIOGRAPHICAL INQUIRY

We begin with two quotations: first, "Autobiography is at once a discovery, a creation, and an imitation of the self" (Olney, 1980); second, "There should be a sign above every classroom door that reads, 'All teachers who enter: Be prepared to tell your story.'" (Paley, 1989, p. vii). The first quotation is appropriate because we see the process of becoming a teacher as an autobiographical project—a discovery, a creation, and an imitation of the self—a process embedded in an examination of past experiences within the context of current and future actions. The second quotation reflects our beliefs not only about teachers but also about all educators. As educators, we must know who we are—our story.

Personal, autobiography-based inquiry forms the overarching framework of this book. Based on the belief that personal-professional inquiry fosters understanding, we highlight the role of ongoing inquiry into self, contexts, and relationships. Through autobiographical inquiry teachers establish a foundation and develop a framework for lifelong learning about their work and roles as teachers. We concur with Pinar (1981), who states that the autobiographical method permits "reflexive awareness of one's participation in the affairs of the world, a reflexivity which captures the mutual determinacy and mutual creation of both self and situation." It permits such awareness because it "reconstructs the past, as it lays bare the relation between self and work, self and others which has prevailed in the past" (p. 185).

AUTOBIOGRAPHICAL (REFLEXIVE) INQUIRY AND TEACHER DEVELOPMENT

Becoming a teacher or other kind of educator is a lifelong process of continuing growth rooted in the "personal." Who we are and come to be as teachers and teacher-educators is a reflection of a complex, ongoing process of interaction and interpretation of elements, conditions, opportunities, and events that take place throughout our lives in all realms of our existence—the intellectual, physical, psychological, spiritual, political, and social. For us, making sense of prior and current life experiences in the context of the personal as it influences the "professional" is the essence of professional development. Thus we situate professional inquiry in the context of personal histories. We believe that knowing ourselves as persons is very much part of knowing ourselves as professionals. The better we understand ourselves as teachers, the better we understand ourselves as persons, and vice versa. Because we see the practice of teaching as an expression of who we are as individuals—that is, an autobiographical expression—we assert that to understand teaching in its complex, dynamic, and multidimensional forms, we need to engage in ongoing autobiographical inquiry.

More specifically, we see autobiographical inquiry as valuable for several reasons. First, and perhaps foremost, autobiographical inquiry and its representation provide a *process* by which teachers can gain insights into themselves as developing professionals. Through the reconstructed articulation of prior and current life experiences, teachers have opportunities to pull out narrative threads that hold together the interwoven fabric of their past, present, and future lives and their personal and professional selves. Second, and related to the first use, is the value of autobiographical articulations as a way of recording one's professional development. Developing autobiographical accounts that begin with past experience and continue into the present is a useful way for teachers to examine their practices and developing orientations, important in forging ongoing professional development. Third, autobiographical writing is a powerful vehicle for enhancing learning. Writing about personal philosophies, theories, principles, and skills related to teaching and education are helpful in discovering and examining the extent and substance of one's continuing learning. Other values of autobiographical inquiry include its usefulness as a method for more "formal" research, either on one's own practice or, under certain conditions, in collaboration with other researchers. We mention the role of autobiography as a formal research method only briefly here because the focus in this book is on autobiographical inquiry as a form of self-directed professional development.

FORMS AND EXAMPLES OF
AUTOBIOGRAPHICAL (REFLEXIVE) INQUIRY

To provide a better sense of what we mean by autobiographical inquiry and to publicly acknowledge that we engage in the same practices that we advocate for others, we provide excerpts from some of our own autobiographical accounts that illustrate the place and influences of our personal histories on our present thinking and research. We each do this quite differently, as is evident in the examples we present. Gary's excerpt is from a lengthier account he wrote with the intention of illustrating by personal example the complexity of teaching and teachers' perspectives and practices and of honoring the place of experience in educators' lives and work. Ardra's excerpt is taken from a larger autobiographical writing project that she undertook in an attempt to understand the personal history–based roots of some of her teaching practices.

An Example of Gary's Autobiographical Rendering

Who am I as teacher? As environmental educator? As outdoor educator? As teacher-educator? I am an artist; I am a teacher. Of the two, neither role (or the experiences which find articulation in them) comes before the other, but each informs the other. That I mainly engage myself in the affairs of teaching—I usually get paid a salary to be a teacher—does not detract from my avocation as an artist. That I am known as a teacher is important to me. But equally important, in *some* contexts I wish to be described *only* as an artist; other times, I desire to be described only as a teacher. Yet, when you talk of me as "teacher" you also talk of me as "artist" although my artistry in teaching is vastly and conceptually different from my work as a two-dimensional artist. Still, the visual artist in me is also evident in my classroom teaching self.

Some say that teaching is an art. For me that is so. I increasingly recognize that my teaching practice originates from both my heart and my mind. It is an artistic expression of the heart, a thoughtful expression from the center of my emotional being. To be a teacher is to commit to a thoughtful expression of heartfelt emotions and perspectives about particular intellectual, social, physical, or spiritual knowledge and experiences. It is *not* merely an intellectual, academic pursuit. Nor is it an endeavor in which the aim is to stuff as many beans as possible, and as fast as possible, into the heads of students! Still, the question lingers, Who am I? Who am I as teacher?

I am also a reader, a scholar, a writer, a researcher; but these academy-like labels or descriptions of my work do not help people understand *who* I am, *what* I stand for, and the general tone and scope of my (teaching) work. Nor do they help provide answers to the many *why*? *where*? and *how*? questions that an inquiring colleague might pose. A reading of some of my scholarship—particularly that published work which is called autobiographical and reflexive "self-study"—may provide some insights into these matters. Even so, the scope and substance of that scholarship is limited, as are the possibilities for insights. Questions posed to some of my students may yield further insights. But their views of me are limited by experience and context. I perform many elements of my work, for example, many functions as "teacher," far from and beyond their visual and intellectual sight. What they see and hear, what they experience, is the public pronouncement of my teaching self. The private but preparatory work of teaching goes on behind the closed doors of my office and home, and within the confines of my mind; it occurs when I am working, eating, relaxing, painting, and driving, for example; it goes on long before and long after I interact with students in classrooms or in other learning contexts. So, is my teaching self separated from my other selves? What is it that really informs my teaching and my teaching self? What is the connection between my personal self and my professional self?

Who am I (as teacher)?

Gardener and dishwasher describe some of my many activities around the home; husband and lover evoke some elements of my roles in relation to my companion, partner, and wife; disciplinarian and companion connote some of my roles with my children; friend and comforter characterize my relations with family members and a few people beyond the family circle; son and handyman are the roles I so easily fall into when around my aged mother or in her townhouse home; canoeist and hiker indicate some of my active pursuits in the out-of-doors; traveler and explorer romanticize my movements over the planet we call Earth; colleague and innovator make known only some of my many roles within the halls of academe; librarian and bibliophile symbolize my lifelong care, collection, and love of books about humans' responses to the natural world; learner and student imply my on-going quest for knowledge and understanding, personal growth and professional development; helmsman and navigator denote my long-time if not, now, latent interest in sailing; consumer and shopper indicate my need to purchase goods and services and my reliance on the manufacturing and retail marketing indus-tries; and, citizen and taxpayer define, respectively, my relation to my country of origin—Aotearoa New Zealand—and my obligation to the state of my present residence—Canada.

Each of these roles hints at elements of my self; I am all of these selves, and more. I am inferring, here, the notion that the nonprofessional roles one assumes are intimately connected, although not always clearly, to professional identity as well as to a more holistic view of self. Yet, having briefly told these things about myself, relatively little may be *known* and *understood* about me, especially about my work and orientation as a teacher. But, what may be inferred from these roles is that I have, as a teacher, particular kinds of knowledge on which to draw. Car-rying out a role infers, in the "role player," the development of knowledge about that role and its various activities.

Such articulations, such naming words—labels—used to describe my vari-ous roles, are also the labels assigned to many other individuals; others are also gardeners, husbands, disciplinarians, friends, and so on. Defining myself as a gardener, for example, suggests that I have particular kinds of knowledge and skills. I know some of the principles of garden design; I know how to till the soil, especially by spade, fork, and rake; I know how to prune most fruit trees and vines; I can identify many garden pests; and I know how to make compost and to use fertilizer, for example. There is much specialized knowledge and many skills that I do not have presently but may learn as I have the need. But there are even more labels that could be applied to me. A teacher educator, progressive educa-tor, alternative educator are terms, for example, that may in a very general sense describe my roles, perspectives, and practices. Through particular understand-ings about the theories behind these terms or their application further insights may be gained about my espoused and practiced beliefs. But because such terms are relatively vague in meaning when used to cast an individual, they are next to worthless in portraying who I am as teacher.

There are at least 6,000 other teacher educators in North America. There are probably fewer who might label themselves progressive educators, and consider-ably fewer again who might call themselves alternative. Having said this, I acknowl-edge that such terms may help categorize me, if that is the intent. With such labeling, however, my distinctive self—my physical being, my style, the articulation of my ideas into practice, my fears, my aspirations, my strengths, my weaknesses, my mistakes, and my achievements—merges quietly into the mass of ideas, faces, and bodies that comprise the throng of intellectual inhabitants of universities and schools. With such relatively superficial descriptions I become a nameless profes-sor, a featureless instrument of students' learning within the extensive bureaucratic and intellectual activities associated with educational institutions. Yet, governmen-tal, societal, and educational bureaucracies often revel in rendering people like me and others, especially students, featureless. I am not featureless. But who am I?

All of these various expressions of experience and roles contribute to knowledge about the substance of my teaching self. The place and influence of these multiple roles and experiences—for they are often difficult to separate—on my teaching and my teaching self are not easily discernible from mere observation of my practice. They do, however, provide slight light-letting cracks into my being. They provide a particular frame, an incomplete picture. Yet the knowledge, skills, and experiences associated with these various past and present roles are revealed in my daily teaching-related work. Their metaphorical meanings are also especially evident: I am a gardener, I help cultivate (inquiring) minds, providing support for new growth; I am a husband, I am wedded and committed to my teaching (and scholarly) work; I am a disciplinarian, I lay out and make clear the consequences of particular actions; I am a friend, I listen and respond deeply to both expressed and unexpressed personal needs; I am a son, I display, as a scholar and teacher, evidence of a particular intellectual and pedagogical lineage; I am a canoeist, I intimately know the foaming white water of the wild, swift-flowing rivers of teaching, teacher education, and professing; I am a traveler, I accompany and walk the same pathways as my students because I aspire to practice what I preach, to be led on the kind of journeys I only imagined; I am a colleague, I value the relational element of teaching and learn alongside those whom I teach; I am a learner, I engage in lifelong learning with full knowledge of the wonders of the natural and built worlds around me; I am a helmsman, I am steering, sometimes erratically, my career and voyage of self-discovery; I am a consumer, I devour the knowledge and understandings articulated by both students and theorists; I am a citizen, I acknowledge my responsibility as a member of planet Earth; I am...

As I articulate these elements of *my* self, I wonder about others, especially school classroom teachers, for I was once one: What features of self do they reveal? Are they comfortable revealing? Are they allowed or able to reveal? What features of self do others, such as school administrators and parents, look for in them? How are teachers known? How are they described? What makes them unique as individuals? But, back to me—to my self—for the moment, back to the reflecting pool, for the purposes of expansion and explanation of my story—come argument.

There are various other ways in which I am featured, described, or distantly known. And each of them contributes some part to piecing together the living, breathing collage. Some people, agencies, or organizations claim to know me through variously delineated and assigned numerals. The postal agency knows my street address—a number. The local police department knows of me because of a recent burglary of our house and because of a past traffic violation. I have been assigned a number. I have some other "official" numbers attached to me as well, for instance: a passport number, an alien number (foisted on me by the United States Immigration Department), a landed immigrant number (assigned to me by Immigration Canada), a taxation number, a social security number, a driving license number, various teaching certificate numbers, and so on. Such identifying numerals, although they provide access to some very specific and composite (biographical) facts about me, do not reveal "the real" me—they do not get to the heart of my being—any more clearly than many of the other more accessible and obvious "biographical numerals" attached to my life—some of them being my age in years, height in centimeters or inches, weight in kilograms or pounds, years of schooling, years of teaching experience, years married, hairs on my head, and so on. Even the academic descriptors of my life as student—such as course numbers taken for credit, hours of coursework taken, course grades assigned, examination percentages or grade attained, and program or degree grade-point-averages—and scholar—number of articles and books published, number of conference papers presented, number of courses taught and students advised, and so on—tell relatively little about my work and orientation as environmental and outdoor educator, and as a teacher and teacher educator. I am *not* quantifiable in ways that make inherent sense to me or, I guess, to others. What I am saying is simply this: numeric descriptors of teachers as persons leave much to be understood.

What really *matters* about and to me, and what really describes my teaching self, can be summed up in one word: experience—*my* experience, had over a lifetime. A multitude of life and work experiences, in concert with the meanings I have ascribed to them, have shaped and molded me into the person I am as teacher—and the person I am as visual artist. Becoming a teacher has been and is a lifelong endeavor; becoming a teacher (among other things) is my lifework to date. (I say this despite what young students might think of their teachers, or of me for that matter. And I say it despite the fact that my career is checkered in focus and energy. I have not always been, or wanted to be, a teacher.) Teachers who seek ongoing personal and professional development and renewal are not static beings. I, like them, am continually changing, remaking myself as I search out the meanings of experience in the worlds of society and classrooms and look to the future. I am who I am. I am who I am becoming.

That I am who I am is also a reflection of the many roles and descriptions I evoked earlier. The ways in which I am known, the roles I variously hold and play, also, at once describe elements of and provide minute glimpses into the experiences of life that have shaped my responses to the world around me and have influenced my personal and professional perspectives and practices. I claim the primacy of experience in both the articulation of my own practice and in the observation of the practice of others. I also claim the primacy of experience as that which has molded my intellectual response to the many theoretical positions I have studied, come to understand, used in my formal research, and developed through my research and scholarship.

Ardra's Autobiographical Account

Ardra's inquiry took a very different form from Gary's and is accordingly represented quite differently from Gary's. The account that follows is Ardra's attempt to understand the origins of her practice of student-centered teaching. She begins with a brief explanation of the focus of her inquiry followed by a story rooted in her experience as a young child. She concludes with a short analysis of the experience and its connection with her teaching practice.

I approach my work with students as an opportunity to learn. I very much believe that all members of a learning community come to the situation with vastly diverse and rich experiences that inform individual and collective learning in very different ways. As teacher, my experiences and knowledge of a topic may be informed differently because I have had opportunities to focus my attention in different ways. That is not to say that my knowledge is superior to others; it is just different, mainly due to different circumstances. I do not see it as my responsibility to pass on what I know. My main responsibility is to facilitate others to first uncover what it is they already know and then to provide opportunities and resources (personal, experiential, literature, etc.) for them to enhance that knowledge.

My students tell me that I am a "good teacher"; I think I am. I love teaching. I invest myself in my teaching in a very authentic, all-encompassing way. I give myself up to it. I love developing and planning courses and classes. I love thinking and writing about my teaching. I have a tremendous appreciation of the students. I enjoy being in class with them. I work hard (and very successfully, I think) at creating an optimum context for learning. I find teaching energizing and exhilarating. I learn so much. And yet, often during and after classes, for several hours or even days, I experience a profound discomfort from not knowing with certainty how the classes have gone. Regardless of how affirming the students are of my teaching perspective and approach, and of their learning experience, I regularly come away from class with a feeling of dissatisfaction with how I carried out my role.

Recently, at the end of one of my half-year courses, the sense of dissonance between my perception and the students' reported experience of the course was so strong that I couldn't shake it. Toward the end of the last class, while we munched pizza and ate carrot cake, I shared with the group a reflective piece I had written the night before which I hoped captured the essence of our mutual learning experience. I asked for comments, and they launched into a free-for-all about the various ways in which the course had positively affected them as learners and knowers. From their comments—throughout the term and during the last "assessment" session—I felt reasonably certain that I had achieved the objectives that I had set out for the course. And yet, I came away with that same uneasy feeling. I ruminated, struggling to understand my dissatisfaction. What is it that keeps me questioning myself and the way I assume my role as teacher?

We Don't Eat 'Til the Fat Kid Dances

"Aunt Dot" was one of my mother's closest friends. She and her sister, Margie, were single, middle-aged women. They shared a small but comfortable two bedroom apartment, and both had what my mother called "big government jobs." They had a niece, Angela, whom they doted over (as unmarried aunts are sometimes prone to do). I never knew Angela very well but because Aunt Dot and Margie were such close friends with my mother, and because Angela and I were close in age, one year I was invited to Angela's birthday party. I think I was nine or ten.

I was always shy among children I did not know, possibly because I spent most of my formative years either in the company of adults or playing by myself. I always felt alienated from other children and I did not know how to become a new group member. I worried that they would not accept me and that I would not know how to play what they played. Being somewhat overweight and feeling self-conscious about it added to my anxiety. So, I felt uneasy about going to Angela's party.

As usual, my mother was happy to "show me off" to other mothers who would be there. She spent hours fussing to get me ready for the party, choosing the "right" party dress and fixing my long braids just so. My dress was black velvet, gathered at the waist with a slightly full skirt. The shawl collar, in three shades of rose nylon, extended from shoulder to shoulder and about six inches down the bodice. A nylon flower in the deepest of the three shades of rose was pinned at the waist slightly off-center. Although I loved the dress—the softness of the velvet and what I thought was a very grownup look overall—I didn't like the way *I* looked in it. I thought the nylon trim attracted attention to me and my chubbiness. I arrived at the party already feeling very self-conscious and reluctant.

Then, birthday parties were held at home, videos were not yet invented, and television did not have such a central role in children's lives. Entertainment at birthday parties was in the form of games like Pin the Tail on the Donkey, Bingo, Post Office, or Spin the Bottle. Kids usually gathered in the parlor and played some of these games while mums and aunts prepared food in the kitchen. Presents were typically opened at the dining table before or after the birthday cake was served.

For some reason, before the adults were ready for us to eat, we had either exhausted all the games we knew or weren't interested in playing them. Wary of the potential for ten idle but excited children to wreak havoc, one innovative adult (I believe I purposely repressed her identity) suggested that we have a talent show. I froze in terror. The thought of standing alone in front of people with my rose nylon acting as a spotlight on my plumpness was terrifying enough; having to *do* something that was supposed to pass for talent was almost too much to bear.

I was overwrought with anxiety the whole time the other kids performed whatever talents they thought they had. I couldn't imagine what I would possibly do. Except for the baton twirler (I think that was Angela) I can't even recall what the other kids did; I was too preoccupied with worry. When my turn came I insisted that I didn't have any talents or tricks and couldn't think of anything to do. Everyone's urging attracted attention from the kitchen. The next thing I heard was my mother's well-intentioned and confident voice, "But Darling, why don't you do some ballet? After all," she said proudly, "you must have learned something after all these years." I hadn't.

There was no way out. I stood, walked to the front of the room in complete and utter embarrassment, looked out at what seemed like a sea of taunting faces, and proceeded to ever so slowly move through the five ballet positions: First,... second,... third,... fourth,... fifth. There. But my "performance" took only about thirty seconds. It wasn't enough. "Come on Dear. Show us something else." I didn't know anything else. It wasn't stage fright. I truly didn't know anything else that I thought would pass for ballet. "Come on now. We're waiting to eat." Out of sheer desperation I assumed the third position (right foot ahead), slightly bent my legs, and jumped up, changing legs to land in third position (left foot ahead). I was sure the room shook when I landed; I was certain I could hear the china rattling in the dining room cabinet. I wished I had cracked the floor and fallen through. The audience (kids and adults) waited for me to continue. There was no noise from the kitchen because I was the last act of the night before we hit the birthday table.

I fixed my gaze on a spot on the far wall, gritted my teeth, and jumped again. And again, and again, at an increasingly frenetic pace, all the while conscious of the impact of my weight on the floor and my pink flower bouncing up and down, with my nylon collar hitting me in the face every time I went down and it went up. I was too mortified to stop yet I knew I couldn't go on forever. I knew that when I did stop people would feel obliged to clap and/or comment on my pathetic exhibition of "talent." All I could do was endure the humiliation of being front and center, the focus of attention, holding an audience captive until they had a chance to escape.

As I continue to think about and assess my teaching and how I assume my role in relation to learners in a teaching-learning situation, I ask myself several questions. They serve as personal standards by which I judge the appropriateness of my practice in a given situation. With respect to the way in which I assume my teaching role, and with acknowledgment that different teaching-learning situations demand different roles, I ask myself: Was I dancing front and center? Was that appropriate? Did I perhaps push some reluctant other to take the stage? Was the learning context such that students felt at ease and safe to be the kind of learners they are?

TEACHING AS AUTOBIOGRAPHY

Teaching is an autobiographical act. To teach is to construct an autobiographical account, to develop a living text. The autobiographical nature of teaching is an acknowledgment of the power of lives lived, the primacy of experience, and the potential for ongoing self- and other-generated (re)examinations of practice; such (re)examinations of professional practice are performed in relation to formal and informal theories about the nature of learning and teaching, and the ongoing self-directed professional development opportunities open to teachers.

Teaching *is* autobiography. To be a teacher is to commit to ongoing autobiographical acts (which are viewed and experienced by others). Teaching acts represent articulations of a life work in progress. Strung together, like beads on a string, the day-to-day teaching events become episodic evidence of changing perspectives and a growing life in relation to society and the world at large. To teach is to be involved in lifelong reflective inquiry. Most teachers are intimately curious about the world around them, about "their" subject matter and its place in the world, and about children as learners. Moreover, teachers are inherently interested in developing satisfying practice and professional lives. Teaching *is* inquiry, especially inquiry into self. Jersild (1955) noted that to be a teacher is to examine and know oneself. In order to teach, one must know oneself—first and foremost. It is, perhaps, impossible to effectively teach others without first knowing oneself.

Teaching is also a lifelong project. It represents a continuum of learning about schools and teaching, a continuum of experience. It is a lifelong endeavor because learning about teaching never ceases. The experiences gained as members of families and pupils in schools is augmented, expanded, shaped by that learned in formal preparation for teaching programs. Such programs set new teachers in particular professional directions (usually bounded by particular theoretical positions, guided experiences, or implicit and explicit ideologies) and, together with experiences in school contexts, these experiences shape the early professional development of new teachers. Teachers learn on the job and they are regularly required by school administrators and bureaucrats to formally adopt "new" practices and procedures. Formal professional development is built into the work periods of teachers while informal development opportunities take place at the hand of living a vibrant, interesting life. Our contention is that these informal opportunities are the crux of optimum professional development—and they cannot be mandated by school bureaucracies. The process of continually redefining oneself as teacher marks "authentic," ongoing professional development.

DEVELOPING QUESTIONS ABOUT TEACHING: BEGINNING AUTOBIOGRAPHICAL (REFLEXIVE) INQUIRY

The following questions (and other related ones that you may deem appropriate) are intended to facilitate your reflexive inquiry. The questions are "big"; that is, they do not have easy or simplistic answers. In a sense they might appropriately guide careerlong reflexive inquiry. The questions are intended to guide, frame, and inspire your inquiry. We present them in clusters that variously focus on self, teaching contexts, professional relationships, and ongoing professional development. We invite you to consider these as overarching questions to guide your reflexive inquiry.

- Who am I as teacher? How did I become the teacher I am today? What have been the prime socializing influences on my career development, specifically my professional understandings (or some specific focus on them)? How do I characterize my fundamental world views and how do they (or not) resonate with my professional self and my professional practices? What are my fundamental perspectives on teacher education and professional development? (And, How have they changed over time?)

- What are my foundational understandings about schools and classrooms (the places where teachers teach and students learn)? And, what are the origins of those perspectives? How do I resonate with the institution (or building, department) within which I work? How have the institution's goals and processes shaped my professional development?

- What are the fundamental social, cultural, political, religious, and historical forces and events that have shaped the nature of my experience of schooling and classrooms over the course of my lifetime? How do these influences play out in my day-to-day conceptions of teaching? How have they influenced the development of my teacher self?

- Who are my students? How do I know them as learners? How do *their* socialized preferences for learning influence my professional practice? How do I understand students' learning needs, aspirations, and goals? What are my needs as a teacher (of learners)? How do I (or, do I) meet my own learning needs? How are my professional development needs understood by my peers and others with whom I work?

- What do I *really* teach (what characterizes my professional work with students)? *How* do I teach (what are the forms, patterns, rhythms of my teaching)? What characterizes my professional work with colleagues? How do others view my teaching? What teaching methods are most appropriate for my students and for me? What are my professional aspirations? How do I (or, do I) articulate my professional development needs to close peers? To administrators?

- How can I (continue to) forge my professional and pedagogical development? How do I inquire into my teaching in an ongoing manner? How might my professional development and practice be informed by my ongoing inquiries? What do I think about traditional means of inservice teacher education? How do I respond to opportunities for professional development?

Having posed these questions we turn now to a presentation and consideration of modes and methods of reflexive inquiry to guide explorations of these and other questions.

RECOMMENDED READINGS

Ashton-Warner, S. (1963). *Teacher.* New York: Simon & Schuster.

Ayers, W. (1989). *The good preschool teacher.* New York: Teachers College Press.

Graham, R. (1991). *Reading and writing the self: Autobiography in education and the curriculum.* New York: Teachers College Press.

McEwan, H., & Egan, K. (Eds.). (1995). *Narrative in teaching, learning, and research.* New York: Teachers College Press.

Mitchell, C., & Weber, S. (1998). *Beyond nostalgia: Reinventing ourselves as teachers.* London: Falmer Press.

Pinar, W. F. (1994). *Autobiography, politics and sexuality.* New York: Peter Lang.

Pinar, W. F., & Reynolds, W. M. (Eds.). (1992). *Understanding curriculum as phenomenological and deconstructed text.* New York: Teachers College Press.

Thomas, D. (Eds.). (1995). *Teachers' stories.* Buckingham, England: Open University Press.

PART II

RESEARCHING TEACHING THROUGH RESEARCHING THE SELF

Consistent with our central tenets that teaching is an expression of the "personal" and understanding teaching is an ongoing autobiographical project, we begin our explorations of methods with a focus on the self. We assert that understanding oneself as teacher is foundational in the initial and ongoing development of professional practice. As Pinar (1981) so eloquently puts it,

Understanding of self is not *narcissism; it is a precondition and a concomitant condition to the understanding of others. The process of education is* not *situated—and cannot be understood—in the observer, but in we who undergo it. In its extreme formulation, truth itself lies in the relation of self to situation, knower to known, in the mode of consciousness which allows the situation to articulate itself, allows the qualitative to surface, the problematic to be resolved. (emphasis ours, p. 186)*

Thus in the next three chapters we consider ways of addressing the question, "Who am I as teacher?"

Maxine Greene (1978) wrote:

Each of us achieved contact with the world from a particular vantage point, in terms of a particular autobiography. All of this underlies our present perspective and affects the way we look at things and talk about things and structure our realities. (p. 2)

This is the premise from which we work when we encourage teachers to explore their teaching and themselves as teachers, and it is the premise of Chapter 3, Personal History Inquiry, in particular. If we were to turn Maxine Greene's declarations into questions, they would form the basis for Chapter 3, in which we consider ways of researching teaching through understanding autobiographical or personal history roots. In this chapter we implicitly pose the following questions and suggest ways of addressing them:

- What biographical influences underlie your perspectives?
- What is the vantage point with which you achieved contact with the world?
- How do your biographies affect the way you look at and talk about things?
- What are the personal history roots of your structural realities?

Patti Canzoneri and Jerry Diakiw, both teacher-researchers who have engaged in intensive personal history explorations, offer illustrations and reflections on personal history inquiry and its role in teachers' ongoing professional development.

Teaching is a dynamic expression of the self. As such, it is important to understand not only the personal history–based roots of practice but also the ongoing, day-to-day expressions of the "personal." In Chapter 4, Researching the Self through Journal Writing, we consider the use of journals as tools for ongoing reflexive inquiry. Margie Buttignol and Anna Faraone draw on their own experiences of journal keeping and, alongside their reflections, we present ideas and issues associated with using journals for self-understanding.

Self-understanding is not limited to knowing one's biographical roots and their influences; neither is it limited to understanding reasons for one's actions. Self-understanding also entails understanding one's ways of knowing and their expression. In Chapter 5, we encourage a holistic exploration of the teaching self through alternative, text- and non-text-based forms of inquiry and representation. Our assumption in this chapter is that knowledge is multidimensional and therefore much of what we know resides outside the realm of language (at least traditional, declarative prose). Along with Margie Buttignol, Carolyn Jongeward, Deirdre Smith, and Suzanne Thomas, we explore ways of researching teaching through a variety of forms of artistic expression—figurative prose, poetry, and visual images, for example.

Because reflexive inquiry is by definition rooted in the self, the methods for researching teaching that we explore in these three chapters and the understandings gained through their use provide the foundation for all other methods and insights. In other words, from a reflexive inquiry standpoint everything starts with and returns to the self.

3

PERSONAL HISTORY INQUIRY

with contributions by
PATTI CANZONERI and JERRY DIAKIW

We teach who we are—a simple but profound statement. And yet how many teachers, either in their initial preparation programs or as part of any professional development opportunities, have been challenged or encouraged to explore the question, "Who am I as teacher?" This question is at the heart of personal history inquiry. As Ayers (1988, p. 22) asserts, "Teachers have a special responsibility for self-awareness, for clarity and integrity, because teachers are in such a powerful position to witness, influence, and shepherd the choices of others."

In this chapter we explore the role of personal history exploration in understanding oneself as teacher. We suggest ways of eliciting personal history information and writing personal history accounts. Patti Canzoneri and Jerry Diakiw provide excerpts from their personal history writing and reflect on issues associated with personal history inquiry. Patti is in her ninth year of teaching. She currently teaches grades 7 and 8 English, history, and special education in a large coeducational elementary school in central Canada. Jerry is a retired superintendent of schools and lives in Toronto, Ontario.

WHY PERSONAL HISTORY ACCOUNTS?

Becoming a teacher is a lifelong process of growth rooted in the personal. Making sense of prior and current life experiences and understanding personal-professional connections is the essence of professional development. We come to know our teaching selves through explorations of elements of our personal histories.

By personal history accounts we mean stories of life and experience that have influenced personal-professional understandings and practices of teaching and learning. Each of us has a rich and interesting personal history and, whether we are aware of it or not, our histories come with us to our daily professional practice. Our experiences of growing up in families and communities, our experiences of learning in formal and informal settings, our experiences of being in schools and other educational contexts as students all contribute to who we are and what we believe and do as educators.

Typically our personal histories remain unexamined yet powerful influences that we treat as, well, "history." We tend to see our personal histories as separate from professional practice and relegate our pasts to our personal archives. "That was then, this is now." In this chapter we argue that through personal history exploration you will find the keys to unlock your understanding of yourself as teacher. In remembering, re-creating, and writing about your prior experiences associated with learning, schools, classrooms, and teachers you can make known the implicit theories, values, and beliefs that underpin your teaching and being a teacher. In the following passage Jerry reflects on the meaning personal history writing had for him as an educator.

Autobiographical writing has been a valuable approach for me in exploring the nature of my life and for revealing my personal and professional knowledge and practice. Stories of one's life are a way of "structuring experience itself, laying down routes into memory, for not only guiding the life narrative up to the present, but directing it into the future" (Bruner, 1988, p. 538). This type of reflective writing has permitted me to explore a holistic view of my entire personal, educational, and career experiences—a life viewed in its full context. Through "telling and living, re-telling and reliving" (Clandinin & Connelly, 1994, p. 9) the meanings and significances of our lives begin to emerge and help us to understand ourselves, how we came to be who we are, and where we are going. This process of revisiting the stories of my past and exploring connections was instrumental in clarifying and revealing the basis of my development as a superintendent. Bateson (1994, p. 11) argues for the importance of story in revealing peripheral vision and drawing connections and patterns:

> Wherever a story comes from, whether it is a familiar myth or a private memory, the retelling exemplifies the making of a connection from one pattern to another: a potential translation in which narrative becomes parable and the once upon a time comes to stand for some renascent truth.... Our species thinks in metaphors and learns through stories.

Through an exploration of our life history we provide the opportunity to surface those singular events, to select those powerful moments that reveal how we came to be who we are and who we are yet to become. It is through this process that I came to understand some of the powerful elements that guided me as a principal and superintendent. As Eisner (1993, p. 5) argues, "getting in touch is itself an act of discrimination, a finely-grained, sensitively nuanced selective process in which the mind is fully engaged." What we choose to include in our narrative begins to select what it is that has profoundly affected who we are. We are like archaeologists sifting through the debris that surrounds our lives, uncovering the treasured or symbolic artifacts from which we can begin to construct the meaning of our lives. From these stories our values and beliefs emerge and we can confirm how congruent they are with our day to day practice because we often operate on an unconscious set of beliefs. The beliefs that guide and shape our actions as individuals and as educators, then, can emerge out of the stories we tell.

Patti shares her perspective on the value of personal history writing.

Many of my students ask in history classes, Why should I learn about the past? What relevance does it have to the present or more importantly to the future? A history teacher always patiently tells his or her students that we must know from where we have come in order to understand where it is we are going. In this same way, as teachers we need to examine from where we have come as learners and understand how that plays out in our classrooms on a daily basis. I remember listening to a professor speak of the importance of acknowledging our implicit theories, and my immediate reaction was that I didn't have any. Of course this was just my own neglect or inability to reflect on and analyze what my true beliefs about learning and teaching really were. I operated on an act-react basis without careful consideration of the motivations and driving forces behind my teaching practice.

Writing about who I am as learner and as teacher has allowed me to understand my actions in the classroom. This new understanding then, can serve as the impetus for change, improvement, or simple affirmation. We can use the past to inform the future. Years from now, my actions of today will be the past and from them I will continue to learn. It is like a cycle that continues to spiral, developing us both personally and professionally if we let it. This is a very powerful notion to me.

ELICITING PERSONAL HISTORY INFORMATION

Although for the most part our personal histories are private mental constructs, most individuals possess observable evidence—artifacts—of elements of their personal histories: photographs, report cards, awards, school projects, creative writing efforts, craftworks, artworks, old textbooks and readers, trophies, school yearbooks, and other memorabilia. These artifacts of experience may serve to jog your memory about experiences and perspectives that have shaped your thinking about being a teacher.

Patti explains how she proceeded to "gather personal history data" in preparation for making sense of it through writing.

When the topic of my inquiry was clear there was so much to consider. The first issue that emerged for me was how to collect data. What would my sources of data be? Memory, of course, must be a primary method of collecting information and this concerned me somewhat. How would my memory serve me? Would time have muted things in my mind? Would I only remember selectively, in other words, what *I* wanted to remember? I had to get this matter out in the open immediately and acknowledge it. I needed to balance this with other sources of information so I searched for other data.

During a recent move, I had discovered a treasure album from my childhood that contained information about me as I moved from kindergarten through university. My mother started this collection for me, recording information such as the names of friends, teachers, hobbies, interests, aspirations, and special events. There was also space for a photograph from each year and a pocket for report cards, certificates, or other relevant collectibles from each school year. I spent hours going through this, smiling fondly at the memories, thinking back to the years I spent in both elementary and secondary schools. I read the comments teachers had made on my report cards and found poems, stories, and articles I had written for school. I found certificates and awards and remembered those people and activities from those formative years. These were a source of data to me and presented a very special collection that defined who I was and the person that I had hoped to become.

There were other sources of information as well. When I moved cities and left a teaching assignment, my students gave me a special gift, which was a book in which they had all written. I treasure their comments and as I read each one over, I realized that in their honesty and sincerity they were telling me some powerful things about my teaching. Photographs of my students, of school events, and of other staff members served as another source of data. As well, I reviewed all of my lesson plan books from each year of teaching. I looked back through my own high school yearbooks, at the pictures and the things that friends had written. I also spoke extensively with others in an informal way about my learning and my teaching. I spoke with my parents, friends, former colleagues, my husband, and others who had been there at key points in my learning or teaching career. These conversations served sometimes to affirm my beliefs and memories or to illuminate things that had slipped below the surface of my memory. Together, these other items reinforced my memory and formed a foundation from which to proceed.

I also read widely on related subjects. It was important for me to understand the power of narrative accounts and to read about how others had successfully incorporated this strategy into their own professional development. I read whatever I could get my hands on that dealt with reflective practice and personal, narrative writing. This reading created an openness to the process and served as an inspiration to believe.

Memories are triggered in unusual and sometimes unexpected ways. Jerry's main strategy for eliciting personal history information was to always be ready with pen or pencil and notebook or scrap of paper for those times when he was inspired to clarify his thinking by examining elements of his life history. He explains:

I was born in 1936. I lived above a hairdressing shop run by my father and mother, an aunt, and two uncles at Queen and Seaton Streets in Toronto. The smell of finger-wave solution and the scorched chemical odor of a permanent wave still trigger an eruption of memories of playing in the shop. Like many children of immigrant parents I spoke no English until I went to kindergarten at Duke of York Public School, nor did I need to. Playing on Seaton Street, I wasn't even aware that English existed. There were so many Ukrainian families on the street that it was not unlike a tribal village in the jungle or circle of tents in the desert, so oblivious were we to the surrounding population. So safe was our Ukrainian community that I could play all day on Seaton Street while my parents worked. If I didn't come home for lunch it hardly mattered; I simply ate with all the other kids at the home where we happened to be playing. Warm, wizened old "Babas" shrouded in black seemed to be everywhere.

On Sundays and feast days, the Ukrainian tribe trudged to the Holy Eucharist Ukrainian Catholic Church on King Street near the Don River. Today, fifty years later, when I exit the Don Valley Parkway from the Richmond Street ramp and pass over the former site of the church, I am flooded with memories of weddings, plays, christenings, and religious celebrations. I swear the smells of incense, wax, and the stale odor of the basement hall are still there twenty years after the hall has been demolished. I sometimes still hear the priest's deep, booming voice chanting, *"Hospody, pomylui! "* as he swings the cadillo of smoking frankincense on a golden chain.

At eight, I survived the terrors of Saturday Ukrainian School where I was threatened with life in eternal hell if I didn't agree to become an altar boy. I remained steadfast under relentless pressure from two very large nuns. My parents were never able to get me to return to Ukrainian school after the nuns forced me to try on altar boy robes to show how beautiful I looked in them. They promised me a life in heaven where as one nun said, "You can have an apple any time you want one." I can still see her bulbous scrubbed face framed by her white habit as she leans close to mine and whispers this holy secret.

When I was five, I was hospitalized with a serious case of strep throat. No one understood me in the hospital as I whined and complained in Ukrainian, and my condition deteriorated. Frustrated, my father whisked me out of the hospital vowing never again to speak Ukrainian in the home. And my parents never did, except when Ukrainian friends came by from the old neighborhood. I slowly became aware that not all Canadians spoke Ukrainian.

So began one of the reflections in my notebook, an attempt to pick up the threads of my life experience that defined who I am and that shaped and directed my personal and professional life. Late in my professional career as a school superintendent, I came to writing as a way of understanding my developing interests and convictions. While I never kept a formal journal, I had occasion to write in my daily notebook—on sheets of paper, or on the computer—thoughts, poems, or reflections that helped me clarify my thinking. Sometimes I would simply write a sentence or two. At other times I would write several pages or even a poem. The more I did this, the more I found insights into what I was doing and why I was doing it.

Wordsworth wrote, "The child is father to the man." So, I began to reach back into my youth to sketch stories that seemed to tumble out. I began to examine my life in its fullest context in a random, casual way. But eventually these jottings and notes began to reveal several themes.

There are numerous other ways to "remember" elements of your personal history. For example, you may choose to take a chronological approach to remembering and work your way through your school days year by year, grade by grade, or teacher by teacher. Or you may focus your remembering on certain themes or critical events in your early (and later) school life. Perhaps when you think of early learning experiences you think of nonformal educational contexts. Maybe your understandings have been profoundly influenced by some of your experiences outside of school— camp, family outings, family life in general, church, organized groups such as Boy Scouts or Girl Guides, friendships, or your own solitary wanderings. These are all meaningful starting points for your personal history inquiry, and any and all of them will provide useful and important insights into who you are as teacher. Although you may feel a bit uncertain at the beginning about how to get started, once you do, the hardest part will be to stop! For additional ideas refer to the Research Activities section at the end of the chapter.

WRITING PERSONAL HISTORY ACCOUNTS

Writing personal history accounts, for some individuals, may be a difficult and perplexing task. For some people the idea of writing autobiographically is enough to freeze the creative juices into an ice jam. What does my life have to do with anything? What can I possibly say about myself that is of any value for others and for me? How can writing in the first person count as knowledge? What do I include and what do I leave out? What is safe? How do I want to represent myself? These are but some of the questions personal history writers typically ask at the outset.

And then there are those for whom the prospect of writing anything of any kind brings on varied manifestations of any number of mysterious crippling illnesses. Anne Lamott, a well-published fiction and nonfiction writer, herself admits to experiencing regular bouts of severe hypochondria and chronic procrastination throughout the writing process. But, she adds, because writing is really "a matter of persistence and faith and hard work.... You might as well just go ahead and get started" (Lamott, 1994, p. 7). "Plug your nose", she says, "and jump in" (p. 4).

In the following segment Patti shares some of her thoughts on the writing process.

There have been so many incidents and people in my life that have shaped and affected me as a learner and a teacher. How would I possibly narrow it down? How would I know what to include and what to leave out? There were so many ideas swimming around in my head and for me the only way to begin to sort them out was to immerse myself in the process of writing. As I progressed, my work took its own form and shape. As I wrote, I knew what needed to be included and what perhaps was not as relevant. Trusting in the process was crucial here. Because of my need for structure, my approach was a chronological one. This allowed me to deal with one chapter of my life at a time and brought some order to how I would proceed. There were days and even weeks where I could not write at all and other times where I could not stop writing. I needed to acknowledge this, accept it, and listen to my inner voice.

I have heard others speak of the emptiness they feel when trying to capture in print what the essences of their experiences really were. They speak of words becoming impoverished on the page, losing and reducing the experience by writing about it. I have read about alternative forms of journal writing that are not so structured and clearly defined—poems, artwork, cartoons, sayings, and snippets of writing. I have always written that way. The process of being able to consolidate the snippets, the pieces, by writing a personal history account allowed the words and ideas to come to life on the page. Writing about my experiences enriched them for me, allowing me to truly explore and find meaning. I could experience it, understand it, and interpret it. I was able to articulate some things that I had never consciously considered before. This type of writing has been described as "authentic conversation with oneself" (Holly, 1989, p. 163), and it meaningfully served this purpose for me. My excitement grew as I proceeded and my trust in the process and in myself grew.

There is no *one* way or *right* way to write a personal history account. Even the two examples in this chapter reflect quite different styles and writing forms. As Patti indicates in the following passage, what is most important in writing personal history accounts is finding a form that "fits."

My personal history account involved researching self. I explored those events, people, and experiences that had been pivotal in shaping my attitude toward learning and teaching. In exploring these issues, I hoped to move closer to an understanding of myself as a teacher. As I began to work through the initial stages of the project—thinking about issues, collecting sources of data, and formulating questions—I realized that there were so many important things for me to express and explore. I started with issues and people in my childhood and moved through the crucial time periods in my life right up to the present.

I work best when I am comfortable with not only the topic but also the format. I needed to find the right voice, the right fit. I was reading an article on ways of eliciting teachers' self-narratives when I came across the idea of unsent letters. The author described a man who had been the headmaster of a school, writing letters he wished he had been able to write to parents, explaining his point of view as head of this school. In doing so, the letters became a part of his whole understanding of the practice of education (Diamond, 1991). I was immediately drawn in by this idea. The idea of writing letters to those people who had been present through my experiences as a learner and a teacher, and were perhaps pivotal in some way, gave me a voice—a form. An unsent letter allows one to write with passion, honesty, and depth.

In another reading, a woman had written an unsent letter to her mother who was on her deathbed, explaining the painful reasons she had chosen to attend class that day instead of going to her mother's side (Cooper, 1991). This letter was full of emotion, pain, and honesty. I could not imagine another format that would have allowed the writer such freedom and such expression. Unsent letters became the format with which I would approach my writing. For me, the fit was right.

The following letter, written to her husband, is an example of one of Patti's unsent letters. In her personal history account she also wrote letters to family members, former teachers and professors, friends, former colleagues, former students, and to herself.

This letter involves a particularly difficult period in my life during my second year of teaching, which was also our second year of marriage. Surprisingly, it was not a difficult letter for me to write, despite the fact that it dealt with a painful time for me in my teaching career. Instead, writing the letter allowed me to finally put this troublesome period into some kind of context. Writing the letter allowed me to reflect on this time in my life with some clarity and perspective. It was the first opportunity I took to delve into exploring reasons why everything happened the way it had. The passage of time and the opportunity to write and reflect brought some enlightenment.

Dear Mike:
 How many years until retirement? Thirty-five? Could I do this for thirty-five more years? What happened to all of the joy, you ask? It was gone as fast as it had appeared. My second year of teaching took everything I had to give and left me deflated, depressed, and in search of another career. To date, this was the hardest experience I have gone

through and the most frightening. I have never felt so out of control, so lost, so weakened. It started at the end of September and lasted until just before Christmas. It was only with your strength, support, and un-questioning belief in me that I survived. Our marriage was young then but you were there for me and somehow I made it through. Though I did not realize it at the time, and would not realize for a long time after, the experience of falling apart made me stronger, wiser, and better able to cope with the world of teaching and beyond. But oh what hell it was!

At the end of the previous school year my department head had been led to believe that because of enrollment numbers I would be transferred to another school. Therefore when he made up the sched-ule, he accommodated everyone in the department as best as he could, leaving open a less than desirable full-time schedule for someone who would come in and take my place. When he found out later that it would be me remaining, he felt badly but believed at that point that there was nothing he could do. I accepted this. Now looking back, with more expe-rience and a better understanding of how things work, I realize that per-haps things could have been changed. However, I was just thankful to be working in the same school and I was still full of the joy and excite-ment of simply being a teacher. I could handle it. I had had a great first year and expected nothing short of continued fulfillment and happiness in my second year. I was another year wiser, no longer the rookie. I had a year's experience and could conquer the world, so it felt. I had six se-nior English classes all at maximum student enrollment. Most of the lit-erature to be taught was completely new to me. I think the only piece I had ever read myself was *Macbeth*. I had lots of work ahead of me.

In addition, I would be teaching two general level grade 11 classes. This in itself normally would not be of great concern; however, this partic-ular year there was an extremely disruptive, hard-to-handle group mov-ing through the system at this grade level and they would be all mine. To say they were discipline problems would be an understatement. They were a difficult group, mostly males, ranging in age from fifteen to twenty-one (I was all of twenty-three myself), with an amazing and complete host of social problems including alcohol and drug addictions, family abuse, attempted suicides, living in group homes, and police records, just to scratch the surface. Academic work was not their strength and their work habits were practically nonexistent. As I reflect on this group, I real-ize I am not exaggerating; in fact it is difficult for me to accurately convey all of the things with which these kids were dealing. Was I worried that summer? Of course not. I taught summer school for extra money and experience, and slowly read through all of the literature I would be teach-ing. It would be a great year. How wrong I was!

It did not take long for reality to set in. It was the end of September and I was supposed to be involved in the Challenge Cup, which was a city-wide event for charity in which different teams competed in a type of crazy Olympics. It was great fun and hundreds of people were involved.

I had been asked to be on the school's team and I had looked forward to a fun and eventful day with my colleagues. I never went. It was the beginning of my difficulties that week. I was overcome with a feeling of fright and apprehension. I did not want to go to school. I did not want to plan my lessons, something in which I had previously found such pleasure. I was filled with an impending sense of doom and depression. It crept up on me slowly and manifested itself in several sad ways. I had trouble sleeping and eating. I cried all the time, frightened of some unknown entity. I did not want to go on that day and laugh with my colleagues and pretend that everything was fine. I called a friend and told her I was sick and also called in sick to school on Monday. I was falling apart and did not understand why.

It is difficult to convey exactly what I felt during this time. My heart ached. It was a heavy, heavy feeling like a dark cloud had taken over my life, allowing me to see only fear and pain. One of the most difficult things to deal with was my lack of understanding of what this was all about. Teaching had always brought me such happiness. I was so fortunate to have a job. Why would I allow these negative feelings to take hold of me now? I searched and searched for answers and came up with none. You tried to be patient with me, to understand me, to be my support. How I must have scared you in those days. I scared myself. I started reading the job classifieds desperately looking for another job, anything to get me out of that hell. I did not know which way to turn and without the love and guidance from you and from my parents I know I would never have survived.

I remember teaching *Death of a Salesman* to my grade 12 classes at the time, moving through my lessons mechanically and ineffectively. (Ironically, my life seemed to be writing Death of a Teacher.) Another teacher caught on to what was going on and approached me to see if I was okay. I told her what was happening and she urged me to take care of myself first, to take some time off. With your help, I decided to see my doctor and get some medication to calm my nerves in the hope that I could start to deal with what was at the heart of this matter. I did that but took very little of the medication, instead managing somehow to snap out of it. I do not know exactly what caused me to bounce back just as I do not know exactly what started all of it in the first place. My students were the same, my schedule was the same but somehow my strength was growing and my confidence began to rebound. It was never quite the same that year as it had been before and it was still a year full of challenges and frustrations but the doom, the cloud had lifted. The weight left and has not returned to me in the seven years since that time. I now laughingly refer to it as my "breakdown" though I was far from being "broken." But I am also able to see it for what it really was.

I had no professional support system in those years. I had no person in the educational system to bounce ideas off of, to share frustrations with, to reflect with about my day-to-day experiences. I had not been taught to nor was I equipped to reflect on my practice and my actions in order to truly understand myself or my teaching. Instead, I had only my joy of teaching and discovered sadly that this alone would not equip me to handle all that was before me. I hid my ignorance and fear from others, always smiling, pretending that I had a handle on everything. I did not want to appear out of control. I was a good teacher and did not want to compromise this standing in any way. But, a good teacher would not be falling apart. A good teacher would enjoy teaching. It was a year of real discovery—discovery about self, about strength, and about the support of a strong marriage.

The year went on. I remember collecting 150 independent study assignments the day before Christmas holidays. Some of them were twenty pages long. We lived in the apartment and it took me four trips from the garage below just to get them all in. I remember piling them beside our bed, between the bed and the wall, for there was nowhere else in our one-bedroom apartment to put them. What an enjoyable holiday season that was! Though I had no illusions about getting them all marked over the holidays, it was a most unpleasant reminder every night as we went to bed about what lay ahead of me. Looking back now, I realize that my inexperience made these times more troubling. Never would I now collect 150 assignments all at the same time. There was no reason for this yet, again, I was not at a place to know any differently. I have learned that to be effective in the classroom I must have a healthy balance in my life. It is the times where I feel overwhelmed by schoolwork and marking that I begin to resent my job. I have learned that I do not have to mark and read every little thing that my students write and I continue to read about and develop strategies related to this. But at that time, that was all I knew. That was the only strategy in my repertoire that seemed appropriate.

We purchased our first home at the end of that school year and that joy was mixed with the overwhelming feeling of trying to move, unpack, and still get my lessons prepared for Monday. It all worked out of course. At the end of the year I was declared "surplus" in the school since enrollment was declining, and I was eventually declared "redundant" in the system. This whole process was very foreign to me but I instantly despised the terms—"surplus" was bad enough, but "redundant"? For months I had no idea what would happen to me. It seems like every week I received a new letter with a new placement, ranging from being split between two schools, being in a permanent supply teacher pool, to finally being reassigned to another Board. These were difficult times for us. The uncertainty was hard to handle, but again your support helped me cope.

Remembering all of the painful moments also causes me to remember all of the pleasurable ones. Despite the tough learning experiences that came out of my beginnings as a teacher, there were also tremendously rewarding and fulfilling times. I am sometimes surprised that anyone found my teaching very effective that year but, despite the difficulties, I realize that I still had a lot to give. When I see former students from that year they recount fond memories. Reminiscing with them about that year reminds me that, though my memories tend to dwell on the "down" times, there were plenty of "up" times too.

I will always remember that day in July of that year when I picked up the phone and received news of my new placement. I was to be transferred to another school within the city. There was a full-time schedule there for me consisting of English and one class of history. History? I had not taken that subject since I was in grade 9. At the time, however, it did not matter. I needed to know that I had a place. I needed to belong somewhere. The old feelings of anxiety and uncertainty returned to me. What would I teach? How would I fit in? But the dark cloud never returned. Despite the anxiety of beginning something new, the old joy sparked again and the sense that I had found my way through a difficult year served as a reminder that I could handle what lay ahead. It would be just like starting over, only this time a little wiser.

Patti

In addition to finding a form of writing that will work for you, it is important to attend to matters of time and context. Writing of any kind can be time consuming; personal history writing can be even more so. After all, look at the material you have to work with! Rather than be daunted by the time commitment, we suggest you try to make your personal history writing part of your normal daily routine—in much the same way as you might incorporate exercise or reading or television. Even if you can find only an hour in your busy schedule, try to set that time aside and jealously guard it. Make your exploration of your life a priority; give it the space it deserves. Sometimes it is easier to sustain your commitment if you designate the same time each day, every other day, or even several days a week. You may want to invest in a special notebook if you prefer to write longhand. If you like to compose using a computer, setting up a separate folder or disk is a way of acknowledging the importance of your writing.

Some people prefer to work alone throughout the inquiry process and others like to share their work with colleagues or friends. If you prefer the latter or think you might try it out, it is important to be mindful of the importance of developing a learning context that is conducive to writing and discussing elements of and understandings associated with personal histories. Although we will return to the notion of collaborative work later in the book, we mention a few important points here. It is helpful to think of the following as principles to establish for yourself and for working with others in personal history inquiry:

- Create, open, safe, and respectful learning environments.
- Accept and openly acknowledge personal experience as a vital source of knowledge.
- Acknowledge and model the value of relational learning.
- Share both written and oral forms of personal history accounts.
- Discuss the process, substance, and value of the various phases of personal history inquiry.
- Help each other to identify connections between personal history experiences and teaching practices.
- Acknowledge the difficulties associated with writing and perhaps consider alternative structures.

How you write and *what* you write are important only in the extent to which they help you make sense of the personal history influences that guide your teaching beliefs and practices. For both Patti and Jerry writing was a clarifying process. Jerry explains:

From my reflections I have identified a number of themes or threads concerning my life history that surface above all others. These narrative threads reveal preoccupations, whether conscious or unconscious, that I have had all these years. These preoccupations are issues such as equity—gender, race, and class; the geographer in me; the hero's journey; innovator as Truk mariner (Truk Islanders are Micronesians from the Western Pacific); the teacher in the superintendent; and reading, writing, and talk, to name a few. They are rooted in almost everything that I do. They either have driven my personal agenda or are at the forefront of my professional actions. Often I have been unaware of how much they have affected me until I have exposed them through reflective writing. Yet they shaped me irrevocably and infiltrated my professional practice.

Patti describes how she was able to make sense of her personal history writing:

I kept a running journal while writing my personal history account. After I finished my personal history writing for the day, I would then turn to writing in my journal. Here I would document my response to and reflections on some of the things that had surfaced in my personal history writing. In the journal I could deal with the emotions, feelings, struggles, and revelations. This was a very important part of the process of making meaning and seeing connections. As I reexamined my journal later, I was amazed at the real understandings that emerged there. For me, this was an integral part of the process.

PERSONAL HISTORY AND TEACHER DEVELOPMENT

As we indicated at the beginning of the chapter, the primary purpose of personal history inquiry is professional development. Again, "we teach who we are" and we need to take responsibility for how we grow. For Jerry and Patti, understanding connections between life and work have been edifying. They have gained profound insights not only into themselves as educators but also into themselves as learners. In the segment that follows Patti acknowledges how the process of self-inquiry changed her view of professional development.

In my eight years as an educator I have always been particularly concerned with professional development. My belief in lifelong learning shapes and directs my practice in the classroom. I believe that it is essential in the field of education, as in many other fields, to always continue to learn, to seek answers and clarifications, and to be open to new ideas and ways of knowing. I have always sought to learn more, believing of course that in simply searching for the answers we discover more about ourselves and those around us. My vision of what constituted professional development for teachers, however, was shaped by what my experience and exposure to this venue had been. We needed to rely on the "experts," read their works, follow their policies, and implement change because it was prescribed from above. We needed to attend sessions with these experts so that they could teach us to teach better. Those with the most experience would surely know more than those of us new to the field.

One of the most profound changes I have experienced is in viewing what professional development for teachers truly is. My personal history inquiry project led me to a new vision of professional development. The issue of "voice" has become so important in my life as I have discovered that "knowing" comes to us through so many different paths. Of course there is a very valuable role of expert, considering those theories and readings and using them, *in part,* to shape our own ways of knowing. But the key to my revelation is that they form only part of what our knowledge is. What I have discovered is most important, however, is our reliance on and understanding of self, for I believe that it is central to everything that we do.

Developing voice and a sense of self as a source of knowledge came as a result of my personal history research, which allowed me to come to terms with and fully experience the power of writing and narrative.

There are many reasons for our behavior, but we rarely step back to ask ourselves, "Why did I do/feel/think that?" Present circumstances, habit, external influences, our biases, and unrecognized needs and motivations can move us to behave in ways that are sometimes at variance with more deliberate aims. We are vulnerable when we question ourselves. We sometimes feel threatened by change and the discomfort that accompanies the dissonance arising from the difference between our images of ourselves and our behavior. To write introspectively means to march, if haltingly, through barriers to self-discovery, into our pasts, and to the motives and circumstances that influence our behavior. (Holly, 1989, p. 75)

The power of personal history inquiry is that it has allowed me to explore my implicit theories—those ideas that shape my notions of what teaching and learning are really all about. The project even took the process one step further and allowed me to deeply examine what had come before and how that had shaped what was now. My hope, of course, is that this new understanding will continue to shape and influence what is yet to come.

In shaping how I came to view my inquiry project, I refer to a quote in Mary Louise Holly's book, *Writing to Grow,* which draws on the work of Maxine Green and Alice Walker (1982):

There are many ways that the journal can help the author make sense of the experience. Writing is an antidote to the aesthetic that slowly beclouds us as we step into routines that protect us from the many demands of teaching. As Maxine Greene (1982) points out, "persons must be aroused to self-reflectiveness; they must be moved to search," to wide awakeness (6).

The search is an age-old inquiry into what it means to be human. Who am I? Why am I here? What is life? Knowing oneself is a humbling process; and wisdom is a lifelong pursuit, as Alice Walker so poignantly sets out in *The Color Purple.* (Holly, 1989, pp. 80–81)

Alice Walker's words are ones that cause readers to stop and think about the meaning of life and the importance of asking the big question of a life. In asking the big questions, the answers to little questions often tumble along as if by accident. Even so, the big questions remain, always to be discovered.

I see my personal history account as asking about the big things and wondering about the big things and in doing so discovering more about the little things that together shape who I am as learner and as teacher.

Jerry, through a reflection on some of his writing, makes explicit the connections between his personal history and his professional development as an educator.

My early life as a son of immigrant parents, particularly my experience as a student at Upper Canada College in Toronto—a "prestigious" private boy's school modeled on the British Public School—profoundly affected me. During the mid-1940s I was living with my family in an infamous hotel, in the "seediest" section of Toronto, where my father managed the beer hall. It was home to many prostitutes and a hangout for a well-known gang. Through a strange circumstance I became a student at the College, a school for the privileged, wealthy Anglo-Saxon elite. Those early days had an indelible effect on my life. In a series of entries in my notebook I reflected on this experience:

What a strange quirk of fate, what a bizarre shift in cultures! My five years at the college were a combination of joy, boredom, humiliation, and anger. I reveled in the sports and other extracurricular opportunities that were mandatory at the college. But the appalling boredom and monotony of my classes, then, with teachers droning on hour after hour, hardly justified the college's reputation. Parents paid exorbitantly for this reputation and students didn't dare question the teaching staff. Most were without any teaching credentials other than that they had attended a British public school like Eton or Harrow.

In many ways, away from the school, I acquired status. On learning of the school I attended I was conferred an unwarranted elevated social status by adults, not unlike the way some adults defer to an Oxford or Harvard graduate. Yet, until I entered Upper Canada College I never realized how Ukrainian, or rather, non-Canadian, I was. Attending the College exposed the socio-cultural hierarchies to which I had been oblivious. For me this privilege was not without its price and not without a significant impact on my life.

In 1957, two years after leaving the College, I served in the Royal Canadian Navy's summer officer training program. I arrived at the officer's mess in Montreal, shouldered my duffel bag to my assigned quarters, and introduced myself to my roommate, Milton Zysman, who was stretched out on his bed reading.

"What kind of name is Diakiw?" he asked.

"Ukrainian" I replied.

"Ah, another Black man!" he boomed.

I looked at him, stunned, as lights flashed in my mind and memories tumbled and unfolded like a kaleidoscope. I had never thought of it that way, yet he had exposed a central truth about the way I felt and the experiences I had had. What did a Ukrainian and a Jew have in common with a Black man? Why did I feel it was so easy to identify with a Black man? While the differences in experience were vast, we had all known intolerance, prejudice, and second-class status. For

Milton and me this status was confirmed by law. Our parents had immigrated to Canada when the rulings under the Immigration Act of 1923 classified North-western European Immigrants as "Preferred," Eastern Europeans, including the Ukrainians, as "Non-Preferred," and Southern Europeans and all Jews except British subjects as "Special Permits Class."

That day that I arrived at the naval base in Montreal I no longer spoke or un-derstood Ukrainian. I was born in Canada and had never visited the Ukraine. I had had no association with the Ukrainian Church since the age of nine or ten. I be-longed to no Ukrainian clubs or organizations or celebrated Ukrainian holidays or festivals. I was almost not Ukrainian at all, except that my identity was defined and affirmed for me by English Canadians. *They* defined the group to which *they* had determined I belonged and that group was somehow inherently inferior.

I was not exposed to this supposedly inferior status until I went to Upper Canada College, where I was confronted by the impenetrable wall of White Anglo-Saxon Protestantism. I was never personally insulted except by one master who regularly kicked and pushed me out of my seat, shouting about how I was born out of my mother's deep black Ukrainian swamp. Otherwise I was treated as an equal and was fully accepted into school life. No door or opportunity, seemingly, was closed to me. And yet I felt like an alien.

In being accepted, I came to learn how my culture, my parents, my family life-style, my past were not accepted. I hid these from my classmates; I don't think they ever knew who I really was. As such they revealed their feelings and attitudes through subtle and unconscious distinctions. The distinctions were relentless: eth-nic jokes, derision about the way ethnics talked or dressed, the language they used to talk about immigrants, the belittling of other cultures. A remark about a Jew, Ital-ian, Black, or Hungarian painted me with the same brush. They accepted me as one of them but when they joked about "ethnics" they defined and belittled me.

At the College we were trained to emulate "proper Englishmen" so that we could take our positions of power in the country, a tradition of which the College was most proud. We were taught Latin and the classics, the true mark of an edu-cated man. We committed to memory during daily Church of England prayers such patriotic English hymns as *Jerusalem*—"Nor shall my sword sleep in my hand till we have built Jerusalem in England's green and pleasant land." I learned about the empire and about all the "pink bits" on the map. Through the Upper Canada College Cadet Battalion's affiliation with the Queen's Own Rifles I learned of that gallant regiment's history in creating, defending, and protecting the British Empire. Prince Philip, our royal patron, made periodic visits to the school to affirm our connection to the top. My classmates and I learned about power, and that power was in the hands of English Canadians. And although it is true that our country has opened up to share the power with other White cultures (for example, by instating a Ukrainian governor-general), my classmates still dominate in every corridor of power.

School was not an environment in which I was able to talk proudly of my heritage. I retreated and assimilated as fast as I could. I was very ashamed of my background. I was particularly embarrassed about my parents. Not until the end of my last year did any classmate visit my home. Only then did I begin to under-stand that despite the differences in culture and wealth, my parents were among the best.

My parents, on the other hand, were prejudiced against the English. The most scathing insult in our home was to behave like a "bronco," the slang word to describe an overbearing, arrogant, or opinionated English person. My mother always warned us never to marry a "bronco" because they would always throw into your face the fact that you are not a real Canadian. All three sons married "broncos."

At Upper Canada College and in the years that followed, I began to understand the impertinence of the "dominant culture." I came to understand and sympathize with angry Jews who stereotype Gentiles, with Blacks who lash out against Whites, with radical feminists who demean men. Reverse discrimination, the slow-brewing reaction to inequality, is often accompanied by anger and hostility. The feelings that emerged out of this period of my life have deeply affected me. I often feel this experience had the overtones of our Native Schools where Native children were isolated from their culture, forbidden to speak their language or eat their food, and were inculcated with White man's values, religion, language, and culture.

These experiences at the College caused a remarkable paradox in my life. As I wrote about them and reflected on their impact on my life, I began to realize that the struggle within me had gone on for decades. For although I have striven throughout my life to be part of the establishment in many ways—from the conservative "blazer and gray flannel" manner of my dress, to my career moves through the administrative ranks of a large school board—I have harbored bitterness, hostility, and anger about establishments and authority, especially the dominant tradition of English heritage hegemony. It is ironic that by most definitions I am part of the establishment—a White, European male superintendent of schools. Although the College and university education provided me with the skills and language of the power elite, I never really felt like I was an "insider." And although I have maintained many of my College friendships, I am still uncomfortable at their social gatherings. The realization that I could feel marginalized, despite my privileged status, emerged as a commitment to equity issues in my professional life.

I found my own way of dealing with this negative energy. As a curriculum planner and as a teacher I wove equity issues into the courses I taught in geography and history. As an administrator, and after writing about my experiences, equity issues began to dominate my thinking and action. The act of reflection about my life experiences began to influence and shape the direction of my professional life. As a result, I believe that one of the greatest sources of my personal practical knowledge lies in the area of multiculturalism and antiracist education, gender equity, and global interdependence.

This writing of a life, from diary entries from long ago to scraps of paper or occasional entries in my day notebook, has been instructive in revealing versions of who I am. The act of extracting these versions of my past affirm an identity, which in turn has shaped my actions and my future. By perusing and exploring previous reflections in writing, personal history writing provides an important lens through which one can examine lived experience. I have found powerful threads of my personal tapestry deeply entwined in my evolving identity. My early experiences at Upper Canada College as well as the many other experiences that I have explored have become some of the "markers" on my loom on which my tapestry has been created.

ISSUES AND CONCERNS

As is apparent by now, personal history inquiry can be both a demanding task and a personally and professionally rewarding experience. As Jerry comments,

The process is a complex activity, rife with contradictions and dead ends, but invigorating because of the many twists and turns and surprises. "Sometimes a narrative which seems to fit into one category metamorphoses into another. These are all ways of learning, by encountering and comparing more than one version of experience, that the realities of self and worlds are relative, dependent on context and point of view" (Bateson, 1994, p. 12). I grappled with the multiplicity of threads of my prior and current life experiences that coalesce to form the patterns of my practice.

But as Patti notes, there are also issues to be addressed throughout the inquiry process.

When the focus of research is *self,* it can seem so terribly "subjective." I needed always to attend to balance in my writing. To remind me of this I kept a picture of a balanced scale above my computer as I worked. It was important for me not to lose my "objectivity"; not to become so wrapped up in myself that I could no longer step back and analyze or make sense of things. I did not want to produce an account that celebrated only my strengths as a teacher and focused only on the high points of my experience. Nor did I want to allow a very negative orientation to permeate the writing; neither one of these would be an accurate representation of my life. So balance was important.

To assist in maintaining this balance, it was important to consider another very important issue in any type of research—*who* is this for? In answering this question, I was actually stating what the real purpose of my research was. The answer to this question was very easy—it was *just for me.* My purpose was to search, reflect, and discover and then to use these discoveries as a way to inform my future practice. Keeping this in mind throughout was essential. If this were true, then I had no reason to be anything except totally honest. A colleague once asked, "If you see what you don't want to see, what do you do with it?" So I thought about that. What did I do with it? For my purposes, I acknowledged it, explored it, and used it as a way to grow and think about the future. Again this goes back to "Who is it for?" The following idea helped clarify this notion for me:

Writing about our lives and documenting how we adapt to the pressures we encounter as educators enables us to identify patterns in our behavior. It is almost like reading about someone else. As we reexamine our journals, we can become increasingly more self-accepting and less judgmental. Once we see the broader context within which we acted, our behavior makes sense. What might now be viewed as a mistake seemed logical at the time. With self-acceptance comes self-trust. (Holly, 1989, p. 72)

The idea important to me here is that in examining "what I don't want to see," I must acknowledge that at that particular time that was where I was and what I knew. That is okay. It then leads me to think about where I am now and where I want to be in the future. I believe that in considering this, there is real growth.

As I wrote, there were themes that began to emerge. Things that I wrote about from my elementary school years surfaced later when I wrote about some of my teaching experiences. The things that were important to me as a learner during my younger years were things that I brought to my own teaching. Understanding the family and social contexts that had contributed to those ideas allowed some important revelations. After reading over parts of my account I found myself thinking, "Deal with this stuff!" Further writing and reflection allowed me to do that. When asked now if, with my new knowledge, I would do things differently today in a similar situation, I can only respond, "I hope so." This is my challenge: Use what I have learned in my research; use it to understand, to inform. I cannot think of a more important purpose for research.

From our own experiences of autobiographical writing and from working with other teachers, we as authors raise some additional issues and concerns associated with personal history research. We outline them here not to deter you from engaging in personal history inquiry but to suggest that you proceed with caution on your personal history journey.

Personal history inquiry is by definition intrusive. And so there are questions and issues related to self-disclosure. What do you acknowledge? What do you write? There may be events and perspectives represented that you may find disconcerting or even painful. You may encounter elements of prior experiences that represent contradictory perspectives to elements of your current life, career direction, or philosophical orientation to teaching. *You* need to decide how to respond to such contradictions or disagreeable realizations. Remember, personal history inquiry is ultimately for *your* purposes and *your* development. You do not need to "go public" with your account; however, you do need to try to be honest with yourself. As Patti says, "Deal with this stuff."

Related to this is a frequently expressed concern over how you will look in print. Again, remember that you are your only captive audience. No one else needs access to your writing. It is entirely up to you whether you share your writing with anyone. You can be author, editor, reader, and critic all rolled into one. You have ultimate authority over the textual re-creation of elements of your life. "So then," you might say, "I can just make the whole thing up." True, but to what end? What we are after in personal history inquiry is self-knowledge—our personal truths.

PARTING COMMENTS

Some say that any act of remembering is a fictional re-creation. Madeleine Grumet, a well-known educator and proponent of educational autobiography, asserts that text revealed through the autobiographical method never completely coincides with the experience it signifies. Interpretation is a "revelatory enterprise.... Intimations, half-truths, contradictions, distractions hover around every tale we tell" (Grumet, 1981, p. 128). Following along with this line of reasoning, do not be concerned about not remembering "correctly" or not getting the "facts" right. And do not worry that in the end you end up with more questions than answers. Patti has this to say about the personal history journey:

Professional growth has been described as "more like finding our way through a forest than driving down a freeway; each of us must find our own path to professional fulfillment. Teacher stories contribute greatly to that process of discovery" (Jalongo, 1992, p. 69). I have found my own path, and my personal history account has been instrumental in this. My story is my reality. My story communicates my experience, and it is this experience that shapes my practice. For, "as William Carlos Williams told his medical students, 'Their story, yours, mine—it's what we all carry with us on the trip we take, and we owe it to each other to respect our stories and learn from them'" (Coles, cited in Tama & Peterson, 1991, p. 23).

The last letter I wrote in my personal history account was to myself. In it I considered the future after writing about the path that had brought me to the present. In it I wrote, "Answers? Most certainly not. But the exploration has been one of the most exhilarating things I have ever encountered." In examining the past and considering the future it is important to remember that "If we measure ourselves by how far we still have to go, we will always feel inadequate. But if we look at how far we have progressed, the outlook is quite different" (Holly, 1989, p. 5).

I know I have progressed as a result of writing my personal history account, and this knowledge serves as an inspiration and as a reminder that learning to be a teacher is a lifelong process offering us the chance to grow and develop. Personal writing has been described as "the author's own Book of Teaching—a celebration of mountains and tides that can cause even its most skeptical author to marvel" (Holly, 1989, p. 174). The mountains and tides in my own learning have been numerous and have allowed me the opportunity to marvel at the world and my place in it. For this I am thankful.

RESEARCH ACTIVITIES

The following are some additional suggestions to assist you in your personal history inquiry:

- Why did you become a teacher? What was it about teaching that drew you to the profession or, perhaps, what circumstances led you to a teaching career? Explore these questions in light of your personal history.

- Identify a positive teaching practice or philosophy that you express in your practice and/or admire in yourself or others. Explore its roots, why you admire it, how you came to hold that view, and so on.

- Recall special relationships you have had with teachers both inside and outside school contexts. What were the contexts within which these relationships developed? What was the nature of the relationships? What events stand out in your mind? What qualities signify the relationships as special?

- Develop a personal history timeline. Beginning with your earliest remembrances of learning (likely well before the formal start of school), draw a timeline that traces your educational history (again, this is likely to include educational experiences inside and outside school contexts). On the timeline identify critical incidents in your learning life. Explore each of these incidents in detail. This activity may develop into a larger project; be sure to allow sufficient time to explore the incidents.

- Think about positive learning experiences you have had over your lifetime. Select one and try to re-create that experience. Recall and record it in as much detail as possible. Look back over your description and try to identify why it was a learning experience, what made it positive, and why it stands out in your mind.

- Focus your attention outside school and identify some memorable educational experiences. These might have occurred, for example, during family field trips or vacations, in church or Sunday school, through activities associated with clubs or organizations, or perhaps while on your own or with friends. Write about some of these experiences and their significance for your learning (and teaching).

- What were some of the values and attitudes toward education expressed in your family? How have these influenced your thinking and practice?

- Interview (or have conversations with) family members, old schoolmates, or even some of your teachers. Ask them what they remember about you as a student. Encourage them to recall specific events or stories that stand out in their minds either about you or about the era in which you were a student.

RECOMMENDED READINGS

Connelly, F. M., & Clandinin, D. J. (1988). *Teachers as curriculum planners: Narratives of experience.* New York/Toronto: Teachers College Press/OISE Press.

Diamond, C. T. P. (1991). *Teacher education as transformation.* Buckingham, England: Open University Press.

Knowles, J. G., Cole, A. L., with Presswood, C. S. (1994). *Through preservice teachers' eyes: Exploring field experiences through narrative and inquiry.* New York: Merrill.

Ledoux, D. (1993). *Turning memories into memoirs: A handbook for writing lifestories.* Lisbon Falls, ME: Soleil.

Schubert, W. H., & Ayers, W. C. (Eds.). (1992). *Teacher lore: Learning from our own experience.* New York: Longman.

Winsey, V. R. (1992). *Your self as history: Family history and its effects on your personality: A research guide.* New York: Pace University Press.

Witherell, C., & Noddings, N. (1991). *Stories lives tell: Narrative and dialogue in education.* New York: Teachers College Press.

4

RESEARCHING THE SELF
THROUGH JOURNAL WRITING

with contributions by
MARGIE BUTTIGNOL and ANNA FARAONE

We begin this chapter on journal writing with Gary's reflection on his early experiences with journal keeping.

I do not remember writing a journal in elementary or secondary school apart from some isolated instances associated with preparing to write short stories and essays, a requirement of teachers. In those infrequent occasions, I simply took brief descriptive notes of my daily activities. These, indeed, were brief excursions into the realm of journal writing, distant memories that I only vaguely recollect.

By the time I left high school I was searching for the meaning of the universe and my place within it. For a brief time, sporadically and with daily and weekly inconsistencies, I kept a journal, encouraged by a close friend who maintained that writing would produce insights into the questions that I posed. Occasionally we exchanged journals. Less frequently, we talked about our entries. I was mostly embarrassed. Her writing seemed polished, and indeed it was beside my fumbling, inexperienced, and less confident hand. I had great difficulty with writing, putting my thoughts on paper. Finding the time was the least of my difficulty. Mostly, I just did not like to write. But, glimmering deep in the pages of my mind were new insights into myself and the world, gleaned from the experience of struggling with the words of my thoughts, my fears, and my aspirations.

As a young architecture professional in my early twenties, faced with the indomitable task of examining the professional practices of teachers before developing a design brief for constructing new classroom units within an educational institution, I again resorted to writing a journal. The journal served as a vehicle to organize my observations of teachers teaching and students using classrooms, to develop design criteria, and to sequence and categorize my thoughts about the practices of architecture and education. This experience, complemented by extensive rereading of the journal entries, convinced me to make a change of career from designing schools to teaching in them.

As a relatively new and enthusiastic teacher, I was given the opportunity to explore the substance of my educational convictions—as I initially supposed I was destined to do—in a tropical South Pacific island country far from my homeland of Aotearoa New Zealand. With the reality of living and working in resource-deficient third world countries, in exotic places and with colorful people, but with the daunting task of developing and operating a largely self-supporting, kindergarten through grade 10 residential school, I again took up the less than habitual practice of journal writing. This time it served as a record of my local travels, my work patterns, and my thinking about teaching in difficult and often perplexing conditions. Mostly, the journal was a brief travel log, interspersed with thoughts that were often no more than relatively superficial reactions to memorable people and the colorful landscapes and complexities of tropical cultures. Least often, it contained deep analyses of the dilemmas of maintaining and expanding a school on a shoestring budget. I also wrote about the contradictions and discontinuities arising from the colonial mentality that pervaded the educational bureaucracy. And often the entries focused on the crises faced, events that at times seemed to occur on a daily basis—the broken water pump, cyclone damage, clashes of authority, and cookhouse delays.

Immediately before and after my first interlude in the third world, I was an outdoor educator, taking academic subjects such as cultural and physical geography, geomorphology, geology, history, sociology, anthropology, and even architectural/technical drawing, and translating them, and aspects of the secondary school curriculum, into outdoor learning activities. A journal simply served as a detailed record of the kinds of experiences and activities that I facilitated, an analytical account of the outcomes, and suggestions for future excursions. Journal writing became important to me again later during another term working in the tropical South Pacific, teaching in and exploring the unique cultural and physical environments of Papua New Guinea. Again, the journal functioned as a quasi travel log and an educational record, with only infrequent, intensely critical analyses of my own professional practice. Most often it contained very specific stories of experience: the time I momentarily got lost (disoriented) with a group of students in an almost impenetrable rain forest in the Goldie River Valley; the time, when paddling our canoes, we came across a bandicoot (a small kangaroolike marsupial) being eaten alive by a python; or the time we paddled on the crocodile-infested waters of Sirinimu Dam.

Given this opportunity to look back on my practices and critically examine them, I see that elements of journal writing were extremely valuable to me prior to teaching at the University of Utah in Salt Lake City in the early 1980s. Elements that were clearly expressed in my early usage included promoting the creative writing and telling of personal stories, searching for meaning, structuring observations and intentions, recording and interpreting, and enhancing program development. Indeed, these functions, all of which are central components to the concept of reflection, were witness to important personal and professional developments in my life, and the writing brought into focus, as does constructing this narrative, my otherwise ambiguous thinking on many key and crucial issues.

So in the early 1980s, after a sometimes tortuous and circumlocutious professional journey, I eventually found myself responsible for preparing prospective teachers for certification in the state of Utah. Committed to making productive connections with the preservice teachers in my charge; to understanding their needs as learners; to predicting their difficulties and successes; and to knowing more about the effects of my instruction, guidance, and counsel, I turned to journal writing as a tool to enhance my practice as a teacher educator. I simply wanted to better understand my practice.

Journal writing, like all other forms of self-directed professional inquiry, is a vehicle for understanding oneself as teacher. Unlike personal history inquiry, which reflects a particular route to professional understanding, journal writing as a form of research is open terrain. It offers a place to explore the planning and outcomes of curricular, instructional, relational, and other classroom activities. It is a particularly good place to record reactions to some of the pervasive and central issues surrounding education, such as racial and gender inequities; financial and resource inequities; political and social influences and demands; issues of empowerment, authority, and autonomy; and so on. The scope of your journal writing is *only* limited by the contexts in which you are working, the time you have available, your imagination, and your energies.

The basic premise of our view of journal writing as a form of researching is quite simple: We see writing as a problem-solving or thinking-through process. As busy practitioners, you have little, if any, time in the run of a day to stop and think about what you do. You quickly act and react to situations, expressing your knowledge through action, in practice, but not necessarily through words. With the multiple, pressing demands of students, parents, administrators, colleagues, and community members (not to mention personal demands), teachers increasingly are challenged to *do*; little emphasis is placed on thinking, challenging, or questioning educational policies or practices. The pace of teaching life is frenetic. We see journal writing as a way of slowing that pace—an opportunity to pause, reflect, reenergize, and as Anna says, "reform and transform."

In the sections that follow, Margie Buttignol and Anna Faraone share some of their perspectives on journal writing and their journal-writing experiences. Margie is a special education/resource teacher in a large coeducational high school in central Canada. As part of her responsibilities this year she also is teaching an integrated curriculum pilot program at the grade 9 level. Margie has been teaching for twelve years. Anna is also a well-experienced teacher. Currently, she is teaching French and Italian languages in a Catholic girls' high school in central Canada.

WRITING JOURNALS

For some people, the idea of journal keeping prompts unhappy associations. As Margie says, "Just hearing the words, 'For this course you need to keep a diary,' always enraged me." We have heard of many people for whom keeping a log, diary, journal, or any other kind of running record of personal or professional life was a task of drudgery usually "laid on" by someone else. We know of others who have suffered feelings of violation when their private writings were read by others without permission. Margie's reasons against journal keeping were different from either of these. In the following passage she gives a poignant account of her early experiences of journal keeping, and how eventually she was able to break free of traditions that had confined her and silenced her "very own writer's voice."

I always wanted to keep a diary. In childhood and adolescence I started diaries a number of times and then never wanted to write in them because the book itself, the diary, intimidated me. Usually the diary was a birthday or Christmas present from a friend or relative. They were always small bound books with an image of a girl on the cover. The covers were usually made of padded plastic. I remember one diary. On the pastel blue cover was a teenage girl with her hair in a ponytail. She was wearing a "poodle skirt" that was fashionable in the 1950s and she was standing beside a little record player. Musical notes were floating around her head. I never felt as if I was the girl on the cover, and I hated that lock on the side of the diary because I did not want to have to worry about opening it each time I wanted to write. Having to deal with the key for the lock was another annoyance. I always forgot where I put those tiny metal keys and often found myself locked out of my own diary. In those diaries of my youth, there was a limited amount of space allowed for each day. If it was a one-year diary, there was about a page of space for each day. If it was a five-year diary, there were only a few lines. I thought that I had to write exactly the amount that the book allowed me for each day, and I felt apologetic if there was nothing to report. If I had a lot to write one day, my handwriting had to be tiny so that all of the words could be squeezed in. If I didn't have much to say the writing would be in big letters to try to fill up the space allowed for me that day. I wanted to have secrets to write in the diary, but I never had any secrets important enough to write about. Instead, I enjoyed writing letters, making scrapbooks and collages as a child. I did them for fun. Diaries were no fun for me at all! The idea of having to find the key, open the lock, find the right page, write in the size of space that someone else had decided I needed was much too restrictive. So after a few attempts at keeping a diary, I just gave up. That was about thirty years ago.

I wish now that I just could have thrown those diaries out when I realized that they did not work for me. Instead, I put them away in the back of a drawer in my bedroom dresser. Every time I came across these unused diaries they were a painful reminder of my silence. I thought that there was something wrong with me because all of my girlfriends and girl cousins said that they used their diaries every day.

After my mother died when I was fourteen, I found her red diary in the top drawer of her dresser. It was there where it had always been along with a bundle of love letters from my father, my aunt's blonde braid, some rosaries, our baby teeth, holy medals, war medals, lacy handkerchiefs, makeup, gloves, and some costume jewelry. My eyes fixed hungrily onto Mummy's red diary. It was in the very back corner of her drawer. Had she left it there for me? I picked it up and pushed the button on the side—and the lock opened. Hoping to learn something more about my mother I tenderly leafed through the lined pages. I put the diary back into the back of her drawer, guessing that Mummy could not use formal diaries either. The pages were mostly blank with the odd entry noting an appointment or a date. I wonder now how much I am like her. Lately, I have decided to fill my blank pages with my discoveries.

I did not have my very own writer's voice—until very recently, that is. I never even thought that I could have one. Only real writers write in books. How could I have ever thought for a moment that I…I learned, rather I was trained, to write in a rational formulaic way, in school, for school. And that is where my writing stayed—as a school subject—that is, apart from my personal letter and note writing, which was always a passion. "To write properly you must always start with the topic sentence, then go to the body, and end with the conclusion….You must always follow this sequence in this order if you are ever going to learn how to be a good writer." I can still hear teacher-after-teacher-after-teacher, year-after-year-after-year recite these words like a solemn litany. In school, teachers tried to teach me how to write and edit at the same time and I found this an utterly impossible thing to do. I felt as if I was expected to be perfect the first time around. "After all, your writing is supposed to be you" I was told in not so many words by the teachers of my past. Fearing that they betrayed a chaotic and unlearned mind, I was often embarrassed by my disorderly written eruptions. I never knew what would come out on paper until I got it out. I never understood the poetry that we learned about in school. I hated those vapid rhymes that we were forced to write. "Pay attention to the rhyming scheme. AA BB AA…," the teachers would all say. I always wondered how you could apply a formula to writing prose and poetry, but who was I to be thinking about things like that when I couldn't even properly follow the rules for writing?

Once in grade 10 we had an assignment to make an anthology of our ten favorite poems. Not having any favorite poems, I figured that I needed to find some that I could pretend were my favorites. So I did what I thought I was supposed to do and found nine conventional rhyming poems that I did not understand at all. The tenth poem was by Ezra Pound. I do not even remember what it was about now, but what I do remember is that Ezra Pound spoke to me with his poetry. Because it did not rhyme, I wondered if it was really poetry. When I was assembling my anthology, just to be safe, I buried Ezra's poem in the middle, sandwiched between those safe rhyming ones. I even cut some dark images and words from magazines and glued them into a border around my Ezra Pound poem. The other nine pages of my anthology I left blank—apart from the text of those contrived-sounding rhyming poems, that is.

Throughout my formal education, I learned to follow all of the rules about writing well, very well. My writing developed just like those teachers thought it should but I always saw it as so superficial, so mechanical, so empty, and so not me. One teacher talked about "creative writing," but juxtaposing the words "creative" and "writing" was too much of a contradiction for me to grasp. If a teacher had allowed me to write a letter, much more of the real me would have appeared on those Hilroy pages, I am sure. I never expressed my self in school. I did not see the point in taking a chance and risking being humiliated in public in front of my peers and superiors. I just did what I was told to do. It made life easier for me at the time. I could regurgitate facts on paper exceptionally well, but I could not write about who I was or how I felt.

Carl Jung kept a diary as he was developing his theory of collective consciousness. Into this book he recorded his images, dreams, fantasies, themes, and all of the connections he saw between them. He even wrote conversations between himself and his anima, which he felt represented the "female" side of his mind. Jung's anima looked like an old man and he named him "Philemon." My husband Rudy told me that, in Italian, *anima* means soul. I wonder what was happening to my soul in school as I was learning how to write the "right way."

Just hearing the words "For this course you need to keep a diary" always enraged me. It always felt like yet one more thing to do. I never could do it "the right way." I see now that I needed to discover "my own way."

Paul Gauguin, the painter, did not want his intimate journal to be a book. All through his journal he repeated the phrase "this is not a book" to remind himself that the form he needed to express himself was more like painting, experimenting, taking away, adding, and following his intuition to discover what would happen by chance. Like Gauguin and Jung, I needed to have a diary form free of traditional conventions and rules—no locks and keys to keep me out. Like Little Red Riding Hood I needed to wander off the path and see what I could find— even if I, by chance, came across something scary like the big bad wolf. I wonder now if that dreaded creature is part of me?

Artists use sketchbooks; writers use diaries and journals. I have put both forms together in my sketchbook. Who do I think I am!

Sometimes my writing is neat, sometimes it is so messy that I can hardly read it. Sometimes I write very large and sometimes very small. Sometimes I draw. Sometimes I doodle. Sometimes I tape in things that I find in a newspaper or magazine, or notes from friends. Sometimes I write single words, sometimes I write lists. Sometimes I just write about how I am feeling. Sometimes I write unsent letters. Sometimes I write poetry and it does not even rhyme. I never plan what I am going to do. I see what I have done after it appears on the page. It is always a surprise. I think of my book as a sketchbook, made up of my mind notes. Like Carl Jung, I am getting to know my own anima. My only rule is that there are no rules in my sketchbook. Anything goes. I always write the date of my entries, but I do not see this as a rule. Everything about me goes into one sketchbook. It would not make sense to me to split up my different roles or the different parts of my life into different books. Through my sketchbook, I am practicing my writer's voice. And I realize that I have more than one.

When I was selecting my first "sketchbook" I had a few requirements in mind. Size was probably the most important consideration. The book had to be small enough to fit into my purse because I needed to carry it at all times to catch my fleeting thoughts. It needed to have an "everyday" look so that I would not be afraid to scribble and scrawl in it. It needed to be durable so that it would not fall apart. It needed to have a flexible binding to that I could photocopy pages easily. The pages had to have a smooth writing surface so that my pen could just glide effortless over it. I did not want anything that was predated, sectioned, or fancy looking. Like Jung, I also did not want anything that looked like a textbook. A Hilroy 300-page, six-by-nine-inch, lined, spiral-spine notebook was my choice. It has lined pages even though I would have preferred unlined. I bought the first one at Business Depot for $1.99. Besides the lines, the only other thing that I do not like about the Hilroy 300-page model is that it is divided with colored poster board into "five subjects." When I get to one of these colored sections I write on them like another piece of paper.

For me, the writing tool is just as important as the choice of the writing format. I like minute, sharp, black lines that run smoothly onto the paper. The feeling of flow is very important for my expression. Sometimes my writing trickles out of my pen like water in a creek, sometimes it swirls like water in a whirlpool, sometimes it bursts to the surface like water in an underground spring, sometimes it cascades like water over a waterfall, sometimes it swells like a tidal wave, sometimes it meanders like a river, sometimes it blocks like the water in my garden hose when it gets bent, sometimes it has deep undercurrents and powerful cross currents. I need the feel of the flow. I detest the feel of that scratchy confrontational relationship that some pens have with paper. I have tried a number of fine black markers and uni-ball pens over the months and by far, the best one to date is the Pilot Hi-Tecpoint V5 Extra Fine. I was sold on the Pilot Fineliner but the Hi-Tecpoint Extra Fine is even better because it has an ink reservoir for the overflow, and so I can write holding the pen bottom down, as when I am writing in bed. One day I misplaced my Pilot Extra Fine and I had to use a uni-ball pen that I had in my purse. I was drawing so furiously in my sketchbook that the sharp tip of the uni-ball ripped right through the paper! I have not used any color in my sketchbook, yet. But, last week I found myself trying out fine colored markers with tiny tips like paintbrushes, and some felt markers called Overwriters, made by Crayola.

In those diaries of my childhood, I felt a terrifying pressure to write every day and to fill every page as the form rigidly dictated. With my sketchbook I make entries whenever I want to. I try not to panic when I do not have time to get everything down as images and ideas and thoughts drift through me. I have learned that the same idea comes around again and again. If I am unable to capture it one time, I will the next, or the next, or the next after. The silent time between dates in my sketchbook also speaks to me.

Breathe in through the nose, breathe out through the mouth—inspiration, expiration. Closing my eyes and doing this simple exercise before writing helps me to focus on the present and empty my mind, all in the matter of a few deep breaths. Turning off the computer screen to that I cannot see the text as I type allows my writer's voice out. With the screen turned off I cannot fall back into the trap of trying to write and edit at the same time. I learned that skill all too well in school.

Writing or typing with my nondominant left hand releases a childlike writing voice. With my new writing I feel like a child who is just learning how to speak.

Margie's message is loud and clear: Find your own way; find your own voice! To be meaningful and helpful, a journal needs to be what *you* want it to be both in form and function. Once you make the journal work for you (instead of the other way around) and allow it to reflect who you are, you are likely to find that it becomes a channel for your creativity and for deeper explorations of self. As Anna indicates in the following segment, being open and flexible can lead to unanticipated discoveries.

Last year when I was meticulously planning my dream project—a Toronto-Nice exchange with my grade 12 French class—I kept an ongoing record of my practices and my reflections on those practices. What started out to be one way (among many other methods) of documenting my exchange experience, in the end became a document that holds the essence of a personal journey describing a teacher's call for adventure and eventual transformation. Even the format of the journal itself changed; I progressed from brief notes in point form randomly recorded to formal writing during the predeparture stage and finally to audio tape-recorded monologues for the rest of the experience and the school year. In many ways, the outer search for a preferred or comfortable mode of journaling parallels my inner search of my "self" as an educator.

What is the exact format of my so-called journal? And is it a "journal"? As stated earlier, I went from capturing small fragments of experience (or "moments of being," as Virginia Woolf would say) in written form to complete sentences in written form, and finally stopped at the spoken word, which represents over two-thirds of the entire record. Are the audiotapes a journal, a conversation or dialogue or interview with myself, a form of autobiographical writing, storytelling...? And what happened during the transcription of the audiotapes? Was it a form of "retelling" or "reliving" that complicates even more the centrality of myself as participant, researcher, and critic? Who am I in the text and in the field?

When we speak of journal keeping we are speaking in the broadest sense of the term. It is not important that you follow a particular convention; what is vital is that you adopt the spirit and concept of journal keeping—that you find a suitable forum to engage in systematic reflection on your teaching. Whether you use a conventional loose-leaf notebook, a commercial "diary," a sketchbook, a video- or audiotape recorder, a computer, or whatever, the important thing is to find what works to get you started. Like personal history writing, the hardest thing about journal keeping is getting started. Once you make the commitment, however, you will realize how much you really have to say and how much you can learn about yourself by taking the time to articulate your thoughts, values, and beliefs about teaching.

USING JOURNALS FOR SELF-UNDERSTANDING

Ledoux (1993) compares the journal with the scientist's laboratory—a place to experiment with ideas and methods. This is a liberating notion if you think of a laboratory as a creative place—a playground rather than a proving ground. If you allow yourself the physical, temporal, and psychological space to explore ideas and events in your teaching life; if you place yourself in your "laboratory" for some time each day to play with ideas and styles of recording, chances are you will come to appreciate and rely on the developmental value of journal writing. Not only is journal writing likely to enhance your development as a teacher, you also are likely to develop your creative potential as a writer, or visual artist if you choose nontextual forms of articulation.

Journal writing serves different purposes. It is likely that the purposes for which you keep your journal will vary according to your needs. It also may be true that the frequency and intensity of your journal writing will ebb and flow as Margie described earlier. It is important to allow your journal writing to develop its own rhythm; however, it is equally important to maintain some level of activity even when your perceived need to write is low. Understanding, after all, does not result only from exploration of problems or perceived critical events. There is much to be learned from an examination of the mundane elements of our practices and lives. In the following passage Anna examines both her reasons for keeping a journal and the ways in which the journal helped her to lay out and grapple with elements of her personal and professional self.

At the start I believe that I had several reasons for keeping a journal. First and foremost, I wanted to learn more about myself. Second, in a Proustian sort of way, I wanted to revisit my past and compare my experience of arranging an exchange for my grade 12 students with my own 1982–1984 France exchange experience. I wanted to heal or celebrate, and not extricate my learning from that of the students. Also, it was a kind of dialogical relationship or "relational knowing" (Hollingsworth, Dybdahl, & Minarik, 1993) with my students since I also asked them to keep a journal during their stay abroad.

Throughout my journal tapes I speak in many different voices: the teacher who talks about curriculum, teacher development, and learning; the researcher who is concerned with the documentation and recording of the exchange phenomenon; twenty-four-year-old Anna who compares her various visits to France; the student/colearner who goes through some of the same kinds of experiences and learning as the students; Anna the child who revisits some of the old issues with her family; Anna the wife/companion who discusses matters of love, sex, and family.

Furthermore, with all of these different hats I fluctuate between my "active self" and my "reflective self" (Baldwin, 1990, p.7), walking and watching, being the participant and the researcher-observer. "Together these two selves create consciousness: the awareness of ourselves within our own existence" (p. 7) and so I speak of the "voices within" for "conscious people are aware of the influence and guidance available through…inner whispers. The directions for our quest most often come from within."

The "writing helps [me] to distinguish between [my] different voices, making aspects of [my]self become more audible and possible" (Diamond, 1993, p. 511), validating my chorus of voices and constructing myself multivocally. But by storying and restorying, by writing narratively we can sort out whose voice is the dominant one (Connelly & Clandinin, 1990). For me, it's the teacher I would like to be:

> This whole trip, everything has helped me to clarify my goals even more. Things are just becoming more and more clear and this is what I want to do, continue to develop special relationships with students. I want to leave my mark. I don't want to be a mediocre teacher. I don't want to be a teacher that kids forget. I want to do something special for them. (May 28/94)

As I examine my embodied language of images, metaphors, and personal philosophies, I understand that my practice is about much more than *just* teaching a second language. I view learning as a whole process embracing the whole child who is an active participant in his or her own learning:

> I am offering this opportunity to my students. I am not responsible for their having a great experience. That is their responsibility! (Feb. 23/94)

My passion for including a component of experiential learning into the second language curriculum comes from my holistic perspective:

> It's not about learning a second language. It's about life, learning, love, relationships, people, friendship, respect, human emotion, human bonding, growth…discovery of oneself. It's about all these important things

that we put aside, perhaps in a classroom, that are more important than the course of study. (April 29/94)

The more I understand my own story, the more I understand my students and move closer to them, involving them more in curricular decisions and accepting their vulnerability. I begin to look at teaching (in the context of an exchange experience) differently. At the end, all I have to say is, "I really love those kids…I know I'm doing good work" (June 2/94).

Margie comments on the role journal writing has played in her quest for self-understanding. She highlights one of the most challenging difficulties inherent in autobiographical exploration—doing what anthropologists call "making the familiar strange" so as to understand it from a distanced perspective.

It is hard to examine your own beliefs and assumptions about life because they are a part of you. It is even more difficult to examine the myths that we create about ourselves. Greek myths, Roman myths, Medusa, Athena, and the myth of Sisyphus—I thought "myths" was just a subject that you learned in school! We do not stop to ask ourselves why we do the things that we do—we just do them. I find that most of the time I do not have a rational explanation for doing something a certain way—it is more of a feeling way of knowing. All of these things about myself and more I am learning through my writing.

JOURNAL KEEPING AND TEACHER DEVELOPMENT

One of the main purposes of this book is to promote attitudes and practices of reflexive inquiry as a form of professional development. Journal keeping is central to both the inquiry and development processes. Whether you choose journal keeping as a form of inquiry in and of itself or use a journal as a research tool in other modes of inquiry (for example, to record personal history or classroom observation data), the journal has an important role to play in professional development. In the following section Anna describes some of the ways in which journal writing has enhanced her learning. Note her reference to self-directed professional development, a concept we believe is essential for truly meaningful professional growth.

My journal has helped me, the teacher as learner, to gain access to alternative meaning perspectives for interpreting my reality. And this is central to transformation! Throughout my "mind conversations" (Baldwin, 1990, p. 6), I allow myself movement into a world of multiple perspectives as I shift from the comfort of remaining the teacher that I am to the challenge of becoming the teacher that I would like to be.

If "the journal illuminates the self" and "the individual self illuminates the collective self" (Baldwin, 1990, p. 28), then I have succeeded in beginning with the personal, the need to understand myself, and proceeded toward understanding myself in my teaching culture. And from this grounding I am approaching an understanding of the whole concept of teaching in general. This introspection has taken "the human image from the self to the culture instead of imposing a human image from the culture onto the self." I now have a better grasp of my blending of the personal and the professional in my teaching role.

To "do research" on yourself through journal writing seems one way to solve the subject-object split frequently found in traditional research, but I believe that the power of this form of narrative lies precisely in understanding and integration—"a bridging of the inner mindscape and the outer landscape" (Cooper, 1991, p. 99). The process is cathartic as well as introspective. My Toronto-Nice exchange emerges as a play of interdependence between the students, the curriculum, and the teacher. There are also numerous dialectics for me to grapple with: theory and practice, process and product, creativity and technique, linguistic and non-verbal communication, intellect and intuition.

Belenky and her coauthors (1986) found that many women reported the use of a diary or journal to facilitate the process of finding their voices and to validate speaking from an intuitive sense, or "from the gut." Through this they gained some power over their own lives and a growing sense of self. These women grew personally and intellectually as they "found their voices." Like them, I can attest to the same kind of transformation. The development of my voice is a way out of my initial despair into a kind of personal power that transforms my alienation from the teaching culture of my school. I describe in my journal the agony I feel in the conflict between my hopes and dreams about what my experiences in the field of student exchange should or could lead to, and the pressure I feel to remain an instrument for the continued rigid oppression of a very traditional principal entrenched in a very patriarchal system.

I try to integrate my own needs, values, and desires with the conflicting expectations of students, administrators, parents, community, and cultures. My struggle between the needs of those I care for and my own needs, as the one who is caring through the whole exchange experience, becomes very loud and clear. Now I know why I survived the experience after having organized the mammoth task all on my own. To some extent the journal worked to combat my energy depletion by reminding me of who I was in the whole exchange process; it helped me to focus on and attend to my own personal needs. Journal writing places us in relation to ourselves so that we become both the one who is caring (or one-caring) and the cared-for (Noddings, 1984). This revelation came as a big surprise to me.

In my constant attempt to comprehend the personal benefits and gains for myself as the teacher/organizer of the exchange experience, I finally grasp the meaning of the intrinsic advantages when I begin to look at the experience as a form of teacher development. And so I come to a deeper, broader, and richer understanding of what I do. I begin to look at teaching (in the context of an exchange experience) differently, seeing it in a new light, coming to appreciate its complexity more than I have done as yet. At times I feel worse, at least temporarily—more doubt-ridden, puzzled, sadder perhaps—as my newly won insight tells me that the battle for the inclusion of exchanges in the second language curriculum is a long and difficult one. I think that this mode of development is probably what Jackson (1992) calls "the way of wonder" or "the way of altered sensibility." What begins to change is indeed my perception of my hard work in this field; I see it differently and I speak too of changes in the value I attach to the work. "We come to appreciate it, even to treasure it, we become attached to it" (Jackson, 1992,

p. 67), and this clearly explains my distress at bidding adieu to the hallway display or to the last group of exchange students exiting the front doors of the school as they go off on their last Toronto excursion.

Perhaps I engaged in self-directed professional development because now, several months after the exchange, I find myself taking more responsibility for "blowing my own horn" to make coherent and public the ways in which I am developing as a professional. I am teaching other teachers about what excites me about student exchange programs. Through a literal "change of climate," an exchange provides "a climate of change" for both students and teachers. Through cultural confrontation, it is the ultimate integrated activity, which allows the interface between the personal and the professional for teachers and students in their holistic learning. My journal has made my own beliefs and implicit theories more explicit and visible for me. This reflection tool has contributed to my journey of ongoing development as a teacher. In the end, "it is in balancing the journey that the journal can be of greatest help" (Holly, 1989, p. 28).

ISSUES AND CONCERNS

One of the most common problems associated with journal writing (or any kind of writing, for that matter) is writer's block. Sometimes writer's block is related to fear of articulating certain thoughts, events, or remembrances or devaluing our experiences. Even if we are certain that no one else will see what we write, we can spend hours censoring prearticulated thoughts often to the point where the material we eventually allow ourselves to write is diluted beyond recognition. It is important to be reminded that you are writing for your eyes only and that honesty is an important precursor to real understanding. Dave Hunt (1987, pp. 82–83) has some helpful suggestions for overcoming "internal resistance" to examining your own thinking and practice. For overcoming internal resistance he suggests the following:

- Send your critic away.
- Don't worry about "going public"—write for yourself.
- Try to bring out what is, not what should be.
- Remember, self-knowledge is a first step toward change.
- But also remember, the decision to change is up to you.

Writer's block can also emanate from particular negative associations with conventional forms of journal writing (refer back to Margie's assessment of her resistances to journal writing). It may be helpful to experiment with different styles of writing and different writing media. Try, for example, removing the blocks by writing in nonconventional forms (such as in all lowercase letters, with no punctuation, in point form, without lifting your pen or pencil from the paper, using your nondominant hand, and without looking at your text on the monitor). Fluency also comes with practice. Just as in physical activity, sometimes a warmup exercise facilitates the writing process. For example, begin your journal writing session by making a simple list of things that recently happened. If you write at the end of the day recollect in writing everything you did from the time you woke up in the morning. You likely will find that, in the process of list making, you are drawn to one or two events that you will want to further explore. When that happens, the exercise has served its purpose. Let yourself go where your thoughts and fingers take you.

Finally, establish and enforce the one rule of journal writing—there are no rules!

Some people find it helpful when journal writing is interactive. If a dialogue journal format is used the writing process becomes the vehicle for extending the conversation to others about the perspectives you hold. The interactive component of the journal writing process comes about when you present your writing for another person or persons to read and respond. The interaction or dialogue that ensues is initiated by the intersection of *their* experiences with *yours* as they question, ponder, and comment on your narrative. In one sense such a close relationship with a reader is a risky business, but if you agree to a format, focus, or range of topics for discussion, and address issues of confidentiality and trust, you may be able to proceed in a very productive and agreeable fashion. The conditions or principles for sharing personal history writing we identified in the previous chapter apply here as well.

PARTING COMMENTS

We conclude with a comment from Anna that we encourage you to consider as you ponder the merits of journal keeping in your professional (and personal) life.

When NASA was recruiting teachers for the Space Shuttle Challenger in 1985, 11,000 teachers applied. Part of the application package was to write a proposal for a project to do in space. Christa McAuliffe, a high school history teacher from Concord, New Hampshire, was chosen to be the first private citizen in space because her project was very simple compared to many other proposals. The Public Relations Director was highly impressed by the clarity and simplicity of her rationale. She stated that she would keep a journal, because according to Christa, "much of American social history had been recorded thanks to personal diaries, mostly written by women" (television documentary on Christa McAuliffe aired on *Arts & Entertainment Biography,* September 23, 1994).

Christa's story underscored for me how something so simple can be so complex, and I was reminded of the fact that the simple things in life are often the most valuable. Like Christa McAuliffe's journal, a huge quantity of women's diaries, letters, journals, memoirs, and autobiographies written from the nineteenth century to the present have both created and recorded history. These records for future generations reveal the real stories of women and teachers as they simultaneously validate the experiences and transformations of those who are recording them.

RESEARCH ACTIVITIES

The following are topics or themes that might help you get started and continue with journal writing:

- instances in your classroom that you identify as "real" learning
- preconceptions or stereotypes that have been challenged or changed as a result of your experiences with students both inside and outside your classroom
- the most rewarding aspects of teaching; the most challenging
- your school as a workplace
- relationships with colleagues
- students with special needs
- your classroom and school and issues of gender, race, and class
- working with parents
- coping with stress
- highlights of the day, week, or term
- your professional development needs
- your disconnections in teaching: the things that cause you grief, the things you do not understand
- things about teaching that excite you
- tensions and excitements associated with beginnings and endings of professional work

Also return to the several groups of questions listed near the end of Chapter 2, Teaching as Autobiographical Inquiry, in the section entitled, Developing Questions about Teaching: Beginning Autobiographical (Reflexive) Inquiry. Any and all of these questions are appropriate areas of focus for journal writing.

RECOMMENDED READINGS

Fulwiler, T. (1987). *The journal book*. Portsmouth, NH: Boynton/Cook.

Gish, S. C. (1994). *"Mr. Gish, may I go to the bathroom?": My first year as a high school teacher*. Seattle: Peanut Butter Publishing.

Goldberg, N. (1986). *Writing down the bones*. Boston: Shambhala Press.

Holly, M. L. (1989). *Writing to grow: Keeping a personal-professional journal*. Portsmouth, NH: Heinemann.

Progoff, I. (1975). *At a journal workshop: The basic text and guide for using the Intensive Journal® process*. New York: Dialogue House Library.

Staton, J., Shuy, R. W., Peyton, J. K., & Reed, L. (1988). *Dialogue journal communication: Classroom, linguistic, social and cognitive views*. Norwood, NJ: Ablex Publishing.

5

RESEARCHING THE CREATIVE SELF THROUGH ARTISTIC EXPRESSION

with contibutions by
MARGIE BUTTIGNOL, CAROLYN JONGEWARD,
DEIRDRE SMITH, and SUZANNE THOMAS

In this chapter we explore ways of researching teaching through artistic, literary, and nontraditional forms of expression (with respect to academic and professional work). Our purpose is to encourage you to tap into your intuitive and creative dimensions so as to understand your teaching in a more holistic way. A point of clarification before we begin: This chapter is *not* intended only for those who see themselves as artists or "creative" in an artistic and aesthetic sense; our point is to urge all readers to gain insights into their practice through ways other than traditional linguistic and text-based forms of expression. Eisner's (1979) reminder, focused on teaching, is pertinent to our comments about research:

> *When [teaching] is sensitive, intelligent, and creative—those qualities that confer upon it the status of art—it should...not be regarded...as an expression of unfathomable talent or luck but as an example of humans exercising the highest levels of their intelligence. (p. 155)*

Although contemporary forms of inquiry such as those advocated in other chapters of this book can lead to great insights, even they are limited by the capabilities of traditional verbal language to communicate action and other nonverbal elements of practice.

The philosopher Michael Polanyi (1967) developed a whole treatise on what he called the tacit, or hidden, dimension of personal knowledge. His basic argument was that we know much more than we can say. (By extension, saying what we know or experience only provides readers or listeners with one dimension of that knowledge or experience.) Donald Schön (1983) extended the idea that we know more than we say to the realm of professional knowledge, arguing that experienced practitioners develop a tacit dimension of knowledge that is eloquently expressed through action but not necessarily easily articulated in words. We recall that when we, as classroom teachers, were asked to explicate a particular practice and its depth of professional meaning and pertinence to us, we were often unable to do so. And now when we ask others in the context of professional inservice education courses to do the same, we find that they, too, have the same kind of difficulty. Teachers very often find it difficult to adequately and accurately explain in words what they do in their day-to-day work; the language of action does not easily translate into words. So we are suggesting that rather than trying to find meaning through words, especially declarative prose, you explore alternative forms of inquiring and representing your teaching. For example, say we challenge you to explore your daily intuitions or expressions of intuition concerning your interactions with pupils: How do you describe what it is you do when you exercise or use intuition? How do you access your intuition? What is it?

Knowing, for example, the value that teachers place on intuition—in guiding all kinds of day-to-day responses in the classroom—our bet is that many teachers would automatically make an attempt to portray intuition in other than traditional descriptive text forms. Perhaps you would illustrate it with a gesture, or a sound (perhaps a musical one), or a sketch or drawing or some other two-dimensional art form. A photograph might capture the meaning and process of intuition for you, or a song or tune, or maybe a short movement, even some dance steps, a verse of your own doing, or a text of prose or poetry written by another. You might choose to make a collage or construct some object or create a mime. Perhaps you would use metaphor or simile. Our sense is that your responses would be as varied as there are numbers of teachers.

TEACHING AS CREATIVE EXPRESSION

The age-old debate about whether teaching is a science or an art will no doubt continue throughout and beyond our lifetimes, with either side gaining or losing ground depending on the nature of the current educational reform movements and theories of teacher development. For example, the humanistic reform movement of the late 1960s was more sympathetic toward the artistry of teaching whereas the reforms of the 1980s and 1990s, fueled by international economic competition and the purported potential of technology to revolutionize the world, nudge forward a more scientific orientation to learning and teaching. (Nevertheless, a recent newspaper article in Toronto's *Globe and Mail* written by a professor of education in Manitoba [Levin, 1997] was a reminder that the debates surrounding criticisms of schools and teachers within the United States in the mid-1950s were almost exactly the same as the debates that raged through Ontario during the provincewide teachers' walkout or strike in October and November 1997.) Debate among theorists, analysts, and policy makers continues outside schools while inside classrooms teachers continue to teach amid an array of complex and complicated constraints and contexts. As complexities in schools increase so do the difficulties associated with documentation and interpretation of school programs and teachers' practices.

Teachers bring to their students, classrooms, and schools a complex array of experiences, skills, habits, values, talents, perspectives, and interests. These elements find practical expression in response to the demands of classroom life and the interplay of students' interests and energies. In this way teaching is an act of personal history intersection—the personal history of teachers with the personal histories of students. Teaching is a complex, dynamic, and socially constructed activity, sometimes impulsive, not always logical, often unpredictable, frequently intuitive, and invariably difficult to describe, analyze, and interpret. As teachers and as people we know that the multifaceted demands and exigencies of teaching necessitate a total investment of the self—our scientific, moral, and aesthetic dimensions—into the broadly defined contexts of learning communities. In this way teaching is truly an autobiographical endeavor. To teach is to draw on our creative energies, to respond to situational exigencies with spontaneous acts of mindful and creative expression. For us, "good" teaching is a form of artistry; there is a seamless artfulness to good teaching. The "good" teacher expresses self through artful teaching practice.

Eisner (1979) asserts that teaching can be considered an art in at least four ways: as a form of artistic expression with aesthetic qualities; because of its spontaneous nature, which demands an element of creative responsiveness; because of its unpredictable quality, teaching cannot be dominated by prescriptions and routines but relies instead on innovation and improvisation; and, in the sense that, to some extent, the achievements or outcomes of teaching emerge through the process. Notions of process, then, are at the heart of our intentions for this chapter.

If we characterize teaching as a form of creative expression—characterized as multimodal, nonlinear, and multidimensional–then it makes sense to search for ways of understanding teaching that are also nonlinear, multimodal, and multidimensional. In one way we urge conceptual congruity and consistency between the focus of an inquiry and the processes used to accomplish that same inquiry. We acknowledge, however, that traditional, scientific research has given only a back seat to alternative approaches, especially since the middle of the twentieth century. The recent proliferation (over the last decade or so) of more qualitative examinations of teaching practice speaks to the great need for research approaches to represent a more holistic and integrated understanding of teaching from conceptualization through to articulation of findings. Our task in this chapter is to challenge the norm and encourage inquiry into teaching that is inherently messy, complex, and holistic; that is, authentic, meaningful, and driven by both teacher-generated theories and practices. First and foremost, then, researching teaching through forms of artistic expression, broadly defined, is an avenue for you to explore other than traditional ways of knowing and expressing. It is a way to tap into those nonlinear ways of knowing that likely have been forced into dormancy by the sheer weight of dominant forms of knowledge, inquiry, and expression. Although the scientific method has essentially devalued the place of the artistic in the inquiry process, we urge its inclusion in inquiries into creative practices such as teaching.

As we move around schools we are well aware that there are many teachers who engage in creative ways of exploring their classrooms and teaching practices. We also are aware that many of these teachers and their peers do not acknowledge the power, persuasion, appropriateness, or even presence of their artistic modes of inquiry. The teacher-authors in this chapter, to varying extents, have grappled with the notion of teaching-as-artistry/artistry-as-teaching. In their work, when a foregrounding of teaching or a teaching event occurs, it is responded to through artistic renderings. When the foregrounding of artistry occurs, it is articulated within a teaching event or teaching practice. The two are synergetic and symbiotic in their relationship. Through reflections on some of their dilemmas and examples of artistic renderings of their practice, Margie Buttignol, Carolyn Jongeward, Deirdre Smith, and Suzanne Thomas allow us to glimpse into processes important to them for fostering their particular alternative renderings of self.

Carolyn has worked for many years as a tapestry designer, weaver, teacher, and researcher. She teaches within community contexts, outdoors, and in a variety of institutional contexts. Carolyn is an avid journal keeper and also creates visual images and writes poetry as a means to accessing and expressing her intentions and feelings about her work. Deirdre is a highly experienced elementary school teacher and is currently a vice-principal in a Catholic elementary school. As part of her ongoing professional development she engages in what she calls "intuitive research." Suzanne, with long experience in the Canadian North as a social worker, teaches language arts and visual arts to junior high school students. Margie has already been introduced in Chapter 4.

For many of us, decades of socialization stressing application of "crippling rules" or negative attitudes about the artistic and creative process have effectively sealed us off from our creative selves and much of our human potential. The message that many of us have internalized is that we must choose from one side of the rational-creative dualism. The teacher-authors in this chapter openly acknowledge this. It seems that such an admission is an important first step in using artistic modes and forms to research and understand teaching. We therefore forthrightly address what might be referred to as a predisposition toward a dualism that impedes efforts to acknowledge, connect with, and effectively express other than rational and linear ways of thinking. Margie begins with a candid reflection on her struggle to make the connection between her teaching and her artistry.

From Dualism to Creative Holism

At some point early in my development I began to polarize art from science and scientists from artists. At one pole I saw scientists as rational and objective, concerned with the intellect and knowledge and the "truth." At the other pole I saw artists as irrational and subjective, and concerned with expressing emotions. I thought that knowledge was something "out there" that could only be expressed in words and numbers.

My dad thought artists were crazy but fun. My mom thought artists were interesting people who showed their work in galleries and museums. In my family artists were considered okay as long as the expression was just for a hobby. Among my childhood friends artists were considered flaky. My childhood God thought artists were blessed with genius; I thought that artists were always on the edge of insanity.

I went to school so that I would learn how to think; for me school had nothing to do with self-expression. I had no conception of personal expression of experience through dancing, drawing, music, or sculpture although I cherished all of those things. I determined that school and self-expression were antithetical. In grade 5 I was told by the teacher that I was being "just a little too creative" when I juxtaposed a man's face onto a cupid's body for the St. Valentine's Day card box. The teacher said that I was making fun of the principal. As punishment for my art I had to memorize a very long prayer for the next day.

As time went by I became a "withheld self" in the classroom. That is what I thought was supposed to happen at school. The values and beliefs that shaped my behavior, through often unspoken rewards and punishments, compelled the creative part of me to go into hiding. Outwardly, I became an obedient and attentive student. I stopped asking questions, taking risks, daydreaming, and expressing my uniqueness in school. I kept my hands folded on top of each new desk. Dry repetition, rigid routines, and conformity to rules took away my personal initiative, and along with that initiative went my creativity.

When I was a little girl I never played "teacher" and I never let anyone "play teacher" on me. In my mind "play" and "teacher" did not fit together. Twelve years ago I became a teacher. When I was in teacher "training" at the Faculty of Education, I sat at my desk, hands folded. "Strange that she's talking about creativity in a curriculum course," I perplexed as the professor talked about her creativity research with children. I wondered how she would find enough creative children in schools to study. I was even more confused when she handed me a pink questionnaire inquiring about *my* creativity. As a preservice teacher I needed to learn about "the curriculum," not creativity. I had come to believe that only very special people like Michelangelo and Mozart could be creative. In my mind, creativity and school were, together, an oxymoron.

I now know that to flourish in my work and in my life I need to use intuitive and artistic ways of knowing to complement the rational mode. Personal re-creation and transformation arise from this synthesis. Flowing from this, I have developed the conceptualization of "teacher as artist." My teaching practice *can* be my art. I wonder how to integrate artistry and rationality in my teaching and in my life, and why I have been afraid to use my creative abilities as a teacher.

I believe that the primary aim of education is to facilitate students in becoming authentic human beings. Education is to prepare students for the inevitable tension between inner and outer life; between their own central paradoxes of self-expression and conformity. The "I" needs to straddle the dialectic to achieve creative unity. Daily life is enveloped in paradox, yet schools have been unable to teach students about living and honoring its ways. Living with paradox is constantly adjusting to the dynamic balance *between* the polarities rather than aligning oneself with only one. Some of the everyday either/or dualisms that I have noticed include self/other; process/product; fantasy/fact; intuitive/rational; art/science; self-expression/social control; means/ends; discovery/discipline; existentialism/behaviorism. Why is it that in school we are forced to pick the "right" one, when we should be considering both at the same time?

Margie's poignant account is likely to resonate with many people. Images of teaching as an impersonal, technical, nonhumanistic, noncreative enterprise are deeply etched in our psyches by experiences in schools as students; depictions of teachers in the popular media, especially film, video, and television; and by traditional "training" models of teacher education offered in many teacher preparation programs. It is not easy to challenge and change firmly rooted conceptions about teaching and appropriate practice in schools or notions of the artistic and aesthetic. Yet, like Margie, we assert that to flourish in professional teaching and in personal life, it is necessary to fuse the technical-rational with the artistic elements of one's self and practice. Sadly, it has been artistic elements of research, practice, and self that have been at best devalued and at worst considered as fluff. In teaching, as in life, we strive for a holistic expression that honors all dimensions of our selves. To omit attention to the artistic and creative in practice, or inquiry for that matter, is to subscribe to incomplete conceptions of the self, a point we will not shy away from making again. Of course it also goes without saying that in our attention to holism we infer that the emotional and the spiritual, and other "unnamed qualities," are simply part and parcel of the whole in creative or artistic endeavors.

Suzanne also struggled initially to let go of her predisposition, or perhaps socialized tendencies, toward linear thought and representation. She describes how, with trust and persistence, the reflexive process took hold and allowed her to move into and connect with other realms of her being.

My journey began in an intellectual, philosophical realm manifested by abstract linear, logical questioning. As I entered the reflexive process and moved into a deeper examination of self, the intuitive, subjective realm took over. My instinctive response was to begin writing. The writing took shape in poetry form, and began to move, emerge, and flow naturally from within. Powerful images and symbols surged forth, demanding a release and form of expression. I found myself in a "no rest" state and experienced a change in energy pattern. A very positive force—creative tension. This movement toward self opened a passage for me to discover a concealed inner creativity that had been laid to rest. I abandoned questions regarding the duality of human nature and followed the natural, internal flow of my inquiry.

Whether it is through poetry, prose, movement, drama, mime, meditation, painting, drawing, sculpture, or any other nontraditional linguistic or nonlinguistic form, the important thing is to find a way or ways that will allow you to, as Suzanne says, follow the natural internal flow of your inquiry. In a sense, this is an essential element of researching through artistic expression. Intuition-guided inquiry is a concept not altogether well accepted in traditional modes of research. Here, we celebrate it.

Deirdre introduces the next section with an account of the many ways in which she connects with and finds expression for the teaching self that she needs to understand. As is evident from her description, Deirdre has developed an acute sense of the multiple modes of knowing that characterize her teaching and herself as teacher. She responds to her moods and modes with differently appropriate creative forms of researching and expression.

RESEARCHING AND REPRESENTING TEACHING THROUGH FIGURATIVE AND EXPRESSIVE FORMS

I write poetry about my teaching when I feel an immediate and strong need to record my experiences in this mode. I experiment with color and images when I feel an unrelenting voice urging me to engage with painting modes of artistic expression. I listen to music and dance when I feel a magnetic and spontaneous pull toward this mode of expression. I record, draw, and talk about my dream and meditative experiences as a result of an inner craving to both engage in and process these symbolic modes of knowledge. I create metaphors for my teaching, research, and self-expression. I read books to which I am intensely and immediately attracted. I write stories about my life when I experience a deep need to further understand and connect these narratives to my teaching. I record daily events on a regular basis. I collect these varied modes of knowing in my reflective journal, which serves as a "spiritual container" for all of these creative expressions. These entries help me to understand my teaching practice and enable me to continue to foster my own growth as a facilitator of children's learning and development.

My journal enables me to consciously reflect on my engagement within various creative or intuitive experiences. It is a written record that enables me to re-observe the processes I engage in when attempting to understand and develop particular aspects of my teaching self. I am more able to see the connections between my personal and professional life within this collective text of experience. My journal becomes a mirror for my teaching, my research, and my self. I am able to uncover themes, patterns, deeper meanings, and understandings about my development through this mirror of my practices. My journal also illustrates a heightening of my intuitive sense about the work of teaching. It seems that in exploring my own teaching, I am inadvertently increasing my intuitive abilities.

I construct numerous charts and images that present themselves to me through guided imagery meditation and dreamwork. Much of what I have discovered about myself has emerged through creative expression. I learn and express myself through visual, symbolic, and integrative language modes. To convey what I have come to know and understand through my affective domains lends itself more easily to the language of metaphor, image, and story.

Metaphors as Figurative Forms of Expression

We have worked extensively with both preservice and experienced teachers in facilitating their inquiries into teaching through the use of narrative images and metaphors. Figurative and metaphoric language is helpful both as a way of communicating about teaching and as a way of enhancing personal understanding of teaching. Such figurative and narrative language can also be artistically expressed, whether through two-dimensional artwork, for instance, or through word forms such as in poetry, fictional or nonfictional prose, or other narrative forms. The idea behind metaphorical expression is a relatively simple one.

In everyday life we use analogies and images to help us clarify ideas or make them more meaningful. We try to see one thing *as* another. The word *metaphor* is derived from the Greek "to carry across." Metaphors provide a way of carrying ideas and understandings from one context to another so that both the ideas and the new context become transformed in the process. When we apply this notion to teaching we have a way of understanding and representing teaching that is more personally meaningful and able to more adequately capture the qualitative dimension of practice. Personally generated metaphors of teaching give meaning to the abstract and elusive aspects of classroom practice; they are linguistic representations of mental images. They can capture and communicate the very essence of one's perspective. As vehicles of thinking, metaphors are coherent ways of succinctly organizing and representing thoughts about particular subject matters, activities, or theories. Such metaphors can be captured in words, movement, mime, drama, dance, artwork, or a host of other expressions.

For example, in an effort to understand how experienced teachers "just know" how to appropriately modify and adapt their teaching to individual students and situations, Ardra worked collaboratively with two experienced teachers in an inquiry into their practices. As any teacher knows (and consistent with Polanyi's notion of tacit knowledge—knowing more than can be said), it is not easy to explain the thinking and knowledge that is embedded in and expressed through practice. "I can just tell," "It just happens after so many years of doing it," and "I just know" are common responses from teachers to questions about *why* they do what they do. The phenomenon of knowing is elusive when pursued by unidimensional means; words can be a woefully inadequate way to capture the multidimensional nature of teaching. In their inquiry together, Ardra and the two teachers found metaphors to be powerful and meaningful media for communication and interpretation of practice. The two teachers generated metaphors of their practice that depicted their beliefs, values, attitudes, and goals—in short, their images of their teaching. The metaphors, as forms of figurative expression, helped the teachers and Ardra understand and talk about teaching in a way that more accurately took into account its complex and personal nature. To illustrate, one teacher used a family metaphor to describe her teaching and classroom: "My class is like a family that is united in warmth, but each person in the family is an individual and has his and her own personality and needs to be met inside the family."

When Ardra and this teacher talked about teaching using language associated with the teacher's metaphor, they were better able to apprehend and articulate the essence of the teacher's practice. The teacher spoke of the importance of the students having comfort and security in a supportive and happy environment, the emphasis she places on fostering acceptance, understanding, respect, responsibility, and independence, and of the importance of order, consistency, and cooperation in providing a stable and interactive "family" unit. She spoke of learning as a process of people working together and helping each other as in a family and of herself in the role of a parent.

Likewise, in his work in preservice teacher education Gary has encouraged prospective teachers to express their metaphorical understandings of schools or classrooms in two-dimensional depictions (mainly through drawing, painting, and collage on paper) as a way of accessing fundamental assumptions held about teaching. He often asked teachers to craft word metaphors as a more familiar precursor to expressing their experiential metaphors through art. The range of artwork produced by new teachers has been varied: from simple line drawings with stick figures and a straightforward articulation of symbols to very complex, layered two-dimensional pieces that exhibit considerable technical and artistic expertise with, say, lead and colored pencil, ink pen, crayon (of various kinds), paint, mixed media, or collage; from rapid, spontaneous renderings of experience (with the artwork completed within minutes) to belabored works revealing the joy and pain of experience, something that takes time to work through and articulate on paper. The point is not that the quality of art should match "gallery quality" work but that the spirit of the effort is authentically rooted in and reflects a particular experience. Given that one of our centrally held values as teachers and researchers rests in the "primacy of experience" we imagine that the range of artistic products will be considerable. And besides, the point is *not* to compare each with one another but to convey heartfelt, thoughtful, personal perspectives on the "professional" in relation to the "personal." We also imagine that each artwork will exhibit a particular integrity that lies in the intimate relation between the knower's experience and the form and scope of the artistic rendering.

Gary also has facilitated prospective and experienced teachers in the construction of three-dimensional objects or "models" that depict fundamental educational processes or perspectives. He has used constructions to depict pedagogy or fundamental assumptions about learning, for example. His typical challenge to new teachers includes: "Construct a three-dimensional object that illustrates your core philosophy about education or teaching," or "your expressed pedagogy," or "your expressed view of your relationship with students," or "your role in the classroom." This process, too, relied on the articulation of metaphor as a beginning point. Both of these metaphor-reliant processes have been challenging for new teachers and have been both freeing and enlightening for particular individuals. These kinds of processes invariably lead to the generation of a proliferation of individual and group metaphors for teaching and teachers' work. Perhaps one of their greatest values is connected to the relationship we have seen between the "professional" and the "personal" that has emerged especially out of spontaneous graphic renderings; such spontaneous images have opened the way for the revelation of highly emotive responses to professional work.

Some examples of teaching metaphors we have heard expressed in words and in various art forms include teacher as nurturer, police officer, professor, judge, waiter, tour guide, gardener, ringleader, builder, therapist, physician, and actor. These examples are all associated with roles of adults or occupations. Other examples might be couched in terms of a process, such as teaching as gardening, conducting, acting, helping, serving, guiding, nursing, fishing, coaching, traveling, farming, and knitting. The following language-based metaphor, generated by another teacher with whom we have worked, illustrates the potential of imagery to communicate the personal and aesthetic meaning of teaching.

Coming from a family of musicians, I like to think of teaching in the context of a musical setting. Specifically, I see myself as teacher taking on the role of conductor and the students each as a different instrument. Good instruments are expensive and very precious. The conductor realizes the value of his or her other charges and knows that with the right coaxing, the instruments can bring forth beautiful sounds. Each sound is beautiful, one being neither more nor less beautiful than another. When the instruments work together and are played properly, they produce a flowing melody, a result of each instrument's contribution. When the total sound lacks even one instrument, the absence does not go unnoticed. Although others may attempt to perform as a substitute, none can fully replace the missing one because it is unique unto itself. The conductor has an idea of what he or she wants the orchestra to sound like, and the sheet music provides some order. From there the conductor works with each instrument to ensure its preparedness and to develop the orchestral sound to its full potential, always mindful that each sound is different, bringing its special characteristics, which are vital to the fluidity of the performance.

Metaphors and images of teaching are vehicles for professional development when they are generated and examined for purposes of gaining insight into thinking and practice. Metaphors used in this way are quite different from those used in casual conversations and writing. The point of difference rests in the degree to which the concept is examined. For example, "teaching is nurturing" or "teaching is mothering" are commonly touted metaphoric notions—perhaps overused to the point of becoming stereotypes—and mostly associated with the work of teachers in lower elementary school. But the assumptions behind these concepts are rarely examined. Sometimes when we hear prospective teachers glibly voice these particular notions we immediately seek to question other elements associated with their commitment to teaching and becoming teachers. So, we ask, "Tell us what you mean when you say 'teaching is mothering.'…"

There are also great gulfs between the kinds of personal metaphors for teaching that we encourage teachers to think about and some of the public clichés that we often hear used by weary teachers, the press, politicians, and the public. For example, "teaching is a battle" and "schools are battlefields" are only acceptable concepts for those who believe that teachers work "in the trenches" or "on the front line" and that the role of teacher is to challenge, do battle with, or fight the norms of student behavior. Such conceptions set up confrontational, oppositional structures, rules, and processes that perpetuate destructive myths about children, teachers, and schools. What are the underlying assumptions about learning, discipline, school organization and structure, rules, and curriculum, for example, held by those who use military metaphors? If the work of guiding learning is a battle, what does that imply for the pedagogies employed? If notions of student discipline rest in the rules and rituals of the battlefield, what does that say about individuality and conformity to standards or rules, about concepts of self-governance and responsibility, and about values and practices associated with the development of caring and thoughtful relationships? If schools are conceptualized as battlefields, what does that say about matters of organization and arrangement of people, spaces, and times? If teachers and students strategize to outmaneuver one another, what does that say about teacher-student relationships? If teaching is no less than a war game, who wins and at what cost? Do schools represent "no man's land"? These and other kinds of clichéd metaphors—and their origins and the assumptions behind them—deserve thoughtful examination.

There are several ways to generate or discover existing metaphors or images of teaching. In the Research Activities section at the end of this chapter we offer some suggestions for using metaphors as a method of artistic inquiry and representation.

OTHER MODES OF INQUIRY AND REPRESENTATION

Keeping in mind that the primary purpose of using nontraditional forms of inquiry is to go beyond the limits set by traditional verbal and text-based means, we suggest a number of other modes of inquiry and representation: visual imagery, poetry or verse, short (or long) fictional accounts of teaching, readers theater, lyrical or instrumental composition, choreographed movements, and drama. Space does not permit us to elaborate on each of these here (perhaps that is the next book we write); however, we provide some suggestions and ideas for researching teaching through figurative and expressive forms in the section on Research Activities. As an example, Suzanne describes some of her work with students using media of poetry, music, and mask making. She follows this with a reflective account and illustration of how she used poetry to make sense of and represent her teaching.

I am led by internal questions and a new pathway begins to emerge. As a new member of the intermediate division [of my school], I observe that a growing number of students are removed from classrooms, sent to administration for disciplinary action, and expelled from school. It appears that this is becoming a perpetual movement. I believe that as teachers we are lacking a real connection with students and I question how we can tap into their inner strengths, resources, and creativity.

My reflexive inquiry continues to transform itself.
Transmuting its mold, shape, form,
    textures, patterns,
     and rhythms,
       resounding rhythms,

As I breathe life into it.
As it is filled with our breaths.

It becomes a journey that I share with my students,
a movement towards greater self-awareness
through the use of writings, symbols, and art forms.

The process of self-awareness becomes a movement of personal reflections through poetry. In preparation for mask paintings, the students and I begin to write about our thoughts, feelings, and emotions. Creating the setting and tone of our space becomes central through physical layout, music, quality of light, and nature of art medium. We make an initial connection with our emotions through an art exercise introduced by one of the students. Free-flowing body movements translate circular and oval motions to paper. We select feelings to be represented and become more in tune with our physical and emotional states. The atmosphere becomes peaceful, reflective, and contemplative. We wait until everyone is prepared for this quieting of the mind, lowering levels of stress, pressure, tension, and activity. We listen to Pachabel's Canon with reverberating ocean sounds and engage in writing as we become more in touch with ourselves. Our voices begin to echo and resonate through poems about self, interconnectedness with nature, cycles of life, death, and rebirth.

Cycle of Life
Throughout the stages of this journey, each transitional
movement reflects a moment of creation and birth.

As we give it life.
As it is born.

We have come into existence as in birth through
the discovery of the "child within."

The students tell me they are now ready to paint their masks.

I follow the child.

I follow the natural order of ideas that emerge from my inquiry, and
complete the process of internal gathering, external observations,
and data analysis.

I refine and re-create my teaching beliefs and practices.

To empower
to allow for empowerment
To communicate
to release thoughts, feelings, and emotions.
To awaken all senses
to plunge into a world of imagination.
To confirm self-expression.
to reveal visions and dreams.
To break through
obstacles of linear thinking.
To nourish
the intuitive, holistic way of knowing.
To stretch and extend realms of experience.
To create new worlds yet undiscovered.
To expand self-knowledge, awareness of self.
To flourish and move toward self-actualization.

To honor the child.

This reflective process has enabled me to
See through my heart
Hear through my eyes
Feel through my soul
All senses have become intensified
And are unified as one.

VISUAL REPRESENTATIONS
OF THE TEACHING SELF

"A picture is worth a thousand words," so the saying goes. Consider yourself a visual
artist for a moment, a person who works with the medium of paint on paper or canvas for the express purpose of conveying meanings or representations of emotions or
feelings, objects or concepts. Perhaps you also explore the meanings of social events

or conditions. Perhaps you critique or deconstruct social issues. And maybe you retreat from the city from time to time to gain inspiration. So, while traveling within a rural landscape, for example, you come upon a distant "natural" scene that triggers your artistic emotions. You decide to sit down and paint that which draws your attention. In the fashion of a realist (objectivist or representationalist) artist, and with a flick of your wrist, you use broad brush strokes to capture the essence of the scene framed by your painterly eye—considering matters of balance, forms, textures, colors, and hues. There are many ways and perspectives to view and represent the landscape that has taken your eye, and you have chosen one. In the sweeping strokes of color and texture layered upon the canvas you can either create loose representations or photographic, minutely detailed images. The first choice demands that you be artistically responsive to the totality of the viewed, experienced landscape, that you take in and express the panoramic scope of the scene before you; the second narrows your focus to specific elements within the landscape, perhaps a cliff, rocks that comprise the face of the cliff, a fissure within the cliff wall, or the agglomerate or grains and crystals that make up the rock. Or perhaps you focus on a copse of trees in the foreground, the form of trunk and the bark or leaves of a tree, the vein and structure of the leaves. Or the stream in the middle ground vies for your attention. Or is it the patterns of rocks and water flow, the pebbles in the stream below the surface, the gently flowing eddies that appear to be whisked away by the current that provide competing inspirations for your art? All these elements, and many more, are representative of the greater landscape; the closer you are to the objects of your representation the more detailed and complex they appear. The matter of form and complexity of representation, then, are issues at the fore of your thinking.

The scope of tasks for the eye, mind, and hand of the painter varies as you position yourself within the expansiveness of the terrain, as you locate yourself within a concept called landscape. What is it that you intuitively bring to bear on the task of imagining and representing the landscape? What is it that you know as an artist that allows you to make judgments about your choice of subject matter, your positioning within your surroundings, your particular gaze, your artistic process, your...? What is it that allows a viewer of your work to instantly recognize the art as yours (besides the way it is "stamped" with your physical signature)? So, why is the essence of your signature instantly recognizable? Imagine yourself being painted as a person within the expansive landscape. What would that be like?

So, try to shift your painterly eye to a different landscape now; imagine the power of an image produced if the same kind of attention and perspective you have just given to the natural landscape were given to either classroom landscapes or internal landscapes (or mindscapes) of students or teachers. Imagine the depth and texture of the image and the nature of a viewer's response. What can it communicate that words cannot? In the following account, Carolyn vividly illustrates this point. She provides a detailed description of the process of representation in which she engaged as artist-teacher-researcher. The narrative detail is intentional given the limitations of the printing process for this book. We would be better served by illustrating her process, but we cannot, given the predetermined form limitations of this publication. Carolyn endeavored to understand the learning and creative processes of adult students to whom she was teaching a course in "creativity." What is most significant in her account is her eventual surrendering to her artistic self and her artistry as a natural and sensible form of expression. In her account, Carolyn provides considerable detail of the artistic process, the thinking going on in her own mind as she sought artistic expression in the form of "portraits." After reading her account one cannot help but wonder whether the kind of insight she gained into her students and their learning could even have been possible through more traditional means.

While researching adult learning and creativity in one of the courses I teach, I had the idea to make a "visual portrait" for each of the student-participants. The process was significant for me, both as an innovative method for research interpretation and representation and also as a means to maintain my own connection with visual intuitive ways of knowing. What follows is an account of my process of making three of the six visual portraits. For each portrait an emergent process deepened my understanding of the students and increased my awareness of visual images as a way of making meaning. Throughout the process several questions were central to my thinking: What do I know of this person? How can I represent this individual's world? How can I make an image to reflect the integrity and complexity of this person? I continually sought ways to make an image that was resonant with each individual.

As I set out to understand students' perspectives through the words they used and the images they made, I entered a process that generated important insight. On one level I worked with materials, techniques, and elements of personal imagery that the students had used. In this sense I made "visual quotes" or references. On another level I found myself connected to feelings, ideas, and attitudes that seemed fundamental to an individual's distinctive creative process. I experienced this depth of connection as an affinity or empathy with another person's way of being.

While I was steeped in the details of each student's story my challenge was to capture in visual form the essence of their uniquely personal process. I looked for ways to integrate different impressions I had about their approaches to creativity and to convey these elements in a unified visual image. And behind this was my own creative exploration, in which I was extending myself beyond what I had previously done with visual art materials and what I had previously made as visual forms. Each portrait was an adventure but tied tightly to the person's world I was exploring.

Focusing on key components of Lillian's creative process, I decided right away to use oil pastels and make a mandala—a circular design containing concentric geometric forms and images and symbolizing wholeness. I had seen how Lillian frequently worked with oil pastels and circular forms. In particular, I knew the circular mandala would be a link with a "stone wheel" Lillian had made. With concentric circles of stones on leather and a fringe of colored embroidery threads, the stone wheel was deeply satisfying to Lillian. She felt successful in completing something that contained many personally meaningful ideas and feelings.

Lillian's experience of creative process was charged with both a sense of vital importance and fear. Her creativity was deeply rooted, and she continually searched for ways to create a unique aesthetic product that revealed her personal inner experience; however, her process was frequently blocked with self-criticism and fear of failure. In her visual portrait, I used black and a stylized spider web (both significant to Lillian) to represent dark fears she had about herself and what she was able to do creatively.

Blues and reds were her favorite colors, which she linked to her emotional nature and feminine sensitivity; however, an exercise done in class had a profound impact because she discovered she was able to open up to parts of herself that she habitually restricted. During a "forbidden colors" exercise, Lillian used yellow, orange, and green, colors she did not like and ordinarily never used. Later, reflecting on how these colors represented to her masculine qualities of self-assertion and intellect, Lillian realized she could begin to enjoy the new meanings and feelings engendered.

In making Lillian's visual portrait, I represented the strong contrasts of Lillian's feelings primarily by creating a dichotomy between the left and right parts of the image. For example, on the left I worked with her habitual colors, blues and reds. On the right, I made a plantlike form using her "forbidden colors," yellow, orange, and green, symbolizing the emergence of her direction of personal growth.

Nearing the completion of this portrait, I recognized a correspondence between how I was feeling and what Lillian had described of her creative process. Initially the image emerged readily and I was excited by what was taking place; however, as I arranged the finishing collage elements, I began to worry about how to do this well. I fussed at length as I was positioning and gluing thin straight and spiral black lines. I remembered how Lillian described becoming obsessed while making something. She always wanted so badly for a project to work out that she was not able to just do it without being afraid that it would not be good enough. As I finished this visual portrait, I found myself dedicating it to Lillian's continued effort to nourish her creative potential in the face of many difficulties and challenges.

Working with color and form to make the portraits, I sought connection with each student, and a meaningful way to represent their experience. Always seeking the best way to express relationships among complex ideas and feelings, I explored how to use color and form to capture what was most important. This often meant working and reworking the portrait until I felt it was right, that is, both true to the student and also unified in itself.

With Susan's portrait I jumped in at the beginning without clearly knowing what I was going to do. I began cutting out images from magazines that connected with Susan's personal imagery—flowers, whales, water, and cliffs. I played with assembling a collage, but left this idea one evening when I started afresh with a spontaneous line drawing. I recalled that Susan wanted to be able to spontaneously and directly create paintings through connecting with her inner experience. After making a large freely looping line I stood back to see what appeared. I was able to see relationships between shapes formed by the continuous line and certain ideas that were important to Susan. I knew I had something essential with which to work.

From this new beginning, I playfully used crayons and watercolors to create a profusion of flowers against a watery ground at the bottom of the emerging image. I wanted to convey Susan's free spirit and joyousness, echoing her own colorful, flower-filled paintings in which she embodied her exuberance for life.

An image of a mask, evident in my initial spontaneous line drawing, connected with a mask that Susan had made for her art project. She painted the mask with two distinct sides to represent her joyous nature and her deep feelings of sadness. I worked on the mask image in the portrait to create a bold symbol that reflected Susan's efforts to be honest and self-revealing in her art work.

Although a sense of vibrancy was evident in Susan's personality and approach to creativity, I also wanted to express a quality that was more subtle and less explicable. A gold arch over a dark blue-black space evolved as I searched for a way to express a sense of magic that Susan experiences while she paints—when something happens that she cannot understand; some inner idea becomes transformed into an image that emerges from a sequence of brush strokes on canvas. In my portrait of Susan's creative process the large golden arch also represents her awareness of a need and desire to connect with something larger than herself. The arch symbolizes a spiritual sense of connectedness that she looks for and sometimes finds in her work at the easel.

I worked many days on Susan's portrait, painting, changing colors, refining the image. I was guided by my intuition, a feeling for the emerging image, and a desire to develop a measure of "truthfulness" in what I conveyed. While working on the upper part of the image I was hesitant. I did not know what to do there and how to paint in the way I wanted to. I recognized a correspondence between the way I was working and how Susan talked about her creative process. She had described how she jumps in at the beginning of a painting and eventually finds herself in the difficult and frustrating position of not knowing what to do. She often has to backtrack to find a place where she can take off from again. In making her portrait, there were times when I had to backtrack and begin again more simply and directly, often eliminating parts of the work already begun.

When the portrait was almost complete I decided to do what Susan often does when she has difficulty with a painting. Unsure about the top area of the portrait, as Susan might have been, I asked for the views of two people I knew would give an honest response. After taking their impressions into account, I tried a new approach and found my way to complete the portrait.

Not knowing what to do can be both disturbing and exciting. Students experienced this in their own creative processes and so did I in making the visual portraits. Like my students I had to discover along the way how to do things and what I wanted to do. I had to find out how elements fit together into a meaningful whole. The outcome of the process could not be known in advance; instead I needed to find a way to proceed by engaging in the process, step by step. My challenge was to be true to the moment, searching for a correspondence between myself, the emergent image, and the person whose portrait I was making.

I started Bob's portrait on a large piece of paper, working spontaneously with oil pastels as if I were having a nonverbal conversation with him. After a while I lost track of who was "speaking" in the conversation. I remembered how much Bob enjoyed a "visual dialogue" exercise in class, which he compared to a "jazz conversation." For Bob, this was an experience of connecting deeply with another person, building a repartee, and wanting to make it last. I gathered images from magazines and photos I had taken from Bob's workshop at home. These included the chassis and tires of a car he was building; a clock face, symbolizing lack of time as his biggest obstacle; a wind surfer, his first major sculptural construction; glacier-covered mountains, the place he most felt at one with himself. I decided to cut the images into triangles and squares and arrange them in a geometric mosaic on top of, and showing through below, the colorful jazz conversation.

For Bob's portrait my guiding idea was the synthesis of a geometric pattern with a lively spontaneous visual image. This integration of order and randomness let me capture two distinctive yet complementary aspects that I saw in Bob, symbolizing the scope of his knowledge and openness. As an aerospace engineer, Bob knew about technical and mathematical aspects of creativity; however, his primary interest in taking my course was to explore spontaneous imagery and nontechnical aspects of creativity. Drawing from my knowledge of geometric patterns, I decided to use the semiregular space-filling pattern that Bob had used in a computer-generated design of thirteen close-packed spheres. I prepared a large number of blue-green triangles and squares to combine with the cut images from Bob's world of experience. I took time to find the best arrangement of these shapes against the background of yellows, reds, and oranges of the spontaneous visual dialogue drawing. Eventually I glued each piece in place, sometimes making changes as I proceeded. Near the top of the image I decided to omit several pieces of the pattern, breaking from the order and leaving more open space.

Along the way the portrait took on a life of its own and I followed an intuitive sense of what needed to be done. I remembered that Bob often used the phrase, "it is a world of its own" to describe his experience of the process by which something comes into being. Bob knew about the risks of creative process, that making a mistake near the end of a long process could mean having to do the whole thing over. I stopped work on the portrait before I risked ruining it. As a final touch I carefully positioned in the center of the portrait a copy of a personal mark Bob used to sign his writings. For him this symbol acknowledged fallibility and contained a sense of irony about the potential for destruction that lies within the passion of creativity. On completion I discovered a lively quality had emerged from the combination of playful randomness and orderly pattern. To me this fit with Bob's appreciation of chaos theory and the paradox of indeterminate determinacy.

I began making the visual portraits primarily in response to my own need to create imagery as a means to explore and represent a sense of wholeness for each student. By the end of the research process I positioned each portrait alongside a written student profile. Together the visual and verbal representations gave a complementary and more complete view of the students and their perspectives. The visual images provided a sense of connection that was very different from the written profiles; they each appreciated the portrait as a unity.

Each portrait was different in content, materials, and approach just as the lives and creative efforts of the students were highly individual. Creating each portrait brought me new challenges and insights but, most importantly, I felt I lived with the individuals' way of being and doing while I was engaged in creating their images. In the end, I created images that embodied my understanding of and feeling of connection with each person. The images allowed me to penetrate the students' symbolic world, a tacit level of representation of experience that underlies outward appearances and points of view. This was possible because I connected deeply with my own tacit experience—intuitions, thoughts, feelings that guided my process. In making each visual portrait I drew out meaningful connections and shaped these into a significant whole, giving an immediate visible form to the wholeness of each student's experience.

I recalled that at the beginning of the research I had a guiding image for what I was setting out to do. In this image I was traveling at night on a large sailboat across the sea. I was on night watch, looking for direction in the movement of wind and water and in the patterns of stars. Then, one day while canoeing I realized that my guiding image had changed. Rather than traveling on a large boat across a vast space at night, I saw myself in daylight, paddling a canoe across a lake. This new image of my research journey reflected a transformation in my perspective. Whereas before much was unknown, now I felt closer and familiar with all the details and facets of the research.

I decided to make a visual portrait of my research journey as a whole, and I chose a circular form to contain the different phases of the story. Working with color pencils, I began the image at the bottom and let it develop in a clockwise direction around the circle. I drew a sailboat against a night sky full of stars. In the darkness of the image, I positioned myself at the bow of the boat looking through a telescope into the distance. Beyond this section I worked on a circular area that I thought of as a "safe harbor." This space contained a web of interconnecting lines that represented relationships among everyone in the class. Above this I placed a rainbow of colors that expressed feelings of hope and possibility that arose from our shared experiences. Next I created a large spiral form to symbolize a lengthy period at the beginning of the research when I looked back through journals and reflected on life experiences in order to make explicit my values and assumptions. Next to the spiral I worked on a shape made up of many little steps and partitions. This section represented the detailed process of making distinctions and comparisons, coding and categorizing during data analysis.

As if moving from dark to light, the image continued to develop in relation to the second half of the research. At the top of the image of my journey I depicted the visual portraits as six differently colored, overlapping, curvilinear forms. Below these forms I drew a "scene" of forest and shoreline, water and canoeist. This represented my view of myself being close and responsive to the many facets of participants' stories while writing their profiles. In a space between the daylight scene above and night sky of the initial image, I worked on an "egg" form containing five symbols that I related to patterns of creative experience, the essence of my research interpretation. Next I created a central design that evoked a sense of opening toward further exploration and unknowns. Finally I worked around the perimeter of the circular mandala in a detailed pattern, creating a boundary to represent the completion of my research.

Carolyn's detailed account provides insights into her creative process as teacher-researcher. We highlight Carolyn's description for a number of reasons, but the prime one rests in the value of explicating the creative process in detail. Carolyn's description helps transcend the gap between image and thinking that is usually difficult for viewers of art to comprehend. Here we are restricted by not having her images on the printed page; nevertheless, her description has use, especially for those who think in imagery but do not formally translate that imagery into artwork. As she notes, the visual images she constructed of the students' creative processes also reflect elements of herself as teacher, researcher, and artist. This is an example of reflexive inquiry grounded in a narrative form. Self-knowledge emerged for Carolyn through a reflexive process of intensive observation and verbal and nonverbal dialogue with her students and with herself. In her account she writes of the connection she made with the students and how she came to understand them and their learning in a holistic way through the processes of inquiry and artistic representation. Central to Carolyn's process of learning about the students was her relationship with them. She would not have been able to engage in the kind of inquiry nor gain the kinds of insights she did without being in close relationship with the students and without seeing her teaching and their learning as a relational act and process. In this sense, Carolyn's account also illustrates a relational, holistic view of teaching, one characterized by dialogue, reflexivity, and unity. Yet, despite Carolyn's obvious "expertise" in artistic representation, she was working beyond her "most expert" mode, that of tapestry weaving. Carolyn's account also evidences a kind of risk taking in art making in which she and her students were willing to engage.

Researching teaching in nonlinear ways requires such a holistic view. As such, there is a close correspondence between the teaching-learning process and the way in which it is understood and represented.

Regardless of the choice of media—chalk; pastels; fingerpaint; acrylic; watercolor, or oil paint; felt-tip markers; colored pencils; paper; canvas; photographs; papier maché; found objects; and so on—the key in creating visual representations of teaching (as with other representations) is to strive for authenticity, meaningfulness, and holism. The idea is to get as close as possible to the focus of your inquiry and represent it in a way that seems most appropriate and meaningful to you and will most authentically capture and articulate what it is you are trying to understand and what it is you are trying to represent.

CREATIVITY AND TEACHER DEVELOPMENT

Teachers' professional growth is often cast in terms of a developmental stage theory-like progression of skills and practices. Evidence of this perspective is abundantly found, for example, in myriad professional development workshops and courses imposed on teachers by authorities in school boards and districts. Consistent with dominant perspectives on learning and evaluation of students, the ongoing learning and development of teachers is deemed by most "authorities" as something that is measurable, controlled, and standardized. Obviously, we are taking a position at the other end of a spectrum of scenarios intended to further professional growth through self-designed artistic means.

Our view of professional growth—teacher development—is this: By attending to and stimulating the creative potential of teachers, ourselves included, we can achieve (ongoing) professional development goals by alternative means. As teachers we are all highly educated about and refined in our observations of the world around us, of relationships, of processes, and of problems. We are not, however, formally "allowed to" or "given permission" (or have time and energy resources) to tap into those most undefinable elements of our experiences, perspectives, or interests. In these hidden or undefinable dimensions, though, lies a wealth of untapped knowledge and resources that can play an important role in our ongoing growth. If nothing else, we are encouraging teachers to expand the dimensions of their expressed thinking by acknowledging the complexity, depth, and breadth of their experience through artistic articulation. In another sense, we are encouraging teachers to access the breadth and depth of their intuitive knowledge for their own use in professional development. This is the same "store of wisdom and knowledge" that teachers access when making tough decisions, or decisions on the run, or in situations in which there are no obvious rational paths or consistent, coherent information to aid decision making.

In the following accounts first Deirdre and then Suzanne present compelling reflections on their processes of researching teaching through artistic modes of inquiry and representation. The power of the inquiry process and its impact on their development as persons and professionals, as artists and researchers is self-evident in their words.

The teaching and researching processes are creative acts of selfhood. I gained deeper understanding of my development as a teacher, learner, and researcher through imaginatively reflecting on my personal history, the substance of my teaching practice, and the teaching contexts in which I engage. My story of utilizing alternative, intuitive approaches to researching my teaching self are based on my views of teaching as a self-directed and intuitive process of ongoing transformation. Participating in an intuitively based self-inquiry provided me with the opportunity to explore and further understand the inner forces that drive, shape, and are integrated into my teaching and learning. These inner forces seek expression through creative, imaginative, and symbolic modes of knowing. Engagement with these forms of nonverbal communication enabled me to more fully understand intuitive teaching and researching practices.

Myths, stories, images, poetry, movement, music, dreams, and meditative experiences give appropriate expression to my nonverbal processes. I draw, dramatize, and put into written form dream experiences and meditative images. I am able then to more consciously and holistically study my inner processes as I reflect on my journal entries. I come to understand the hidden and symbolic meaning of the nonverbal modes of knowing that seem to significantly influence my teaching, learning, and researching.

Through researching meditation, visualization, dreamwork, drama, and creative expression become a regular part of my daily interactions with children and colleagues. I see the power of nonverbal modes of knowing. I consciously realize why I have engaged in such activities since I was a young child and how naturally I have integrated them into my teaching without deeply or consciously understanding the powerful impact of such processes on my teaching.

My intuitive research journey resembles the creative process. It is necessary to respect and trust the inner creative voice of the artist who dances, sings, paints, and sculpts to the tune of the creative energy within. Intuitive teaching and researching enable the teacher-researcher to let the inner light of artistry guide her way. It enables the teacher to more deeply appreciate the creative moments alongside the learner and invites the researcher to more deeply appreciate the creative moments alongside the teacher. These moments of artistic brilliance make an imprint on the soul. There is no better way to study the artistry of teaching than through artistic modes of knowing.

Suzanne once again reflects on the convergence of the teaching-learning process and the researching process. In so doing she illuminates the notion of teaching *as* inquiry—a process and an orientation that drives major elements of her teaching.

As a reflective practitioner I have gained a greater insight into and knowledge of my personal pedagogy and have expanded my visions of effective teaching practices. Through nontraditional methods the students and I have become self-researchers and each has participated in our individual reflexive inquiries. We have used vehicles such as imagery, poetry, mask making, and fingerpainting to explore our inner selves and to express our deeply held truths.

As this inquiry evolved it became an exploration of inner self and the primacy of emotions. Although the journey was traveled together, each of us followed a personal path. Along the way our separate paths merged as we developed a deep level of trust and found ways to share our self-discoveries.

The timing of the experience was of an essence for me in my first year of teaching both grade 8 and visual arts. It has reaffirmed my commitment to work with intermediate level students and to develop, for next year, an integrated language and visual arts curriculum. My principal hears the power of our voices and sees the expanse of our work. He supports me as an agent of change and hopes that I will work as a mentor with other intermediate teachers within our school.

It is clear from their words that Deirdre and Suzanne are highly committed both to their teaching and their professional development as teachers, and that they are passionate about their teaching and researching artistry. Indeed, Deirdre asserts that "there is no better way to study the artistry of teaching than through artistic modes of knowing." Although clearly we strongly advocate alternative ways of researching teaching, we suggest that what is most important is that teachers and other researchers engage in inquiry practices that are consistent with their perspectives, values, contexts, and interests. This of course requires an understanding of one's own views in relation to others'. It also requires a knowledge of the nuances of one's artistic, literary, and nonrational ways of expression. And it requires that teachers (and other researchers) engage in a multidirectional search for evidence and adopt an openness to surprise and a willingness to exclude no element of experience or activity as irrelevant to the search for understanding. For us, then, attention to process is paramount because it allows the work of researching to find its own creative form. In so doing we honor the place of the nontraditional and the artistic in all its forms in teacher development endeavors.

In one sense what we are saying—and it bears repeating now and again—is that researchers or those inquiring into practice must inherently remain true to themselves and to forms that resonate deeply within them so that acts of reflexive inquiry are and remain essentially congruent with who they are as teachers and researchers and as individual people. Who we are as individuals and who we are as teachers—or researchers—needs to make essential sense; the frameworks by which we organize our lives or the lenses through which we view life need to reflect the processes of inquiry that we use in our professional lives.

ISSUES AND CONCERNS

In the beginning of this section Margie continues to grapple aloud with some fundamental issues related to the forced dichotomy of artistry and rationality. She looks to
some of the formal educational research literature and to other educators for inspiration, support, and guidance as she struggles to paradoxically find reasons so she can
"allow" herself to be a teacher-artist. In one sense she is simply drawing on the work
of others to legitimate her processes in the eyes of peers who may harshly judge
"what it means to do educational research." On the other hand, the authors whom she
acknowledges provide her inspiration to forge ahead and be the "teacher as artist"—
and, we might add, the "researcher as artist"—that she desires to be. Margie has
moved on to other literature and other inspirational authors; meanwhile she continues molding the rational with the artistic and acknowledges the ongoing expansive
growth of her arts-based researching horizons.

How do I become a "teacher as artist"? I could not find any specific methods from
teachers, artists, and researchers who have gone before me, only little fragments
of information and advice. Grumet (1983) asserts "that it is an essential property
of art to challenge convention" (p. 32) and cautions me that "terrible vulnerability
accompanies aesthetic practice" (p. 37). May (1974) muses that I need "courage
to create." Grumet also recommends that teachers who see their teaching as art
find ways of "combining seniority with determination, with a reputation for eccen-
tricity, and a little larceny" (p. 37). Diamond (1995) cheers me on with "stop apol-
ogizing and be an apologist." Russell's (1995) words "I think you're onto
something" give me hope that I will find what I am looking for even though I am
unsure of how to recognize it. Barone (1983) warns that school personnel and
the public need to be sensitized to "the institutional constraints and other 'frame
factors' that discourage teachers from facilitating truly aesthetic and educational
experiences" (p. 26). Eisner (1983) describes the art of teaching as "precisely the
willingness and ability to create new forms of teaching—moves that were not part
of one's existing repertoire" (p. 11). Stenhouse's (1984) advice is that art is improved by critically exercising it. Rubin (1985) helps me to know what I need to do
to become "teacher as artist" and that involves nurturing my own natural teaching
style based on who I am as a person. Becoming the "teacher as artist" involves
listening to my own pulse and that of each student—being "mindful" (Langer,
1989; Miller, 1994). I still wonder how to integrate artistry and rationality.

The issue Margie raises represents the crux of our endeavor. Perhaps what is
most important is not how to integrate artistry and rationality per se but rather how to
be true, both in one's teaching and one's researching, to who we are as people, how
we experience the world, and how we know. We sense that for many of us the technical rationality paradigm that has dominated society's views of knowledge and research for so long has effectively cut us off from our other nonrational modes of
thought, knowing, and being. Our challenge is to reconnect with our other ways of
knowing and being. Each of the teachers represented in this book has sought to reclaim authentic, personal ways of knowing that resonate with their essential beings.

In the next segment Deirdre speaks of other kinds of dichotomies associated with the inquiry process. She acknowledges some of the difficulties and challenges associated with engaging in alternative, emergent, artistic, holistic, or intuitive forms of inquiry. Deirdre offers explanations and suggestions for ways of overcoming these challenges and connecting with one's creative energies and resources.

Researching the self through creative means requires the inquirer to respect and trust the intuitive process. This process emerges within its own time frame, which can be difficult for those of us used to establishing time lines or having our lives governed by time lines created by others. Externally imposed time frames serve to hinder and silence the creative process. Instead, the researcher must patiently wait and actively attend to natural moments of experience when a creative spark spontaneously ignites. As the creative energy builds and seeks expression, the researcher needs to physically, emotionally, cognitively, and spiritually respond. In essence, the researcher must surrender to the inner timeline of the creative process. This requires openness and belief in the process. Everything within our rational or Western world view suggests that such a perspective is irrational and ridiculous. This constant lack of support can be a great source of frustration for the researcher who is inquiring into an area of reality that is nonverbal, internal, and invisible.

The intuitive researcher must work diligently to continually access his or her own inner energy. The intuitive process unfolds in a personally meaningful manner. Along the research path the intuitive inquirer will experience exhilaration beyond words and deep levels of frustration; extreme joy and indescribable pain. Commitment levels will alter from being unwaveringly strong to being clouded with doubt. Moments of peaceful silence can change to periods of unrelenting noise. A person filled with a calm centeredness can change into an unfocused, scattered individual. The affirmation of being clearly understood can suddenly become lost within a fog of misunderstanding. An intense sense of knowing can be replaced with a feeling of confusion. The dichotomy of opposites presents a challenge to anyone embarking on an intuitive research journey.

PARTING COMMENTS

Suzanne provides a closing reflection on her experience of the reflexive inquiry process.

Through this reflexive inquiry we (the students and I) have discovered a pure raw creative energy at our core of being. We have been moved by the power of truthful self-expression. We experience euphoria as our senses become heightened, and this feeling is transmitted, flowing outward to others as they connect with the pulse of our energy sources.

An echoing resonance has emanated from teacher to learners. From within the circle, its ripples continue to undulate and extend out into the endless, far-reaching fathoms.

The intricate movements of this inquiry will never be re-created. As the students move on to "new beginnings," I will experience the pain of separation, and yet rejoice that for a time we have joined hands, touched hearts, and moved from the same impulse, as choreographers in this celebration, a dance of life together.

The principles that I have applied and the personal and professional growth that I have experienced will further enhance my pedagogy and will continue to inform my future directions as teacher, learner, and "eternal child."

RESEARCH ACTIVITIES

Activities and ideas for researching teaching through artistic (creative) forms are numerous and varied. The few we list here are intended only to spark your imagination, to encourage you to be playful and to tap into your creativity. The representational forms we suggest are not limited to inquiries focused on your self as teacher; the ideas related to form presented here are appropriate for all inquiry projects and foci. We urge you to think about these and other creative representational forms as you engage with inquiry ideas throughout the book.

• Building on the notion of metaphor as a way of articulating your image of teaching, we suggest the following activities:

  • Listen carefully the next time you and your colleagues engage in a conversation about teaching. Analyze the language you and your colleagues use. What metaphors or images are present in your conversation? What assumptions or messages underlie those images? Does the metaphorical language you use accurately depict your view of teaching? Are there other images and metaphors that would "fit" better?

  • Rent some of the many feature-length films available on video that depict teaching, teachers, and schools. (See Video List, pp. 360–361, in Knowles & Cole with Presswood's *Through Preservice Teachers' Eyes,* published in 1994, for a list of titles. More recent films can be accessed through video catalogues. In a chapter entitled "A Teacher Ain't Nothin' But a Hero: Teachers and Teaching in Film" in *Images of Schoolteachers in Twentieth-Century America,* edited by Joseph & Burnaford, also published in 1994, Ayers offers a critique of some well-known teacher films.) View them closely and analyze the ways in which teachers and teaching are portrayed. What facets of teaching are underrepresented? To what extent do media depictions of teaching reinforce culturally bound stereotypes of teaching? To what extent do the films accurately portray the profession?

  • Carry out a similar analysis of portrayals of teaching in other popular media such as cartoons, comic books, songs, and children's rhymes. For an excellent formal analysis of this kind we suggest you read *That's Funny, You Don't Look Like a Teacher,* by Sandra Weber and Claudia Mitchell, published in 1995 by Falmer Press.

  • Observe and listen carefully to children "playing school." What images of teaching and teachers do they depict in their language and dramatization?

• With a colleague or perhaps on your own engage in an imagery exercise in which you allow yourself to tap into each of your senses in order to generate sensual images of teaching. Find an appropriate way of recording your images and create a sensual portrayal of teaching—what it looks like, tastes like, sounds like, feels like, smells like.

• Generate images or metaphors of teaching through free association or sentence completion exercises such as, "Teaching is..."; or "My classroom is like...." Look over the images you generated and find one that seems to best characterize you and your teaching. Analyze the metaphor for its embedded meanings.

• Express your metaphor in two-dimensional depictions (through drawing, painting, or collage, for instance, on paper). Use some key words or concepts associated with the metaphor to initiate your artistic response, your first line to paper.

• Using found objects (ones you may find in the attic, for instance, or in the home workshop, or in the kitchen, or lying around the classroom or school) and common fixing materials to attach items, construct a three-dimensional object that illustrates your core philosophy about education or teaching. Similarly construct an object that represents your expressed pedagogy or your expressed view of your relationship with students. Your role in the classroom might also be a point of artistic representation.

• Following one of Deirdre's modes of inquiry, record your dreams in a "dream journal." (See Chapter 9 for Marina Quattrocchi's description of how she used dream journals with her students.) Depict them in any form—through narrative, poetry, visual images—and gather them over a period of time to create a dream portfolio. Review your portfolio for themes, patterns, and symbols and engage in a process of interpretation to explore connections with your teaching and your self.

• Some say that all (auto)biography is, in large part, fiction. The idea here is that all acts of memory are reconstructed interpretations highly influenced by our predisposition for selective attention and remembering. Take this notion to its extreme and write a fictional account related to teaching. Give yourself literary license and create characters (presumably teachers, students, and perhaps administrators and parents) and a setting (presumably a classroom and/or school or other educational context), and develop a plot (presumably related to teaching and schools). Clearly, your story will be influenced by your experiences and perspectives but let your imagination run free. You will be surprised at how much you will learn about yourself as you create and write about your fictional teacher.

• Try a variation on the above theme and, instead of writing a narrative, use a (screen) play format.

• Using any medium (watercolor, oil paint, fingerpaint, color pencils, crayon, chalk, paper, cloth, papier maché, for example) try to create some visual images related to teaching. They may be abstract images or highly representational; they may be highly sophisticated or first attempts at visual representation. The point is to try to allow yourself to tap into another way of knowing and representation in order to gain insights into your teaching through another dimension.

• Carry a camera with you for a period of time and snap photographs in the classroom and school (and perhaps elsewhere) in order to create a "photo essay" of teaching.

• Using photographs, images from magazines, printed words or captions, and the like create a collage, perhaps affixed to bristol board, that represents who you are as teacher.

• Use Mitchell and Weber's (1998) *Beyond Nostalgia: Reinventing Ourselves as Teachers* (particularly chapters entitled, "Picture This: Using School Photographs to Study Ourselves," Undressing and Redressing the Teacher's Body," and "Turning the Video-Camera on Ourselves") as a starting point for exploring elements of your experience.

RECOMMENDED READINGS

Diaz, A. (1992). *Freeing the creative spirit: Drawing on the power of art to tap the magic and wisdom within.* San Francisco: HarperCollins.

Egan, K. (1986). *Teaching as story telling.* London, ON: Althouse Press.

Fontana, D. (1993). *The secret language of symbols: A visual key to symbols and their meanings.* San Francisco: Chronicle Books.

Goldberger, P. (1983). *The intuitive edge: Understanding intuition and applying it in everyday life.* New York: Jeremy P. Tarcher/Perigree.

Hunt, D. E. (1987). *Beginning with ourselves.* Cambridge, MA/Toronto: Brookline Books/ OISE Press.

Jagla, V. M. (1994). *Teachers' everyday use of imagination and intuition: In pursuit of the elusive image.* Albany, NY: State University of New York Press.

Joseph, P. B., & Burnaford, G. E. (Eds.). (1994). *Images of schoolteachers in twentieth-century America: Paragons, polarities, complexities.* New York: St. Martin's Press.

Lakoff, G., & Johnson, M. (1980). *Metaphors we live by.* Chicago: University of Chicago Press.

Lee, J. (1994). *Writing from the body.* New York: St. Martin's Press.

Newman, J. M. (Ed.). (1993). *In our own words: Poems by teachers.* Halifax, NS: Braeside Books.

Oliver, M. (1994). *A poetry handbook: A prose guide to understanding and writing poetry.* New York: Harcourt Brace.

Solnicki, J. (1992). *The real me is gonna be a shock: A year in the life of a front-line teacher.* Toronto, ON: Lester Publishing.

PART **III**

RESEARCHING TEACHING THROUGH INQUIRY INTO ELEMENTS OF PRACTICE, RELATIONSHIPS, AND CONTEXTS

This introduction to Part III has a slightly different purpose than the brief introductions to Parts I and II. We take time here to describe elements of the inquiry process from developing an inquiry focus through to methods of inquiry, to information gathering, and to interpretation. The processes we articulate are foundational to all modes of inquiry contained in this book. We describe them here as we move from a more internal focusing on the self to inquiry that involves the gathering of more externally located information.

In Part II of the book we focused on researching teaching through various forms of inquiry into aspects of self as teacher. In the next two chapters, we shift our focus outward to expressions of practice and the contexts within which teaching and learning are situated. We continue with our assertions that teaching *is* inquiry, and understanding and improving teaching come about through ongoing reflexivity—that is, turning one's teaching and all that embodies it back on itself for examination and insight. Also, because we believe that teaching is an autobiographical project, inquiries into elements of practice and contexts are also situated in the personal. In other words, what goes on in your classroom is an expression of who you are, what you believe and value, and how you perceive and facilitate your relationships with students, peers, and parents. It is necessary to understand who you are as teacher. In so doing you are able to more fully understand how you respond to, interpret, interact with, and shape the contexts within which you express your teaching self. You also need to understand who you are as a teacher before you can satisfactorily form significant relationships with peers, parents, and students.

DEVELOPING A FOCUS

Where do I begin? How do I get started? The prospect of researching one's practice can be both exhilarating and overwhelming. Knowing that systematic study will result in enhanced understanding of *your* practice and therefore will be of significant benefit to *you* and your students can be a tremendous incentive. On the other hand, the plethora of possible topics or areas on which to focus can be intimidating. Stop and think for a moment about how many questions come to mind in the run of a normal teaching day as you interact with students, parents, administrators, colleagues (teaching and nonteaching staff), and curricula and as you plan and reflect on your teaching. Any one of these questions is likely an appropriate topic for research, although some more than others are probably more pressing, critical, or otherwise relevant for more in-depth exploration. It is difficult to know where and how to begin, especially if you think of teaching *as* inquiry and the classroom (or school) as a perpetual research site. Perhaps the first and most important thing to do is set aside the notion that you will ever be able to ask and answer all of your questions. And, as you know or will discover, research serves to raise more questions than provide answers. So, it is useful to think about inquiry as a habit of mind and practice rather than as an add-on to your already overfilled itinerary.

Having said this, we recognize that a habit develops from a starting point. There are various ways in which to begin. Some teachers come to the idea of researching their practice with a specific question in mind; most do not. Both for those with clear questions in mind and for those still developing ideas for possible areas of inquiry, we suggest keeping a journal or some other method of recording thoughts and questions that arise in the course of practice and which may eventually provide a focus for your inquiry. Once you make the commitment to thinking and acting in an inquiry mode you will be surprised at how many questions you generate. Not all or even many of these questions are likely to form the basis for focused exploration; however, we suggest you keep an ongoing record of such ideas and questions for a period of time. You will notice, when you look back over your notes, that some of the same questions, or variations on those questions, keep coming up over and over again. These are the questions that are likely to be of most immediate relevance to you and therefore worthy of exploration. Throughout the remainder of the book, the teacher-researchers comment on their respective processes for developing an inquiry focus.

METHODS OF REFLEXIVE INQUIRY INTO PRACTICE, RELATIONSHIPS, AND CONTEXTS

Reflexive inquiry into teaching practice, classrooms, and schools is a straightforward and commonsensical enterprise that requires only a genuine commitment to know and an openness to observe, listen, and seek understandings. The methods of inquiry are simple: looking; listening, asking questions, and listening some more; and collecting and reading artifacts or documents of various kinds. Although we more fully discuss and give examples of these methods in subsequent chapters, here we provide a brief introduction to ways of gathering "external" information.

Observation

Although in one sense you have been observing teaching, classrooms, and schools almost your entire life—first as a student, later perhaps as a parent, volunteer, or in some other nonprofessional capacity, and more recently as a teacher—how much do you really "see" of what goes on? How much time have you spent in actual focused and systematic observation of either your own practice (students in your classroom) or the teaching world around you? One of the most serious constraints to understanding and improving teaching and the work of schools as learning communities is the lack of time and opportunity to stand back and observe.

Teachers are typically lone adults working behind closed doors striving to meet the multiple and pressing demands of modern-day classrooms and schools. There is precious little time, opportunity, or encouragement for teachers to stop and look in a more than superficial way at what they and their students are doing and why. To engage in observation, therefore, requires some deliberative effort and either technical or collegial assistance. Although it is sometimes helpful to have a focus or specific purpose for systematic observation, general and relatively broad observations of classroom processes, student interaction, and behavior, your teaching or activities in the broader school context can be just as informative and often help to identify an area for more focused inquiry.

The key to learning from looking is detailed documentation. Because it is not possible in the midst of action to stop and make observation notes, assistance is often required when the inquiry is focused on one's own teaching. Video cameras make self-observation relatively easy although there is much in terms of subtle nuances that a video camera will miss simply because of its inability to provide a sense of the whole context of the teaching-learning situation. (In Chapter 6 Todd Chisholm recounts some of his experience with the use of video cameras to research teaching.) Often teachers solicit a colleague to act as an observer-recorder. In such cases it is important to clearly explain the purpose and focus of your inquiry and how the colleague can facilitate your research. Because you are mainly interested in having a *description* of your practice documented in print rather than your colleague's impression or interpretation of your practice, it is vital that you develop a recording system that will help *you* achieve your goal.

For example, say you are interested in learning more about the way in which you practice gender equity in the classroom. It is likely that you have very clear ideas about what you *think* you do, how you treat and interact with girls and boys; however, you may want to gather information about how your ideas and beliefs actually play out in your practice. To do so you might negotiate with a teacher-colleague to observe at least one and perhaps several periods of teaching and to record in detail the frequency, patterns, and nature of your interactions with male and female students. At the end of the designated observation period(s) your colleague would be able to present you with detailed observation data or descriptive notes, perhaps even frequency tallies if you requested that kind of information, that will enable you to examine that aspect of your teaching practice in light of your beliefs, values, and espoused theories about gender equity.

Sometimes, with the assistance of either a volunteer, teaching aide, or perhaps a preservice teacher working with you, it is possible to engage in some focused observations of students. In fact, cooperating teachers working with preservice teachers regularly comment that sharing teaching responsibilities affords them invaluable opportunities to sit back and observe students and to see them in a brighter, more revealing light.

Observing, like any other skill, improves with practice. Acuity will develop with regular focusing, adjustment, and readjustment of research lenses. The primary purpose of observation is to gather information that will provide insights into teaching, classrooms, and school life. There is no one right way. What is most important is making the commitment and finding ways that will provide the information you need to better understand your teaching. One of the major outcomes of observation, then, is the identification of questions or areas of focus for further clarification and inquiry. For example, you might be intrigued to know why students responded in a certain (perhaps unexpected) way to a series of discussion questions you posed. You may want to engage in more observation and perhaps involve students in a conversation about the matter.

Conversation

George Kelly, a renowned psychologist with a pragmatic approach to understanding human behavior, used to advocate that if you want to know something about people you should ask them. The same principle applies to understanding teaching. Listening to and talking with students, parents, colleagues, and others in a systematic and focused way can provide invaluable information. We use the word *conversation* rather than *interviewing* because it has a less formal connotation although, in principle, we are suggesting that you engage in conversations with people in much the same way other researchers would use interviewing as a research strategy. Accordingly, research conversations are focused on an area of inquiry and, as information-gathering devices, are documented in some way. Perhaps, by way of contrast though, they are not staged events or formal question-answer sessions; rather, they are more like informal conversations that take place in "natural" contexts.

Nevertheless, these research conversations can range from brief interactions during the normal course of activities to extended interviewlike sessions. Regardless, as researcher you will guide the conversation in the direction of your inquiry, having thought through and articulated a purpose for your inquiry and a set of questions to which you want answers. In a more structured conversation, it may be helpful to use a conversation guide—a list of predetermined questions, topics, or areas to be covered during the session. These same questions guide less-structured interactions but are likely to be less evident and more sporadic. Alternatively, such conversations might be set up by an agreement to keep focused on a particular issue with a provision for free-range commentary.

Depending on your inquiry, it may be appropriate to use either or both methods of gathering verbal data. For example, you might be interested in learning more about students' motivations to learn in classroom settings. In addition to gathering information through observation of students at work (or not) and students' written, verbal, and behavioral responses to particular activities or subject matter, you might engage individual and/or groups of students in conversations about their interests and learning preferences. One way of gathering information would be to involve students in group discussions focused on the topic. You or a helper would facilitate a discussion by asking a few predetermined questions and perhaps several clarifying questions. It is important with this research strategy to keep the discussion focused on the topic without dominating the conversation, much like journalists do in similar situations. The more informal processes associated with focus group inquiries are relevant here.

As with observation, the key to gathering information through conversation is documentation. Because it is essential to capture what was actually said and not just impressions of what was said, a reliable method of documenting verbal data or spoken narrative is necessary. The most effective method to use is an audiotape recorder. In a group discussion in particular it is impossible to attend to, take in, and accurately recall the substance and nuances of participants' responses and interactions. Recording the conversations on audiotape makes it possible, during the session, to more fully attend to the group. Replaying the conversation after the session is often like listening to it for the first time; it is amazing how much the human ear and brain can miss and how memory can distort. And such distortions can occur even over a very short period of time. What is also surprising to many teachers is the amount of "air time" actually given to students (or others involved in the conversation). Many beginning researchers discover, by listening to audiotaped conversations, that they allow far less opportunity for their "interviewees" to express themselves than they thought. It takes time, effort, and practice to, as a famous journalist once said, "ask a question and get out of the way."

Short conversations with individual students are likely to be much less structured; an audiotape recorder might seem out of place and perhaps impede conversation in these kinds of situations. Because of the brevity and uncomplicated nature of such conversations it is usually adequate to rely on one's own memory along with a commitment to note taking. As soon as possible following such a research conversation it is important to find a quiet place to "re-create" the conversation in as much detail as possible, again focusing at this point in the inquiry process on what was said and *not* impressions or interpretations. It is important to develop skills of making notes that, in their detail, will reflect the substance and feelings associated with those conversations.

As with observing, there is nothing complicated or mystical about listening, asking questions, and listening some more. Research conversations can be very narrowly focused or wide-ranging, involve as few as one person or as many as you deem necessary, and range from structured interviewlike sessions to very informal passing interchanges. With practice you will find that researching through conversation becomes a natural part of your professional practice.

Print and Nonprint Material

Documents or artifacts provide the third main kind of data or information in qualitative and reflexive research. Although not all methods of gathering information are necessarily used together in any one inquiry, print and nonprint material such as school and student records, tests, curriculum guidelines, policy statements, school newspapers, student work, journals, photographs, school projects, mementos, and the like often provide important additional insights into aspects of teaching and school life. In some ways the collection of artifactual data is similar to creating a portfolio of materials to document students' progress or your own career development. It is also similar to creating a photographic history of one's family, for example. Document collection may involve a bit of backtracking to gather materials created and used in the recent or more distant past or may involve systematic collection of current materials over a period of time.

Imagine, for example, that you are interested in understanding your teacher-colleagues' negative responses to a recent fund-raising proposal for the school. Because you are relatively new to the school, you are not familiar with its institutional history or the ongoing experiences of more established colleagues in the school. Nevertheless, the proposal sounds like a good idea to you. In addition to talking with and listening to people and observing both in the staff room and staff meetings, it might be helpful to gather some historical data related to fund-raising activities of the past. Staff-meeting agenda during the period of other fund-raising activities, financial statements, back issues of school newspapers in which the activities were reported on, and memoranda or correspondence on the topic might provide helpful insight into the issue. Clearly you would need the cooperation and assistance of the principal or other administrative and support staff, but that should not be a problem given your support for the fund-raising idea. Perhaps, also, the home and school association or other parent groups publish a newsletter; this, too, could be a useful source of information, as might a school yearbook. The documented information you gather will not only aid you in your understanding of the faculty's response but you may also be able to help identify certain issues and problems that lie at the root of the faculty's concerns, which in turn might provide the basis for more productive action.

In a classroom-related inquiry, you would likely collect a different array of print and nonprint material. For example, say you are interested in involving students more in the evaluation process and you want to include more than test scores in an assessment of their performance. Data, in addition to test scores, to help you with this inquiry might include regular self-assessments or reflections submitted by the students; examples of student work selected by them as evidence of their learning; photographs of school projects and work activities; and your regular anecdotal reflections or journal entries about students' work patterns, attitudes, and productivity. Taken together and collected over a period of time, these artifacts would provide a rich accumulation of information to help you assess the usefulness and effectiveness of the new evaluation strategies.

Print and nonprint material, like observational and verbal dialogue data, provide the requisite foundation for understanding the issue or topic of inquiry. In and of itself information is just that, as interesting as it may be. In the process of gathering information you will in effect begin a process of preliminary analysis; however, more complete answers to your research questions will come about through a systematic process of data analysis or interpretation.

MAKING SENSE OF INFORMATION GATHERED

Interpreting research data can be an overwhelming experience, not because it is so difficult but because there is usually so much information with which to work. The task is straightforward: to find out, from the information gathered, an answer or answers to your research question(s). Unlike statistical analysis, however, where data or coded data are entered into a computer database to be translated by a mathematical formula and analyzed by a computer program, the interpretation of qualitative data is more conceptually demanding of the researcher. And, also unlike statistical analysis, there is *no* set formula or prescription, only suggested guidelines. The analysis process we suggest here outlines basic steps that will help you make sense of the information gathered. It is important to follow these as *guidelines* only, adapting them to suit your preferences and the tone, intent, and scope of your research. Also note that although we lay out a step-by-step procedure, the interpretation process is nonlinear and relies much more on complex and intuitive judgments than is suggested by following a lock-step outline.

- Begin by reviewing your inquiry, the intention of your research, and your inquiry focus or research question. Keep these in mind as you proceed.
- Gather all information together and organize it to allow easy access and efficient handling.
- Read over all data to get an overall impression and to get a comprehensive sense of what you have to work with. Devise a system of note taking so that you can record thoughts and impressions as you interact with the information.
- Return to the beginning of the data and reread, more slowly and methodically this time. Highlight key words, phrases, and passages that stand out for some reason (this is where the intuitive judgment comes in). Identify and make note of patterns or themes that seem to emerge from the material. You may want to do a preliminary interpretation of each kind of data (observation notes, verbal data, and documents) separately and then consider the emergent themes together.
- On completion of this preliminary analysis, return to your notes and the highlighted passages in the data and list all of the identified themes or patterns.
- In a way that works best for you (on slips of paper, file cards, chart paper, or by computer) sort and cluster the themes in categorical or thematic groups. Also note anomalies or patterns that do not seem to fit with any others. These apparent contradictions are likely to prove valuable for further inquiry.
- Assign a new name to characterize each cluster of themes. The new characterization will represent all of the themes in each group in an overarching way.
- Revisit the material to check accuracy of new characterizations. Ask yourself, "Does this description or label reflect what is presented by the data?"
- Identify passages in the data that best exemplify the themes or patterns identified; you will likely use these to corroborate your interpretation or provide evidence for the articulation of your findings. Also, try to explain the inconsistencies you find. These often lead to further inquiry.
- In a way that is meaningful and useful to you, report on your findings. You may choose to write a brief summary in your journal or perhaps a more formal account of your inquiry to share with others; or you may choose to represent your work through various forms of artistic expression (see Chapter 5).

It can be quite exciting when similar patterns and messages emerge across data. The whole interpretive process can be exhilarating, kind of like panning for gold. You sift through heaps of sand and gravel to find the nuggets of knowledge that inspired the quest. Insights, understanding, and answers discerned through research have the potential to be highly provocative. Insights lead to more questions, which inspire further inquiry. And the spiral continues. And continues. The process becomes infused with other elements of your professional practice. Researching becomes an integral part of your teaching. As such, it can become quite seamless.

TEACHING AS INQUIRY

The methods and processes for inquiry that we have described here are really nothing more than an explication of what inquiring teachers do in the natural course of practice, albeit what we describe is more extensive and systematic. The inquiry process parallels the cycle of experiential learning familiar to many people (see Figure 1). Experience or practice provides the basis for reflection and analysis, which in turn informs future action. Thus the assertion that teaching *is* inquiry. Engaging in research on one's own teaching and being reflexive about one's professional practice are one and the same when the inquiry begins with and returns to the teaching self. In other words, because we assert that ongoing professional development is essentially a career-long autobiographical project, understanding teaching *must* be framed by one's own experiences, perspectives, values, and beliefs. Understandings of students, colleagues, parents, learning contexts, communities, and so on are filtered through our understanding of ourselves.

In the next two chapters we explore, in a more focused way, researching elements of practice and educational contexts. In Chapter 6 we look at classroom-based reflexive inquiry, including researching elements of practice and understanding students. In Chapter 7 we look beyond the classroom to ways and means of conducting school-based inquiry. In both chapters accounts by teacher-researchers provide the bases for our discussions.

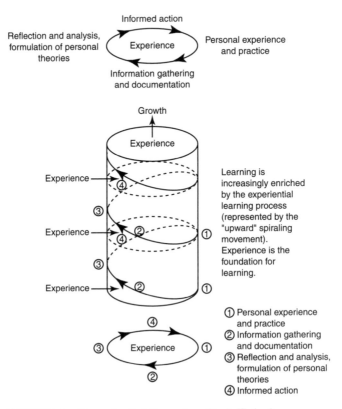

FIGURE 1   Experiential Learning Cycle/Spiral

Source: Adapted from Knowles and Cole with Presswood, 1994.

6

RESEARCHING PRACTICE AND STUDENTS' EXPERIENCES

with contributions by
TODD CHISHOLM and LYDIA LANZA

Teaching is, among other things, relational and practical. Understanding teaching requires an understanding not only of oneself as teacher but also of the relationships that define teaching life—relationships with students, colleagues, administrators, and parents—and the actual practices in which one engages in everyday classroom activity. In this chapter we focus on both the relational and the practical as we explore ways of understanding teaching through reflexive inquiry into students' experiences and elements of practice, the former of which receives very little attention in formal educational research, and the latter of which is the subject of most formal inquiries. We briefly elaborate.

It is ironic that in most educational research involving students the focus traditionally has been on their performance, achievement, motivation, cognitive or affective development, and so on. Very little attention has been paid to how students actually experience school, learning, and teachers. Despite their centrality in schools and classrooms, seldom have students themselves been asked about how *they* experience the educational process, schools, classrooms, and teachers. There are a number of possible explanations for the exclusion of students' voices in educational research, most of which are rooted in traditional notions of scientific inquiry. One argument is that involving students in research in other than passive ways would render the research far too subjective and therefore contaminate the results. Another view is that students are not capable of contributing ideas and perspectives that would be helpful to researchers and/ or teachers. Similarly, children have little voice in school, so why should school and educational research be any different? We adamantly oppose these and other similar viewpoints. Educators and other researchers have much to learn from students. As equal participants in the teaching-learning process, students can inform teachers in helpful and meaningful ways. As Lydia asserts later in this chapter, "Children are often heard in the classroom and the playground; yet, they are seldom listened to.... Educators and researchers must be willing to listen.... It is time to ask the experts."

Just as students' voices have been excluded from educational research, so have teachers'. The focus of most educational research has been on what teachers actually *do* in classrooms from a somewhat distanced perspective as they interact with children to facilitate their learning. Yet most of this research has been based on the assumption that teaching and learning are purely observable and measurable and can be understood in objective, distanced ways. It has only been in the last decade that teachers have had an active role in educational research and have been treated as other than mere research subjects. And it has been only very recently that teaching has been considered by researchers to be a complex, personal, contextual, and moral enterprise. In other words, very recent research on teaching has gone beyond surface-level understandings of observable behaviors to explore the assumptions, beliefs, values, intentions, and knowledge embedded in what teachers do. Even so, it still can be argued that most educational research is not perceived by teachers to be of significant benefit to them or their students. When we ask the question, "Who is the research for?" the answer must include, "For teachers and students." Hence the importance of practice-based, teacher-driven, reflexive research that involves students as a focus of inquiry into teaching and as partners in that inquiry (a concept we explore in greater depth in Chapter 9).

In the accounts that follow, Todd Chisholm and Lydia Lanza address these and other issues related to practice-based reflexive inquiry. They describe elements of their research process, explore some of the issues that emerged at various points in their inquiries, and reflect on what they learned from researching their teaching. Todd's reflections are based on his experiences as a grade 6 teacher. He has also taught senior kindergarten, where he "learned more about teaching in one year than in all previous years combined," grade 5, and grade 5/6; he is currently teaching grade 8. Lydia is an elementary education teacher. Because both Todd's and Lydia's accounts are based on their first experiences of systematic reflexive inquiry, we are privy to some of their initial anxieties, concerns, and uncertainties about being researchers, as well as the satisfaction and personal rewards they experienced once their concerns were allayed. We begin with an impassioned reflection by Lydia on the role of students in research on teaching.

UNDERSTANDING TEACHING THROUGH UNDERSTANDING STUDENTS' EXPERIENCES

All children who experience school can describe how they experience it, and we can learn from them. Children are at the forefront of the place we call school. Who better than they to tell us about the experience? Yet students voices are not being heard to the extent that they could or should be. Why is there such a scarcity of the children's point of view in educational research? One could suggest that conducting interviews and analyzing children's responses is excessively time consuming. Yet Cullingford (1987) states that it "is not so much due to the time it takes to interview and analyze the transcripts, but because teachers are naturally tempted to feel that education is a one-way process, from the stimulus to the response" (p. 333). Educators have tended to view themselves as imparters of knowledge. There is greater emphasis on being a teacher than on being a learner. The traditional role of the teacher has been to deliver the curriculum, test the children, and report whether or not they learned what was presented to them. Learning, in the traditional sense, has been the student's role in the school environment. As teachers begin to place themselves on the other side of the schoolroom desk and become learners themselves, they realize that the school experience is much more complex for both the children and themselves. Until this practice becomes more prevalent, however, children will remain the silent partners of the education system.

It is critical for teachers and researchers to recognize the richness and resourcefulness of children's perspectives. As Erickson (1992) observes, the absence of student experience from the current educational discourse limits the insight of both educators and students. When student voices go unheard, it means that teachers' skills of listening and learning from what is said are neither developed nor utilized.

According to Cullingford (1991), a second reason for the lack of inclusion of children's perspectives in educational research is that there is an unexamined assumption by researchers that children do not really know what they think, and they are so busy taking in information that their only value in research lies in measuring and evaluating what they produce. This suggests that if children's explanations of their experiences in school are not measurable, they are not valuable and cannot be seriously considered. They are not "reliable subjects."

As teachers we know that children's language represents the diversity and richness of school experience. The reality of the school experience cannot be understood in the sterility of the laboratory or under laboratorylike conditions. Viewing students as subjects renders their personal accounts of school experience empirically invalid. Their personal views of school experience, even after analysis, do not provide scientific rationalist models for educational practices. But interviewing children about their personal experiences cannot, and should not, be treated as scientific inquiry.

Neglecting or dismissing children's accounts of their school experiences suggests that children cannot be honest, direct, logical, clear, or articulate. Yet, those who have taken the time to interview children and truly listen to their responses understand that children are capable of and willing to discuss their school experiences in considerable depth and can provide valuable insights into school life, learning, and teaching. Researchers and educators must be willing to listen. It is time to ask the experts.

Later in the book we devote a chapter to researching teaching in collaboration with students as partners in inquiry. In this chapter our emphasis is on the importance of involving students as vital sources of information and insight about teaching, learning, and schooling.

It may take time to fully accept the idea that asking students for their viewpoints and otherwise involving them in classroom explorations constitutes "legitimate" research. It also will likely take time for you to see yourself as a researcher and what you do as "real" research. Reluctance to accept these notions is understandable. Years of socialization in the dominant scientific paradigm has instilled in many of us particular views of research as a scientifically controlled experiment often conducted under laboratory conditions and performed by university-based experts. While this interpretation is appropriate for research into the natural sciences, medicine, technology, engineering, and applied science, for example, it is an inappropriate construct for understanding human experience and behavior.

Those who oppose the use of traditional scientific methods for the study of education have fought hard to advance more naturalistic, contextual, and personal methods. It is not easy, however, to change long-held conceptions about what research is, who does it, and how. Kincheloe, commenting on how teacher-researchers tend to regard their inquiry work, observes, "Even after their involvement in educational action research, teachers are reluctant to say that they really did research; even if they admit to having done research they maintain that it was unscholarly or of low quality" (1991, p. 18).

We assert, however, that the kind of research promoted, described, and discussed in this book *is* real research. Moreover, it is useful, relevant, meaningful, and beneficial to those who conduct it and those who are influenced by it. How much more "real" could it be?

CONTESTING TRADITIONAL NOTIONS OF RESEARCH

Both Todd and Lydia struggled to let go of traditional notions of research. The decisions they made from the outset of their inquiries through to the point of analysis reflected this struggle as they thought about how to frame their questions and involve students in their research projects. They were conscious of being pulled in one direction by traditional *research* standards of "objectivity" and hypothesis testing, and in the other direction by their *teacher* standards of being responsive and sensitive to students and involving them as partners in the classroom. They worked through these dilemmas as they became more confident and clear about who they were as teacher-researchers. Lydia explains:

I wanted to explore the school experience through the eyes of the children. As I initially contemplated researching children's school experiences, I became aware that my study was developing into a confirmation of my own personal theories in an attempt to make conclusive statements about the nature of all children's experiences. Once I began to reflect on this, I realized that there is a tendency in traditional research to begin with the answer. If the answer is predetermined, it is merely a matter of finding studies that corroborate the given ideas for the research to be complete. This notion of beginning with the answer led me to question why I would conduct the study in the first place. I wanted to define, test, measure, and validate my views. I left little room for points of view. What I was planning did not seem like an inquiry. There was no mystery here. The study was not likely to generate substantial new insights; it was likely to be only safe and self-confirming. There seemed to be little if any redeeming value in reiterating that which was known. What became interesting, meaningful, and important was that which was *unknown.* In order to do significant research, I needed to begin with a question.

As I reflected on the concept of beginning with a question, the forthcoming research study, which I soon envisioned, became increasingly fascinating. I was about to be engaged in *exploration* as opposed to *reiteration.* My study of the school experience took on another dimension. The children were not only the focal points of my research but my primary source of information. I realized that if I wanted to know about *their* school experiences, I needed to ask them directly. I would not assume, but explore. They would no longer be the passive subjects of a study but the active force leading my inquiry.

Children display a sense of awe and wonder about the world around them. They inquire and explore in an attempt to explain the world in their own terms, and these insights are revealing and deserve to be taken seriously by knowing adults. I wanted to capture the sense of awe and wonder that was natural to them. I needed to explore the school experience with a sense of "not knowing." I needed to question the children, record their responses, and listen and reflect on what they said. Their responses reflected thought, insight, and originality.

Similarly, Todd's research focuses on children's actions. Todd describes how he thought through some of the dilemmas facing him with respect to how to proceed with his research.

I was faced with the dilemma of how to introduce the research project to the students. I wondered about how much to tell them and whether to inform them that I would be videotape recording some of our classes. I consulted several articles on qualitative research methodology and discovered that the authors stressed the importance of actively including participants in the kind of research I wanted to do. My principal, however, questioned how much would be gained by explaining all aspects of the project to the students. But, because I wanted the students to see the classroom as a partnership based on mutual trust and respect and because I wanted to promote a warm and inviting classroom environment, I came to the decision that I wanted them to know everything about the project.

I wondered whether the videotape recording would inhibit their natural participation in classroom discussions but then decided that telling them about the camera was the only logical choice. Not telling them would have made them passive subjects in the research project, which would have damaged the feeling of partnership that I had worked hard to foster in the classroom environment. In my research journal I noted that if I were doing this research according to more traditional (quantitative) research standards, I likely would not have told them about the camera. I would have wanted to control the variability in their behavior. I'm not sure how helpful that would have been.

I believe the eventual success of my inquiry was due to the honest feedback and active participation of the students in my class. Including them and keeping them informed about the project was essential for them to feel part of the process and also further promoted a warm and inviting learning environment.

In the following segment, Lydia engages in a similar problem-solving process as she debates and finally comes to terms with the kind of research she was embarking on and how she would conduct it.

It was critical for me to accept that my inquiry was not an attempt to make a sweeping generalization about the school experience for all children. Rather, it was a genuine attempt to listen to the voices of the grade 2 children in my school as they expressed their ideas and shared their experiences with me. The grade 2 children would be a vital and valuable resource. We had developed a good rapport over the past two years because I had been one of a team of teachers who worked with them in grade 1. And now we were together in grade 2. We would therefore be able to comfortably and confidently join together in discussion as a "circle of friends."

I was no longer concerned with the notion that research must be conducted through experiments, required strict controls, and must result in a conclusive statement or a general scientific truth. In contrast, my inquiry invited an open expression of the children's views with the hope that I would use these insights to inform my personal practice.

Nevertheless, involving students in research does raise several important issues that need to be addressed, particularly ethical issues associated with anonymity and confidentiality. We discuss some of these issues later in this chapter and again in Chapter 9. For now, suffice it to say that seeking the perspectives of students and respecting their participation in both the teaching-learning process and the researching process is worthwhile. We now turn to more practical aspects of the research endeavor as we consider ideas and issues associated with actually conducting practice-based inquiry.

FRAMING AND CONDUCTING FOCUSED REFLEXIVE INQUIRY INTO PRACTICE

Some teacher-researchers have found it beneficial to talk over potential research ideas with others—colleagues, friends, administrators, and other researchers. Although we recognize that the idea of teacher research, or reflexive practice, is not well supported (at least beyond the level of rhetoric) in most school contexts, many teachers have found it helpful to connect with other like-minded teachers. Such a support group might be building based, school or district based, or be made up of like-minded individuals from diverse contexts. As Todd states,

The guidance and suggestions provided by members of my research support group were an integral component of the research process. Not only did the support group encourage me to clearly articulate my ideas and further reflect on the process, but the different perspectives and viewpoints they provided were vital.

For some, inspiration and ideas for practice-based inquiry come from reading accounts written by other teacher-researchers or from more general exploration of educational literature. Todd recounts how he developed a focus for his first systematic inquiry into his practice. The process was not straightforward for him; however, he persisted until he was able to articulate an area of inquiry that "felt right."

Initially, I spent a great deal of time reflecting in my journal about possible areas of inquiry, and I explored ideas with my principal. I narrowed it down to three possibilities: an examination of my teaching to see if I was living up to my espoused philosophy, an examination of the relationship I had developed with my grade 6 students and the classroom climate I tried to create with them, and a study of my emerging role in the administration of the school. In the end, I chose none of these as an inquiry focus.

I found my inspiration in a journal article about a teacher who used questioning to control students' inappropriate behavior. The account related to a concern

I had when I questioned my own students during class discussions. I noticed that I tended to ask questions to ensure that students paid attention. I wondered whether my questioning to control their behavior might be at the expense of inhibiting their participation. This seemed like a fascinating research project and one that I could easily conduct as I read and discussed a novel with the class. This inquiry focus also seemed attractive because it was related to another area that I was interested in researching—how to encourage an inviting yet disciplined classroom environment. Although most of the time students in my class are aware of and sensitive to what counts as acceptable classroom behavior, it seemed worthwhile to better understand how I teach or promote that understanding and how students interpret the fine line between acceptable and unacceptable behavior.

Talking with other interested teachers, I was able to describe a focus of inquiry: whether or not my controlling or refocusing questions increased or decreased participation as I read to the class. More specifically, I wanted to examine to what extent I use questions that control or refocus student behavior and questions that extend or enrich discussions. I also was interested in the students' reactions to these two types of questions and whether my questioning takes away from their enjoyment of the novels I read to them.

Todd framed his inquiry in a way that was right for him. He chose to focus on his use of questioning and its role in establishing and maintaining classroom climate for reasons related to his teaching beliefs, values, and goals. He also focused on an immediate need he had—reading a novel to the class—making it the context for his inquiry work. Framing his inquiry in the way he did, he explicitly tied his research on his practice to who he is and wants to be as teacher. In other words, his inquiry was reflexive.

The key to developing and framing a focus for inquiry is its meaningfulness and appropriateness for facilitating your ongoing understanding of your teaching (and students' learning). There is no one right way or one right kind of question. Accordingly, there is no one right way to gather information in search of answers to your questions. Todd and Lydia chose very different information-gathering strategies. They made their decisions based on their research focus. Lydia chose to set up focus group discussions with groups of students. Todd elected to use a video camera to record himself and his students during several sessions in which he read aloud to the class. He later supplemented the observations with the use of a survey questionnaire to gather students' perspectives.

In the next two sections Lydia and Todd describe some of their procedures and some of the issues that arose during their inquiries. We do not include detailed explanations of other information-gathering strategies; rather, we focus on *their* reflections on and learnings from the process. For further discussion of information-gathering strategies, refer back to the introduction to Part III just prior to this chapter.

Learning from Interviewing

Lydia offers a candid account of how she prepared for and engaged in "interviews" with two groups of grade 2 students. As she indicates, her most important lessons about interviewing came from the children.

It was essential that the questions I developed accurately reflected my area of interest—children's experience of school. Although the questions were initially developed to address issues I wished to explore, they were open-ended in order to encourage discussion. The emergent nature of the questions encouraged the possibility that new insights, themes, or ideas that I may not have considered might surface. It was also critical that the language and/or wording of the questions was simple enough for the children to understand and comfortably respond to. For example, I asked

> What makes school a good place to be?
> What makes school not such a good place to be?
> What do you really like about your classroom?
> Describe a good teacher. What is she or he like?
> Describe a teacher that is not so good.
> Do you ever have your feelings hurt at school?

Having prepared the questions, I was ready to conduct the interviews, which took place over the course of two days. I met with each of two grade 2 classes separately for one-half hour. The questions I developed were used with both classes. I asked the children to seat themselves on the carpet in a circle formation and I sat in a chair at the top of the circle. In order to accurately capture the children's responses, I placed an audiotape recorder with a powerful multidirectional microphone nearby. Taperecording our discussion was essential so that I could actively participate. I needed to focus on what the children were saying so that I could encourage discussion and elaboration on their experiences. In order to be able to effectively probe their thoughts and ideas, it was essential that I concentrate on their words. This was my role in the circle of friends.

Children have a way of making you aware of the clarity with which you express yourself. Prior to asking the formal questions I had developed, we engaged in a brief discussion about the recording equipment and specifically the strength of the microphone. In my role as "imparter of knowledge," I matter of factly explained that when one uses a microphone such as the one we had, "It doesn't matter where you are, the microphone will pick up the sound." A little boy interjected with a straight face, "so, like if you're across the ocean?" My initial response was a smile, a little laugh, and a clarification. "Well no, not that far." They began to laugh but remained serious when I further explained that the microphone could pick up voices anywhere in the *room.* "Oh," they said.

Before we had formally begun, the children had taught me a critical first lesson about knowing your audience and the importance of effective communication. This preinterview event forced me to recognize that if I were to gather the information I desired, I would have to be clear in my presentation and open to their messages. I quickly learned to be careful and concise in what I asked and communicated. The children's powerful first message helped to define my role in the research process. I must see myself as the learner who is eager for their "expert" evaluation of the school experience as a whole. No longer could I see myself as the "great communicator"—the know-it-all. Our roles would be reversed. It was my turn to listen. This was exciting but not easy, interesting yet humbling. I was now depending on them. They did not disappoint me. Their simple explanations led to great insights into almost every aspect of the school experience. My hope and goal was to interact, not counteract or react. The truth of their answers must remain intact.

And so the inquiry began. The exploration soon led me to the realization that "great things come in small packages."

Learning from Videotaping

Using the video camera to record and examine my teaching practice helped me focus, reflect on, and analyze my teaching in a formalized manner that I had not previously done. Watching the videotape also allowed me to recognize some of the skills I used when I read aloud to the class, such as helping students to make connections between events or issues in the novel and their life experiences and helping them to consolidate major issues and events by summarizing with them at the end of each chapter.

Using a video camera as a means to observe the students and myself was invaluable. It allowed me to focus my attention on the novel and facilitate discussion without having to be cognizant of what every student was doing as I was reading. I did, however, have some concerns about using the videotape recorder as an observation tool. Aside from my concern about how the recorder would influence the students' behavior, I also worried about how *I* would respond to its presence. Indeed, though the students quickly forgot (or ignored the fact) that their actions were being recorded, I noticed that when I stopped reading to ask a question I felt very conscious of the recorder's presence. True to my suspicions, I found myself asking fewer controlling questions than I normally would and on the second day I actually turned the recorder off when I was about to give a lecture to two students about their behavior! When I thought about it, I realized that I was worried that the observation was in some way connected to an external evaluation of my teaching. I needed to remind myself why I was doing the research and whom I was doing the research for. Keeping this point in mind helped me to become less self-conscious of my own behavior.

Other technical aspects associated with the use of videorecording as an observation tool became apparent as I watched the images on the monitor. The audio portion of the tape was difficult to listen to because of environmental noise such as chairs scraping and people coughing. Also, the microphone was positioned so that my voice was loud and clear but the students' voices were almost inaudible. There were also problems with the angle and location of the lens. A wider angle lens would have been beneficial so that the whole class could have been captured on tape at one time. I positioned the camera at the back of the room. Although the students seemed less aware of it there, having it at the front of the room might have provided a clearer picture of the students' activities while I was reading the novel to them.

Todd raises several important issues related to using a video recorder as a research tool. Technical issues associated with the use of audio- and videorecording equipment emerged for both Todd and Lydia. There are advantages and disadvantages, problems and issues associated with the use of technical recording devices. It may be necessary to experiment and work through some of the technical problems as they arise. Preferably proficiency in their use would be achieved in advance. The point that Todd raises that merits further consideration is his tendency to be concerned about how he appeared on the videotape. While it is natural to want to show the best side of ourselves when our actions are being recorded, Todd's concern goes beyond natural human tendencies. His concern relates to the association he made between observation and evaluation. It is a common concern for teachers. Indeed, it is one of the largest obstacles teachers struggle to get past when they begin to engage in research on their own practice.

Norms and traditions governing teachers' work traditionally have not been based on notions of lifelong learning or self-directed professional development. These qualities typically are not fostered (although recently there is considerable rhetoric to suggest otherwise). Teachers are used to carrying out their work in the relative isolation of their classrooms and emphasis is placed on doing, not thinking about, practice. For the most part, the only time teachers are observed at work is for performance evaluation purposes, and often the focus is placed on what the teachers are doing wrong or the problems they are having in class. It is no wonder, then, that teachers spontaneously associate observation (even if they are observing themselves) with evaluation and have difficulty reframing that association. We raise this as a point to ponder both to affirm any similar concerns you might have about researching your teaching and to encourage you to acknowledge and then reconstruct your thinking on this matter.

THE EMERGENT NATURE OF REFLEXIVE INQUIRY

As we indicated earlier, research serves to raise more questions than provide answers. It is essential to be prepared for this phenomenon. Contrary to traditional scientific inquiry conducted under strictly controlled conditions and with emphasis on adherence to a priori design and analysis instrumentation, reflexive inquiry (and other forms of qualitative research) is based on principles of an emergent design. Reflexive inquiry is no less systematic than other forms of research; however, the key difference and hallmark of reflexive inquiry is flexibility. This essentially means that instead of having the research design carefully planned out in advance in minute detail with the intention of merely implementing or applying it to an inquiry focus, you will have a basic structure or plan to follow but must expect and be prepared to modify your plan as you proceed. This is another example of how researching is like teaching. It is not important that you implement the design to get results; it is important that you attend to the *process* of researching so that you learn from it. Depending on the questions and issues that emerge as you engage in inquiry, sometimes you might only slightly modify your initial plan; at other times you might dramatically change it. Trust the process and trust your own judgment as teacher and researcher. If the plan is not working, then change it—just as you would in teaching.

Another feature of reflexive inquiry is that, unlike traditional research, it is not a linear, sequential process; it is more spiral or cyclical (remember the experiential learning cycle depicted in Figure 1). Thus the research process requires ongoing reflection, analysis, and responsiveness. In the following segment, Todd describes how, during his inquiry, he modified his research design to reflect his learnings throughout the inquiry/learning process.

As my inquiry progressed and I reflected further on my research question, a different and more meaningful question began to surface. My rationale for asking controlling-type questions was to make sure that the students were focused and paying attention; however, as I explored this issue, I realized that I could not necessarily know by observing that students were in fact paying attention. Were the students who were making eye contact with me really paying attention? Were the ones fidgeting, drawing, or appearing inattentive actually so? I needed to further pursue my assumptions connected with these actions. The videotape would provide the necessary visual record, but I needed to gather information about the students' behavior during my reading and the class discussions following my reading. A member of my research support group cautioned me to be careful about taking recorded observations at face value. She proposed that I involve the students by asking them to explain their behavior. I developed a printed list of questions that included ones about the novel that would help me determine whether the students were in fact paying attention and questions about my questioning techniques and how the students saw themselves participating.

Lydia comments on the generative quality of reflexive inquiry.

At first, my concern was to get the answers to the questions I formulated. After all, this was research, and I had to ensure that I was going to be successful in my inquiry. I soon realized that providing the children with a chance to express their views *was* the answer to my questions. As I began to ask questions and the children began to answer, I suddenly realized that each question was many questions, and each answer gave many answers. The answers I was given often demonstrated greater insight and depth of understanding than I expected. The children surprised me with their ability to express their thoughts about teachers, the curriculum, fellow students, motivation, effective teaching practices, communication, teaching/learning styles, friendship, and other issues that arose during the interviews. When I later reflected more deeply and analyzed their responses I realized that more often than not they were intuitive, intelligent, thoughtful answers and then some. New, exciting, and surprising information illuminated related areas that I was not necessarily inquiring into. The answers were often related to issues that I was not specifically exploring at the time. I realized that this research was not the end but the beginning of many more similar inquiries.

LEARNING FROM RESEARCHING

We return to the question, "Who is the research for?" and we reiterate the response, "teachers and students." The broad intention of classroom-based reflexive inquiry is to further teacher-researchers' understanding of their practice. The research questions derive from curiosities and problems associated with practice and the understandings and insights gained through inquiry serve to inform subsequent practice. Learnings from reflexive inquiry are not generalizable in the traditional sense, nor are any principles or theories developed universal. Indeed, the personal, particularistic quality of reflexive inquiry is one of its most compelling features. Teachers who engage in research on their practice can be certain that what they learn will have direct and immediate relevance to who they are and what they do as educators. The key to learning from researching is to be honest with oneself and open to the surprises that inevitably emerge. Lydia illustrates these points as she reflects on some of what she learned about the process of researching.

In collecting, analyzing, and presenting children's views of their school experiences, I was able to enter their world for a brief time. Prior to engaging them in research, I felt that I had already entered their world, their experiences, and their feelings by virtue of being a teacher. Not true. The children responded to my questions in an honest, articulate manner. They addressed my areas of interest and expanded on them. My role as listener and learner in the circle of friends allowed me to enter their world as they experience it. In their roles as teachers, the children taught me important lessons. In order to be an effective teacher, you must first be an effective learner. In accepting my role as a learner, I needed to be a good listener. In order to truly learn from children, they must be given the opportunity to speak. In my evolving role as a researcher, reflective practitioner, and lifelong learner, I need to recognize that I do not have all the answers. Looking at the school experience through the children's eyes was an eye opener—a revelation. My focus became the process instead of the product.

It is the process of attempting to better understand and learn from a particular group of children at a particular moment in time that is universal. The findings may vary, but it is the *process* of understanding and learning about children in any given classroom that makes this sort of research so important for teachers. It is the process of listening to children speak and understanding their viewpoints that assist the practitioner with informing personal practice. What a teacher learns about his or her own class does not provide a blueprint for other teachers.

The dynamics of a classroom at any given point in time can be explored and researched, yet each year the environment and educators' responses to it change. In responding to a changing environment, educators are responding to their students' needs. Letting students voice those needs and views is the first step to better understanding each other's roles. Questioning and understanding the immediate circumstances of learning and teaching allow students and teachers to grow and change with the environment. A teacher's sense of wonder about what the students might reveal is essential to enriching the school experience for all involved.

Indeed, the power of reflexive inquiry is not in the research findings or outcomes but in the *process* of researching. As Todd points out, it is in the *process* of inquiry that researching and teaching merge. And, it is the *process* of inquiry that provides a context for ongoing, self-directed professional development.

Examining elements of my teaching was extremely rewarding. Although the results of my research were interesting, the discoveries I made during the process were even more meaningful and insightful. The research allowed me to formalize the experiential learning cycle that my practice (and students' learning) is based on and helped me to further develop my teaching skills.

ISSUES AND CONCERNS

Earlier in this chapter Todd and Lydia described some of the technical, procedural, and conceptual issues that they had to address in their respective research endeavors. Issues and concerns of various kinds emerge during the conduct of any inquiry and need to be acknowledged and dealt with. The kinds of issues that seem most critical relate to the ethical and political implications of engaging in practice-based research. All research activities demand a sensitivity to the ethical implications of actions. For example, if you maintain a personal journal or field notes about observations or conversations, it is important to keep them confidential (that is, safely stored) and to not use names or other identifying information that might have negative repercussions for those involved. And after analysis (that is, once you have used the information) it is important to destroy the notes, tapes, or other forms of information that have been gathered specifically for your inquiry purposes. Researching, like teaching, is a moral and ethical enterprise. Clearly, every effort must be made to respect those involved.

From a more legalistic standpoint, the protection of confidentiality of persons involved in your inquiries, especially students, is especially critical if you decide to informally or formally present your work in a public forum—in a presentation to colleagues or other educators or in some published form. It is wise to try to anticipate how you will use the findings of your research before you begin because most school boards or districts require completion of a formal ethical review process for research that will be made public in any way. For research involving students that is intended for public presentation, teachers are usually required to gain informed consent from parents or administrative consent from the principal or other representative authority of the school and district. It is understandable that protection of students' rights to privacy is a concern for those legally responsible for students' care and well-being while in school. And it is understandable that parents and others might be concerned about having students represented on videotape, for example. Even if researchers have the best of intentions, there are no guarantees about how actions depicted on video and taken out of context will be interpreted by other viewers. On the other hand, our view is that reflexive research, for which the goal is improved practice, is more like teaching, and a healthy questioning of the legal assumptions and normalized practices is appropriate. We raise these issues not to deter you from involving students in research but to encourage you to think through the long-range implications of the decisions you make with respect to research design and use.

Having said this, we assert that ethical and moral behavior cannot be mandated. We expect that you will engage in research relationships with students with the same kind of care, respect, and thoughtfulness that defines your teaching-learning relationships.

Earlier in the chapter we made the point that most schools are not outwardly supportive contexts for reflexive inquiry. We return to this issue here as it relates to the political implications of engaging in reflexive inquiry. We do so in order to acknowledge this reality and to encourage you to be mindful about some of the potential political implications of your research work. We also urge you to find ways of creating supportive and healthy professional contexts for yourself so that you can realize your research and professional development aspirations.

Neilsen (1994), in a collection of essays about teachers and teaching, poignantly illustrates the kind of unsupportive context to which we refer. She cites an experience, reported by a teacher-colleague, of an unsuccessful attempt to initiate professional conversations in her school staff room. Neilsen comments:

> *Teachers who bring their new ideas and practices to the staff room conver-*
> *sation threaten to stir up a carefully-cultivated atmosphere of boredom and*

faded ideals. The enthusiastic are called "keeners," the "resident expert,"
or "ambitious." To be an apprentice to life and learning again, to mix the
energy of a beginner with the wisdom of experience, can have the same ef-
fect on a staff as becoming a long distance runner in a community of couch
potatoes: it just makes everyone else look bad.

But a professional community that resists new ideas is often one in which
teachers feel besieged with responsibilities and frustrated in their attempts to
effect change. They are overworked and tired, and the friend they once
counted on for noon hour conversation has a newfound zest for teaching that
they can't seem to share.... Sometimes, as many teachers are learning, it's
just easier to go back to the classroom and close the door. (pp. 102–103)

We have read this excerpt to several teachers to gauge their response; the level of
resonance it has for many teachers is remarkable. Most who hear it are certain that
Neilsen is talking about their school, although some suggest that an addition of a few
names "stronger than 'keener'" would render the description more accurate.

Many teachers who engage in systematic inquiry into their practice and profession do so secretly behind the closed doors of their classrooms or away from their
places of work. We are reminded of a recent conversation with an experienced teacher
about a research project she was planning to undertake in her classroom. This teacher
had been actively engaged in research on her own practice for a couple of years and
the topic she was currently interested in exploring involved other teachers. "Great,"
one of us says, "you'll have an opportunity to work with other teachers in your
school." "Are you kidding?" the teacher exclaims in disbelief at the naiveté of the
statement, "No one in my school knows that I do this stuff. I'd be ostracized. If I want
to do this [study] I'll work with some of my teacher-friends from other schools."

Although it seems as if we are casting schools as professional development contexts in the worst possible light, we are mindful that this *is* an unfortunate reality.
Until the norms that define the teaching profession and teachers' work are fundamentally changed, however, we expect that teacher-researchers will remain a minority in most schools. It is important, therefore, for you to find ways of sustaining your
commitment to self-directed professional development, perhaps through contact
with other like-minded educators.

PARTING COMMENTS

We conclude this chapter with a reflection from Lydia.

A journey of a thousand miles begins with the first step. Until there is some attempt at action, there is no movement. At the beginning of my research journey, I
did not recognize that in order to understand the children, I needed to walk with
them and not ahead of them. My attempt at moving with the children through
their experiences began with the decision that I would be involved in research on
my own teaching. The moving force of the research was the children. As they
guided me through their experiences, I realized that they were leading me to the
destination I thought I had already reached. The grade 2 children were the ulti-

mate tour guides. Their descriptions and discussions of their school experiences were informative and enlightening. The key to tapping into their insights was giving them the opportunity to express their views. It seems so simple yet so far removed from what traditional research about children has allowed.

In the process of changing and challenging my assumptions about children, education, and research, I was able to venture into the children's school experience with a sense of wonder and curiosity that I had not experienced in the past. The children's perspectives on their experiences were personal and meaningful. They reminded me that I am their teacher for a brief moment in time; as they proceed through their school years, their needs and perspectives will change. I learned about their fears, joys, disappointments, and triumphs. I learned about when my role as an educator is central and when it is peripheral. I realized that we each have ideas about the school experience and what it entails. Our ideas differ at times. That is the point. In speaking with the children, I learned about what they were thinking and feeling. When the reality of what they said clashed with the assumptions that I made, I truly learned something.

RESEARCH ACTIVITIES

There is an infinite number of research topics and questions and numerous ways to frame and design inquiry projects. The activities we suggest here represent but a few examples of different kinds of practice-based reflexive inquiry. Together with the examples provided in the introduction to Part III and others in this section of the book, we hope they will provide some ideas and inspiration that will spark a long chain of lively investigations.

• Following along the lines of Lydia's research, engage students in conversations about their relationships with teachers. What are students' perceptions of teachers? What do they see as essential qualities in teachers for developing productive relationships with students? What are the ways that teachers who have good relationships with students act toward them? What are the ways in which teachers who do not have good relationships with students act toward them? Why do some teachers develop productive relationships with some students and not others? Do teachers have particular skills, attributes, or interests that suit them to work with particular students?

• For purposes of better understanding students' experiences of school, design a study that will allow you to experience a day in the life of a student. You may decide to focus on a particular student who seems to experience some kind of difficulty in school or you may want to see school through the eyes of a "typical" student. Negotiate with that student to spend time with her or him (perhaps in your spare periods, lunchtime, or during after-school activities, or perhaps you can negotiate with another teacher or principal for some research time). "Shadow" the student through his or her normal activities. Be a keen observer and respectful listener. Ask questions to elicit information about the student's experience of school.

• Keep a journal or other form of record about the highs and lows, ups and downs, rewards and frustrations of teaching. Over the course of several weeks, jot down activities, events, or interactions that prompted notable responses. Provide detailed descriptions of your feelings at those times. At the end of several weeks look back over your entries and analyze them following the guidelines suggested in the introduction to Part III. What patterns do you see? Are the patterns circumstantial, contextual, or cyclical? What sense can you make of them? How does this information help you understand yourself and your teaching? What strategies might you develop to help you sustain the highs and get you through the low periods?

• Use an audiotape recorder to record an extended period of interaction with a small or large group of students. Transcribe the recorded lesson or discussion exactly as it appears on tape. Carefully read through the transcript and make note of incidents, behaviors, and speech patterns that stand out for you. These notations could inspire any number of subsequent inquiries into aspects of your teaching.

• Return to the groups of questions we presented in Chapter 2 in the section entitled Developing Questions about Teaching: Beginning Autobiographical (Reflexive) Inquiry. These questions could form the basis of any number of inquiry projects. Here we repeat two of the groups of questions that seem most relevant to the focus of this chapter:

• Who are my students? How do I know them as learners? How do *their* socialized preferences for learning influence my professional practice? How do I understand students' learning needs, aspirations, and goals? What are my needs as a teacher (of learners)? How do I (or do I) meet my own learning needs? How are my professional development needs understood by my peers and others with whom I work?

• What do I *really* teach (what characterizes my professional work with students)? *How* do I teach (what are the forms, patterns, and rhythms of my teaching)? What characterizes my professional work with colleagues? How do others view my teaching? What teaching methods are most appropriate for my students and for me? What are my professional aspirations? How do I (or do I) articulate my professional development needs to close peers? To administrators?

RECOMMENDED READINGS

Bissex, G. L., & Bullock, R. H. (1987). *Seeing for ourselves.* Portsmouth, NH: Heinemann.

Burnaford, G., Fischer, J., & Hobson, D. (Eds.). (1996). *Teachers doing research.* Mahwah, NJ: Lawrence Erlbaum Associates.

Cochran-Smith, M., & Lytle, S. L. (1993). *Inside/outside: Teacher research and knowledge.* New York: Teachers College Press.

Goswami, D., & Stillman, P. R. (1987). *Reclaiming the classroom.* Upper Montclair, NJ: Boynton Cook.

Halsall, N. D., & Hossack, L. A. (Eds.). (1996). *Act reflect revise...revitalize.* Mississauga, Ontario: Ontario Public School Teachers' Federation.

Hubbard, R., & Power, B. M. (1993). *The art of classroom inquiry: A handbook for teacher researchers.* Portsmouth, NH: Heinemann.

Jones, G. (1991). *Crocus Hill notebook.* London, ON: Althouse Press.

Winter, R. (1989). *Learning from experience: Principles and practices in action research.* London: The Falmer Press.

7

RESEARCHING SCHOOLS

with contributions by
ROGER FIELD and FRAN SQUIRE

Teachers know that being a teacher involves much more than teaching and facilitating learning within classroom contexts. The roles and personae associated with being a teacher are complex and multifaceted. Teachers' work is defined within a social context; teachers' work is also a personally defined practice. Understanding teaching in a comprehensive way therefore demands an understanding not only of the person the teacher is, the practices she or he expresses, and the way she or he relates with students. It also requires an intimate understanding of both the broader and particular contexts within which all those other dimensions are situated and find expression. Indeed, the notion of context is central to elaborating on and understanding the multifaceted roles and practices of teachers. Religious, historical, political, and cultural influences provide just some of the contexts for the location of teachers' work. In this chapter we focus on researching schools as an important part of understanding teaching and teacher development. Inquiry into and making sense of the complex contexts within which we work as teachers is a meaningful engagement because it helps to explain or give reason to how we experience much of our work.

Anyone who has been inside even two schools knows that even though they may be similar in many overt ways, schools differ markedly in the way they "feel." So, although there is a degree of universality associated with working in schools and being a teacher—say, in Canada, or New Zealand, or Brazil, or Finland, or South Africa, or Cambodia, or Papua New Guinea—there are marked differences in the manner in which teachers' work is defined and takes place. These differences can be explained by the markedly different milieu associated with each location. By milieu we mean the broadest interpretation of locational context. At the school level it includes the people, the curriculum, the materials at hand, and the community. For the purposes of this chapter there are three levels of context that play out in the way schools feel. Ontario schools, for example, have contextually based elements that link them together;

likewise Quebec schools, Nova Scotia schools, Michigan schools, or California schools. These context-specific influences are connected to particular mandated curricula; teachers' working conditions; regional demographics; social conditions; fiscal resources; parental attitudes and involvement; and of course the particular political, religious, educational, and social histories associated with a region, a province, a state, or a nation. Another expression of context occurs at the local level.

The local community in which a school is located has a particular interpretation of the more pervasive, broader contextual influences, and these play out in response to the interplay between various social, status, and economic groupings of families and their connected demographics. The various ethnic and cultural groups within a community, corporate and business influences, the particular energies of parents, not to mention local politics all influence just how schools are defined and express the learnings of students and the work of teachers in relation to the community. The third level of context is defined by the climate or tone of the school. This level of context is a complex interplay of all of the various contextually based influences and the psychosocial and micropolitical characteristics and patterns of interaction evidenced between professional educators, parents, community members, and students.

The ambiance, tone, culture, or climate of schools has been a topic of interest over the past several years for educational researchers and educators who seek to understand the social organization of schools and the influence of school context or culture on teacher development, student learning, and school improvement. As Rosenholtz (1989) notes, in an analysis of seventy-eight elementary schools in eight school districts of one southern state of the United States, the manner in which teaching is defined, performed, and changes is inextricably linked to the social organization in which it occurs. Similarly, Johnson (1990), working with 115 teachers in one eastern state, points out that teachers' perceptions and experience of the school as workplace— the physical features, organizational structures, socio-political aspects, economic conditions, and psychological dimensions—strongly influence their career choices and attitudes toward work. Nevertheless, even with studies such as these, the depth of research-informed understandings about the complex interplay between schools and school climates and society, or between schools and school cultures and local/regional contexts, is quite shallow. Much that teachers know about these topics comes from intuitive articulations of experience. Much that researchers know come from case studies (e.g., McLaren, 1986; Nias, Southworth, & Yeomans, 1989; Peshkin, 1991).

Researchers also have developed typologies to characterize some of the differences among school cultures. Most of these differences have to do with understanding the ways schools work. For example, Rosenholtz (1989) differentiates between "high consensus" or "collaborative" schools, in which teachers and principal work together collegially and in community toward a set of commonly defined and shared goals, and "low consensus" or "isolated" schools, in which teachers carry out their work according to individually defined goals and with no common purpose and generally experience their work with a sense of frustration and waning commitment. Hargreaves (1993) describes four different kinds of school culture; each influences, in a different way, patterns of workplace interaction. "Fragmented individualism" is the predominant school culture characterized by norms of privacy, isolationism, conservatism, and a general lack of enthusiasm for substantive growth and change. In schools characterized by a "balkanized" culture teachers separate themselves into sometimes competing groups or cliques defined and identified by certain attitudes or perspectives, subject matter orientations, professional goals, or personal interests. In schools in which a "collaborative" culture prevails there is a broad agreement on educational values and shared commitment to the attainment of mutually agreed on goals, and teachers and staff work together and interact with a natural warmth and sincerity and with the support and encouragement of the school administration. "Contrived collegiality" defines a recently adopted pattern of interaction. Teachers in schools characterized by this type of culture work together largely by a fiat of administration and usually without the will and commitment to do so.

Characterizations such as these have a high level of resonance for most school people; they can easily identify "their" school as typified by one of the categories Rosenholtz, Hargreaves, and others have suggested, and they usually can offer illustrations to support their analyses. In other words, the idea that schools have their own persona that powerfully influences what does or does not, can or cannot, happen is well accepted. This, we suggest, is a useful notion for teachers to consider as a basis for beginning inquiries into aspects of their own schools. And, when a school-focused inquiry explores elements of the relationship between the school context and a teacher's individual practice and values, the inquiry becomes reflexive. That is, reflexive inquiry is a spiraling and cyclical process that begins with and returns to the self—the experiences and the meanings and assumptions derived from experience—and explores the connections between, for instance, elements of experience and context, and in turn elements of experience and relationships within that context, and in relation to matters of professional development and future or possible action as influenced and informed by the inquiry process.

Understanding the contexts within which we work—the norms and implicit rule systems; the values that guide activities and actions; patterns of behavior and interpersonal relationships; as well as socioeconomic, cultural, racial, and political influences, for example—can provide insights into how we experience our work. Knowledge of this kind might, for example, inform teachers' decision making about the appropriateness of certain kinds of contexts (be they classroom, school, or community) for the enactment of their beliefs, values, and goals.

WAYS OF RESEARCHING SCHOOLS

The methods of external data gathering, such as interview (conversation), observation, and document collection as described in the introduction to Part III represent, in a broad sense, some of the many and varied ways of researching school contexts. There are of course variations on these methodological themes; the strategies can be variously interpreted and employed. For example, in this chapter Roger Field primarily uses observation as a way of engaging in ongoing inquiry into the school where he works. Fran Squire employs the methods of interviewing, observation, and document collection. Both of them, however, use a narrative mode for articulating their inquiries: Roger tells stories of his school through excerpts from his journal; Fran uses stories as metaphoric symbols to communicate the complexity of her school context. Methodologically, the accounts draw together elements of inquiry as articulated in Chapter 4 on journal keeping, Chapter 5 on creative forms of expression, and the introduction to Part III on methods of inquiry into practice, relationships, and contexts. In so doing, they highlight the principles of diversity and flexibility that guide meaningful and personally relevant processes of inquiry.

To honor the power of story as a form of inquiry and to provide a sense of what such an inquiry mode might look like, we diverge from the format we have used in other chapters and present first Roger's and then Fran's accounts of their school-based reflexive inquiries in their complete, uninterrupted form. The stories, we think, speak for themselves, as good stories do.

Roger is principal of a kindergarten through grade 9 small rural school just outside Halifax in Nova Scotia, Canada. Fran, a classroom teacher, consultant, and teacher educator in Ontario for more than thirty years, is currently a program officer in the Professional Affairs Department of the Ontario College of Teachers (a regulatory body established by the government to oversee preservice and inservice teacher education programs, including initial and ongoing certification).

Days (Minutes) in the Life of a School

A Thursday in May

On Thursday morning after announcements, I had a phone call from a woman who had brought two young girls to the school about two months before. She had explained to me at the time that she was the girls' stepmother; she had married their father, who had custody of them because their mother was unstable and possibly dangerous; she and the father had been together for several years; the father had recently "run off" and was possibly in a detox center somewhere; and she had moved here because her mother was here and she needed a place where she could safely live with her own daughter and the two older stepdaughters. The girls had started at my school and seemed to be doing well. I had a sheet with two photographs (one clipped from a newspaper) attached so that we at the school would know what the mother looked like and do everything we could to prevent any contact between her and the two girls. I also had a fax from a law office explaining that the stepmother did in fact have temporary custody and that the mother could see the girls only under the supervision of a child protection agency.

This case was unusual only because of its complexity and the fact that we actually had photos and documentation. In my experience it's usually the mother saying that the father can't see the child, isn't allowed any access, and offering a description of the father—sort of small, ginger hair, no beard. If I ask for a photograph, one often shows up. Sometimes the parents get back together, don't tell us, and we have a situation with a teacher saying, "I'm sorry. Please understand that my instructions are etc. etc.," and the father, frustrated and trying to be patient, explaining that they are back together and he's supposed to be picking up the boy, and there not being a phone, and us trying always to do the right thing for the kid. These things aren't easy, but they are a regular part of my administrative practice.

So, Thursday morning I got the call. The stepmother explained that the mother had somehow got herself a new car (she described the car), and there was a chance that she might drive this way (100 km from where she was living) to try to see the girls. I thanked her for letting us know and looked for the photos. The classroom teachers didn't have them, they weren't in the girls' files because we hadn't yet received the files from the school they had attended in another province, and I was worried the photos were buried in the pile of "current" papers on the left side (and the right side) of my desk. Luckily the information was in the center drawer with the fax, and I made up a quick fact sheet to let all the teachers and supervisors know of the situation. This was done in the morning. Nothing happened at recess or lunch, a couple of teachers commented how tough it was getting keeping track of these things, that the mother looked very professional (especially in the newspaper picture), that the girls were really sweet and how awful that they should have to live like that, and so on. There were other things to be done and I had to look after Joey on his in-school suspension most of the day and meet with his parents after lunch because they had questions about the suspension; I didn't think too much about the girls or their mother's possible visit.

At ten to three the stepmother phoned and said the mother was parked in her new car outside the stepmother's apartment (just around the corner from the school); there was a police cruiser behind it, so could I have the girls wait in my office at dismissal (in fifteen minutes) until she (the stepmother) could come and pick them up? OK, I said. I went to the classroom across from the office and quietly told that teacher, then up to the third floor to tell the older sister's teacher, and came back to the office to look once more at the papers on my desk and to check on Joey, who was trying to make a start on a story about two students who got in a fight in the hall because of a disagreement over a coat hook. I suggested it could be quite a comical story. Joey had to think a little before he could see how it might be a little funny or ridiculous, but he said he'd try to write it funny.

A moment later Tracey, a blonde girl in grade 5, came running to the office and said Mr. F., the music teacher, wanted me right away in the music room. Most of the time Mr. F. looked after behavior concerns and rarely asked me to come to escort someone away for a break from music class, so I wondered if it could be a late Thursday afternoon treat. Tracey had run ahead of me down the corridor to the music room. I didn't bother yelling anything about not running; I knew she wanted to be back in her place when I walked in the door. Mr. F. smiled at me, picked up a tiny wooden chair, and plunked it down in front of the grades 5 and 6 choir group. It was my seat of honor. He positioned his guitar, asked them if they were ready to do it again, explained to me that they had just tried a difficult song and it had really worked (part unison, part three-part harmony), and they wanted me to hear it. So I sat on my tiny chair in front of about thirty grade 5 and 6 kids and listened; each of them was so earnest and focused on getting it right. They sang like angels. I had a lump in my throat and hoped I wouldn't have to say anything too soon. At one point I looked to the side and caught the eye of Julie-Anne, a new girl in grade 6 who has had some trouble making friends. She flashed me a smile and kept on singing. Everyone else was watching Mr. F. so closely that I figured they wouldn't notice the tears in my eyes. They finished, sang a second song, I composed myself, thanked them, and hurried back to the office because I knew the two girls would be there in a few moments, right after the buzzer.

The stepmother was there. She told me that the police had taken the mother away for questioning about how she had obtained the car back in the city and thanked me for my help. The younger girl came from across the hall and asked her stepmother what she was doing there. When she didn't answer right away, I said that she just wanted to come and meet the girls. The girl smiled, the stepmother smiled, the older girl arrived, they went home, I talked to Joey about what came next for him. I went home happy.

June 20

Tonight I came home from the school at about 9:30. It was cloudy but still light enough to see well. The big maple trees next to the Laurie Street side of the school were densely lush. The wind blew through them. They had perfect tree shapes, huge and green, in front of the brick walls. Their leafy life was exactly right to soften the impact of the building, to take the edge off the corners.

I look at the school often—in early mornings when I walk Griff down Laurie and along Alice, later when I walk over with my briefcase, when I return again from lunch, and often I look back at it when I leave. It's a big place that stands proud and I am proud to be the principal.

When I first went there almost four years ago, the entrance had a reddish dirt bank that everyone walked up—hardly anyone used the steps from the parking lot. Marcel told me that in previous years the hallways would be filled with fine red dirt every day from all of the sneakers and shoes that cut across the dirt to get in. I have told him more than once that one of the things I am most pleased with having accomplished is getting the railings put in and the banks sodded and planted. Now there are two healthy young flowering crabs and green grass where the dirt bank was and Marcel's floors are clean. It may not be a really major accomplishment, but it makes a difference to the feel of the place that is important, and I like that feel.

When I heard a lecture about garden and landscape history and design, the one phrase that stuck with me was "the mystery that lies at the heart of garden making." The lecturer talked about gardening as "interventions in the landscape," an idea that I loved, and I thought that the mystery he talked of was the mystery that is at the heart of any human activity, the thing that makes us want to do it. Mystery and heart belong together in the same sentence, in the same body. Mystery is what is worth exploring, even knowing that it must always be mysterious, and the heart of the matter is where it lies.

Alice Street School is, in the simplest sense, my garden—this red brick building surrounded by pavement but softened by large maples and the sloping curves of grass where once was red dirt scuffed by everyone's feet. That's why I stop sometimes, when I am walking home, to turn and look at it, admire the shapes of the trees and the contours of grass. But it is also, more complexly, another kind of garden; to use the beautiful German word, it is a *kindergarten,* a garden of children.

The thing that first struck both Nan and me when we drove by Uniacke District School last summer was a feeling of starkness about the building, and we talked about the need to plant things there, to make it less severe. The school sign, made of metal letters, has been tampered with, and right now it reads UNI-ACKE STRICT SCHOOL. I want to get those two missing letters replaced (though it is a good joke), and I want to have some trees around it.

Yesterday, when I drove around with Jim, the retiring principal, he showed me where the students came from to the school. As we were coming back from seeing the western part of its catchment area, I noticed how a long green field sloped up toward the school, which seemed to be clustered at the top of a rise. I hadn't really looked at it before from that direction, and I thought, "The school on the hill." I said it out loud to Jim, and he chuckled a little and said, "Yes, I guess it is."

I didn't say out loud what else popped into my head the moment I noticed how it sat on the land—the Beatles' song, "Fool on the Hill." If I'd said it, Jim might have figured that's what I'd be as new principal there! I don't think of him as having much in the way of leaps of imagination. Maybe there is a song in it somewhere; certainly their music teacher has some sparks of wit and energy about him.

June 23

Tonight I was walking back up our street with Griff. I had admired again the façade of the school with its bright grass under the streetlight and the lush green of the row of maples in front of the old part of the building. I walked under one of the big lindens on our street and admired the huge leaves just above my head; they were so thick and they always shone under the light as if they were wet. When I touched one it was sticky, and I noticed an area of the sidewalk where sap must have run off the tops of the leaves and dripped.

Back at the corner, a family was getting out of a car, voices murmuring. Then one voice, which I didn't immediately recognize, a child's voice, a bit hoarse, called, "Hi, Mr. Field!" "Hi," I called back, still not sure who it was even though I knew the house and that Aaron lived there. I could make out some of the explanation to the grandparents or whomever it was the child had to explain to, that it was "Mr. Field, the principal of my school." It is a fact of my life in this neighborhood that children will see me and notice what I'm doing and say hi or ask me what I'm up to.

Lately Burton, who is now in grade 7 and getting into all kinds of trouble at the junior high, has sometimes said from the other side of the street or down the hill something like "Faggot Field," never loud enough or clear enough that I can be sure that that's what it is, but always when he is with someone else. I want to ask him what that's about. Earlier today we passed him and Chris (who has been suspended since January from junior high) when we were driving and they were crossing the street. I waved and said "Hi" as we passed, as I always do. I can't figure out what it is with Burton lately, especially since I was always fair with him when he was at Alice (even though we often did not agree on what was OK or not OK). Robert, who was his teacher last year in grade 6 and who also had disagreements with Burton, told me that Burton yells things like "Fuck you, Mr. George" when he drives past him. Faggot Field is not so bad, I guess, but, unlike Robert, I want to know what the deal is, since I don't believe there's a reason for it (except of course to show off to whoever he is with). It's not that I care what he calls me; it's simply that I don't want things to end that way because they don't need to, and because Burton needs other ways to handle things besides hating or deriding teachers.

All of the above is connected to my thinking of the move to Uniacke. For one thing, it is a primary to grade 9 school. That means that the kids who are wrestling with us (the school) and our authority or influence over their lives, and feeling their hormones kick in (especially if, like Burton and Chris, they have taken an extra year to complete elementary and are just that much older), do not just move on to another school and become someone else's problem. So they are still our students in grade 7 *and* grade 8 *and* grade 9 (though Rick has told me from his junior high experience that grade 9s tend to be more settled). I believe that staying in the same school, that is, not having to adjust to a new place and jockey for position and influence with the grade 7s coming from the other feeder schools, would obviate some of those difficulties; however, there is no question about the fact that hormones and a shifting attitude toward the school (and its administrators) will be a part of my life and practice at Uniacke.

Jim told me when I was there on Wednesday that there was a significant difference between the elementary (grades P–5) staff and the middle school (grades 6–9) staff, that the former tended to be more accepting and compliant, and the latter more expressive of their concerns or issues or disapprovals of things. I knew this before but haven't had to work with it; I think it maybe matches the kids and their development.

At any rate, the "Hi, Mr. Field" and "There's Mr. Field; he's *my* principal!" may still be part of my elementary practice, but I sure don't expect it quite like that from the middle school. It just wouldn't be cool!

End of June

Looking back at the last day of school, which was June 27 this year, I have to start with the night before. I had worked solidly through Monday, Tuesday, and Wednesday—the administration and marking days—but stuff just had not all got done. When teachers are in the school, they often need me for something; it's always important but usually it's not what I had thought I was going to do. These are also the days that parents know I am in the school and they call with their concerns, also important, so I often have *my* things that *I* have to do still waiting at the end of the day.

I knew when I went home on Wednesday that I would be back there that night, because some things could not be put off any longer. Thursday was the last day the teachers would all be there, and there were deadlines listed in the End of Year Deadlines Memo from the assistant superintendent (the memo with phrases like "no later than 5 P.M. on Thursday, June 27" in bold type and underlined).

I went to Save-Easy to pick up a few things and was spotted by Taylor, a primary student, whose dad is manager of the store. Taylor made a big thing of seeing me and, when we were in the checkout line, told his mum that my hair had grown since he had last seen me. It was a windy day and my hair did seem a little big. I told Taylor that I had been trying to find the time to get it cut and decided that I'd have to go to Mike's before school in the morning.

I worked that night until five to twelve, came home, slept, got up early, and by twenty after seven was sitting in the chair at Mike's, his first customer of the day. He asked me what plans we had for the summer, so I told him about changing schools and planning to try to sell the house and move. When he asked me where, I told him Uniacke District School.

"Uniacke District School?" he said. "I was just reading about that in the newspaper."

"Uh, oh," I thought, "This is not going to be one of those Picked as the Fourth Best School in North America stories."

Mike explained about there being a complaint from a parent about her grade 2 daughter being held down and kissed by two grade 2 boys, who then exposed themselves to her.

So this is Uniacke District School; this is what I'm going to. The only time Alice Street School made it into this newspaper was at the end of our million word reading promotion two years ago. This was not really a big surprise to me. I had been told about some issues regarding supervision and the need for a fence. It was just one more thing to think about on my last day at Alice Street.

I told Mike that when he reads about Uniacke in the paper next year that I'm going to make sure it's about something good.

August 12

The goldenrod is in bloom, Queen Anne's lace sways by the highway, rabbit's foot clover has replaced the hop clover blooming at the road edge, and it's getting closer to school time. This morning when I woke the sky was a darker blue, the first day of the summer season to look like that. At Uniacke today the P. E. teacher was visiting Jim because he'd noticed the car out front, and Jim is leaving for the Territories in three days. He said he had watched the Perseids shower last night because one of his kids had swimmer's ear and kept him awake and that he had noticed the sky this morning, that the season had changed.

That change in the season, like the bloom on the goldenrod, is a time to bring school issues into sharper focus; it's the time when teachers who dread school (as I have dreaded it at times) start to have school dreams. One of my worst, twenty years ago, had me at the front of a high school class that was L-shaped, so I couldn't see all of the students at one time, with a slippery mud floor. I can't remember if I fell, but I do remember the dread. I had a Uniacke School dream this morning. All I can remember are some efforts being made to fix the school sign and some large shining green letters spelling the name of the school over and over at different angles. No dread, just a dream exploration of one take on the school.

The meeting today with Jim was to go over a few things so that I would not be blindsided or compromised because of not being warned. This is useful, I think, as long as it doesn't set up too much anticipation of difficulty when I meet the people involved. I have been briefed on some of these same issues/personalities by the supervisor responsible for the school and on one specific situation by the assistant superintendent, and I have to be careful in listening to Jim not to seem to know too much already about them as there seems to be a fairly high level of sensitivity at the school about Central Office involvement/interference. I have already been quite clear to any staff members whom I have talked to that our house in Truro is for sale and that we do plan to move from there to somewhere closer to Uniacke. It seems to be important to show I am not a "suit from Truro" and that my commitment is to the school. At the same time I don't believe that I can have as carefree an attitude toward Central Office as Jim did and won't be able to let things slide by quite so easily.

Today I got my keys and Jim walked out of the school. I am now the person responsible, the one who decides. I spent a bit of time looking at a few files on the computer, made a couple of phone calls, poked my nose in a few corners, and left to drive home. It's hard to start before you have people there and things you have to do. The engagement with the school awaits. In the meantime there are some things I can start on.

September 7

It's Saturday morning, end of the first week of school; kids have been there three full days, and it's 6:30. I have been getting up at quarter to six all week, leaving here before seven in order to arrive at the school by eight. The drive is an hour and five minutes, and I have been pulling in to the school behind the same bus each day. It is long but I am hoping to do it only until the end of the month when we move from here; however, this is Saturday! If we drive anywhere today, it will be to go to the beach. We wanted to be up reasonably early because the house is being shown today and we need to clean up, but I left the alarm off so we could sleep in at least a little. To wake up at six and start composing my next memo to the staff while I lie in bed is a little ridiculous! Anyway, here I am, having scribbled notes for the various memo items, and there's finally a little time to do this.

I spent three days during the week before Labor Day weekend working with Seamus, the vice-principal, and Barb, the school secretary, in order to be ready for this school year. It was great! We worked hard and well together, sorted out a number of important issues, and found (I believe) that we could function as a team.

On the second of those days, Seamus sat in my office and asked me what my agenda was. I felt he meant more than the agenda for our next short time together—what we would be discussing or doing that morning. The question stopped me short. I didn't believe I had an agenda, certainly not in the negative sense of a "hidden" one, no specific mission to accomplish at the school. I told him first that I did not come as an agent from Central Office in Truro with a mission to carry out. Since I knew that this school, with its great distance from Central Office and its relative isolation from other schools in the District, had a suspicion of any initiative from Truro (and I was, at least until we moved, driving from Truro), it was critical that I make that clear. Beyond that it was still a very real and important question.

I told Seamus that my first and main agenda was to learn about the school and how it worked and how I could work in it. I said that I didn't want to change anything that was working well and wanted to find ways to address things that people agreed needed addressing. I gave him a copy of my first memo to the staff.

I asked for his opinion of it and told him that I would like him to go over each memo I sent out before I sent it. Since Seamus has been VP here for three years and taught in the middle school for about ten before that, I knew that this would be a great help to me; it was also really important to me that we work as a team, and I didn't want the fact that he had also applied for the principal position to be problematic.

Finally, I told him what I have learned about my administrative practice over the past few years: my agenda is simply me, how I work, how I understand and what I believe about my work, and who I am as a teacher and learner in the school; my agenda is myself. I suspected at the time (and now know) that Seamus is intelligent, hardworking, and highly organized, and that he cares deeply about the kids and wants always to do the right thing for them. We are different people in many ways, but we share some deeply held beliefs about kids, teachers, schools, and the kind of work we do. I know that he is a treasure and that we will work very well together.

This past summer our second son planted trees in Ontario. It was his second season, and he hooked up with another experienced planter (a real "pounder") who had become a good friend. They agreed, since you are paid by the tree, that they would work as partners and split whatever they earned that season no matter how many one or the other planted. Their idea was that if one had a down day the other would work harder to make up for it and that at the end of the day (and the season) it was only their team total that counted. They learned, as anyone who has been part of a working team learns, that by working cooperatively toward the same goal (let's plant as much of this lot as we can, let's get another tray in before quitting, let's take a break only after we do such and such) they enhanced each other's performance remarkably. This Saturday morning, after our first week of school, I realize that that is how Seamus and I are working, and it is a joy!

A happy footnote: Seamus and I were walking back from a tour of some of the play areas, talking about ways we could make them work better and improve supervision and student safety. He told me he had wanted to do something with the triangle between the sidewalks at the main entrance. It had some grass and those little weeds that grow only where people walk on the grass a lot, as well as a fair bit of pounded-down bare earth. He said he had wanted to put in some small trees and maybe a couple of heavy benches to improve the area. Hallelujah, I thought! This guy also wants a garden here. I told him I wanted to do something with the raised concrete planter (now a flourishing bed of weeds) right by the entrance and mentioned the possibility of bulbs for the spring. He said that the staff had tried different things with planting flowers there with very little success but suggested that if we put some Euonymus and other evergreens, we could also have bulbs and probably we could keep the kids off it. I know we will make a good team here (in fact, some of the staff call us the A-team already!), and that this kindergarten, Uniacke District School, will flourish.

Outside the window the sky is deep blue, and the mass of foliage in our backyard is a deep green highlighted with gold from the early morning sun. Time to clean the house and head for the beach!

January 20

Today, at the end of the day, a teacher from the middle school standing at the office counter asked me, "How was your day?"

I thought for a small moment and told her it was a good day. I was thinking about how it had been fairly quiet most of the day and that, except for my last Book Bureau order, everything on today's list was completed. That is always a good day.

The teacher continued, "So how do you find it here?"

"Very good," I told her.

"But do you like us?" she asked.

I laughed. "You know the answer to that!" I said.

She smiled. "Yes, yes, I do." And she did. She knows that I like her, that I like the rest of the staff, and that I look forward to coming to the school each day. Each of these is important to my practice, and the last of them is critically important. I have to like the place I work in. If I don't like it, I need to change it until it is a place I like.

I have been principal of Uniacke District School for almost six months now, since August 1, and we are in the fifth month, at almost the halfway point, of this school year. I survived the fall, with changing schools, selling a house, buying a house, moving, helping to fix up a house, and learning something of how to be principal at UDS. Today Bill Clinton was sworn in for his second term as president. I believe this is around the time in nonelection years that a president usually delivers a State of the Union address. I told someone last week that I felt the need at this point in my position at UDS to do my own "state of the union," a reflection and accounting of my time at the school, to make some determinations about what changes, good and bad, my principalship had brought about and where I might try to go from here.

When I was interviewed for the position, someone on the committee asked me what kind of change agent I was. I have always had trouble with that notion. So often I look at other principals and hear about all of the initiatives they have been taking, all the great things they are doing together with their staffs. And often I look at my own practice and find myself wanting. I am not a kick-butt change agent. I don't find myself leading big staff initiatives. I don't often have accomplishments I can brag about. Yet I think there are ways that I am a good principal. I answered the question by saying that I am a gradual change agent, that I work most effectively by modeling ways to be, ways to understand, ways to learn, ways to know, but that I am also a stubborn change agent.

I never really knew that I was stubborn or perseverant—it took my wife to tell me that—just as my friend and colleague, Wilfred, never knew that he was a "controller" until we took a self-test on management style and he added up his points. Once you know it, however, you should be able to find ways to make use of it without being completely governed by it. And I need to know what to be stubborn about, where and how to persevere, what matters and what doesn't at UDS.

For me, this appointment was only the second nonteaching administrative position I had held, even though it was my fourth principalship, and it was the first one I had gone into with my eyes somewhat open and with some sense of the possibility of defining myself there and doing something. I visited the school over a year ago, when I first knew that Jim might retire. I visited again in June, once for Jim's retirement ceremony and once to spend a day with Jim seeing how things worked. I worked a couple of days with Jim and Seamus over the summer and then worked on my own, once I had my set of keys to the place. It was all a process of acquaintance and familiarization, but I knew that I couldn't get any real sense of the place until it all started to happen.

Now I can look back at the notes I made sitting in the office with Jim and see what they mean, though they were only scribbles and phrases when I put them down. Now I can look at the school and see this thing or that thing that Jim or Seamus mentioned and know what it is. But when I think about coming into the school with my eyes open, I understand that there is very little that I can do or know until I am in it and doing it, and then I can only understand by trying to lift myself out from the everyday and looking around.

The wholeness of Roger's stories stands in contrast to more-formalized accounts of teachers' inquiries into schools. Roger believes that his narrative accounts of experience evidence much that is significant for his ongoing work of leading a small school community on a rewarding and rich educational journey. The accounts evidence at once a documentary function and an analytical function, a problem-defining value and a problem-resolution value; they illustrate the place of personal experience as it influences a community responsibility and mirror the rich, complex experience and thinking that forms the basis for his actions. Fran's story follows.

School Stories as Metaphors for Understanding

The context of setting plays a significant role in teacher development research and yet is often limited to brief comments about the physical attributes of the research site. In my work as a teacher-researcher I have come to see the school setting as an integral part of the teacher's professional knowledge landscape. Using the metaphor of a landscape to describe context or setting allows us to explore the communal exigencies of the workplace environment and gives us different ways to represent lives lived in and out of classrooms, lives shaped not only by personal constructs, motivations, and desires but by diverse political and social pressures. School stories are often told through metaphor or symbols, and the stories take on a life of their own.

Recently I conducted a research study that explored the relationship of a principal, a beginning teacher, and myself, an experienced teacher-researcher, as we moved from a small, collaborative, alternative school to a larger school with a very different culture. As I began my research I discovered that teachers and the principal often shared information through stories about themselves and about their schools. Understanding school stories is important as a form of research because, as Clandinin and Connelly (1995) remind us, "to properly understand the professional knowledge landscape it is necessary to understand it narratively as a changing landscape with a history of its own" (p. 28). To investigate that history I tapped a variety of sources, including historical records such as old newsletters and procedural manuals; listened carefully to solicited and unsolicited staff stories of the school; and facilitated a collaborative reconstruction of stories with Lisa, the principal, and Rebecca, a new teacher. My emerging understanding of the school was a narrative one, built on the fragments of school stories I heard and stories I experienced. The following story illustrates what I mean by a narrative understanding of a school.

The Mural: A Metaphor for Change

> Dominating the front lobby [of Millside School] is a mural depicting a Canadian historical scene. The painting, characterized by tones of dark green and murky brown, is somewhat awkward and amateurish in style. A tall, confident European explorer, attired in a morning coat and plumed hat, strides across the painted tiles, rifle in hand, to meet a scantily clad representative of the First Nations who extends his hand in welcome. The mural speaks of a time past, rife with images and stereotypes of Native peoples and the White man. An incongruous image of the current houses of Parliament floats above the figures.
>
> No one looks at the mural anymore. Posters and art work from various classes often hang lopsidedly from the mural's dark surface. Parents and students waiting for office personnel often lean up against the mural, their bodies obliterating the images. The mural has become comfortably invisible, taken for granted, though its original narrative content speaks dramatically of settlers and Native Americans coexisting in harmony—contentious issues of our Canadian past. Our diverse student body, representing

forty-seven nationalities and living out a different sort of multiculturalism, walk by day after day ignoring this faded symbol of Canadian history.

During the month of February a group of parents from the Parent Teacher Association (PTA) suggested that the mural be repainted to reflect more contemporary Canadian society. The idea was discussed at the PTA meeting and teachers and parents explored possibilities for change. As a participant in that discussion I recall the talk being lighthearted, with many humorous suggestions for a new foyer painting. The arts teacher was delegated with the responsibility for researching the mural's history and whether there was any significant political reason it could not be changed.

The next day a handwritten letter appeared in every teacher's mailbox, an impassioned plea from a long-standing staff member to retain the mural just the way it was. It began, "It came to my attention Friday that a proposal is afoot to destroy a foyer mural." Miss Redfern's letter continued on for several pages, citing artistic, cultural, and historic reasons for the mural's survival. It concluded with the suggestion that another mural could be painted, if desired, in another free space in the school. At the day's end the letter was submitted to the monthly staff meeting. My field notes from that meeting suggest an attitude of bemusement on the part of many staff who wondered what all the fuss was about. Other staff joined with Miss Redfern in vocal exclamations of indignation that a school landmark might be changed.

A day later Miss Redfern canvassed the entire staff asking for signatures on a petition to save the foyer mural. Some agreed completely with Miss Redfern's arguments and gladly added their signatures. Others reflected later that they felt pressured by the personal request and acquiesced out of a sense of duty. Yet another group of staff—more recent members of the school community—had no particular opinion and either signed or avoided Miss Redfern altogether. The petition was then placed in a prominent position in the front office with a further invitation for all teaching and support staff to consider the issue if they had not already done so. The petition garnered over half of the building personnel's support. The PTA chairperson, believing she had offended the staff, quickly withdrew the proposal for change. Administration kept carefully neutral during the proceedings. The proposal for change quickly became a nonissue.

As I observed the events unfolding around the mural dilemma, I wondered whether the mural was about art and culture or whether it spoke more eloquently of tradition versus change. Understanding the mural as a metaphor for the difficult process of change taking place in the school provides a different set of lenses through which to interpret events.

Miss Redfern stood for the school's long history of traditional ways of teaching. She staunchly defended the mural—a piece of that school's conservative culture, a visual representation of values once held by the school community. She rallied her initial support from those teachers with similar long histories at the school, many of whom believed in a teacher-directed, structured way of doing things. Many of us new to the school, who welcomed a change in the foyer, were also teachers initiating changes in the way children at Millside were taught. Perhaps it was more than coincidence that we assumed polar positions on the mural issue.

Was the mural really about conserving art history or was it about the way we incorporate the old and the new? That question of change was a part of the school's current story—one causing stress for many teachers who were being asked by Lisa, the principal, to change their traditional teaching strategies. Teachers at all levels were being invited to move from teacher-centered to child-centered strategies, to incorporate whole language and process writing, to develop cooperative learning groups in their classrooms. When Miss Redfern suggested another place for a new mural to coexist beside the old, I was struck by the notion that perhaps we were not talking about the mural at all. Perhaps we were trying to figure out a way to implement change within a traditional program, creating some space for new ideas without destroying the old.

Through researching I became aware that the context of schools could be represented in many aesthetic written forms and that no single perspective could capture the essence and complexity of a school. Lisa created her own representation through the medium of poetry. She described her experience through an artistic metaphor suggesting that Halverston, the alternative school where she was principal before coming to Millside, was an Impressionist painting by Monet while Millside was embodied by the imagery of Escher. Fascinated, I asked her to say more but the image had faded and words were inadequate to express her tentative thoughts. Months later she hesitantly presented me with a piece of writing that she felt captured the essence of the metaphor.

Monet ...
Escher ...

Monet is soft, gentle, blended
blue green
peaceful
Escher is sharp angular
black
white
mystifying

With Monet, there are dreams, sighs, warm hugs
Escher jolts, shocks, startles
Monet floats, erases the edges
soothes the pain
Escher's bite attracts, repels, pushes, and pulls
both are bold
deep
draw in the mind
both have passion
and now...today...
it is like having two lovers
Monet and Escher
both wonderful

The poem is Lisa's attempt to frame her conflicting experiences in a way that ultimately reconciles their differences by recognizing, respecting, and comparing the particular qualities of each situation. Deriving meaning from experience through a visual metaphor, Lisa creates images that invite us to enter into her experience from an intensely personal and sensory perspective. She invites us to understand the emotional context of each school by leading us into the dichotomous landscapes of Monet and Escher.

Sometimes the ways to represent schools can be filled with humor, humor that pervades our lives in schools but so rarely makes the transition to the printed page. Here is another school story about a symbol for change that has become a flag for caution for my husband, Ken, a principal with our Board (District), and one of his out-of-town colleagues, Catherine Douglas. The story was originally told to Ken by Catherine when he was an exchange vice-principal at Catherine's school. The central message in the story is, "Don't move the fridge." How this apparently incongruous phrase directed their subsequent leadership actions is described in the following account.

While Catherine was a second year vice-principal, a new principal was appointed to her school at Christmas. Over the holiday break the new principal came into the school, inspected the staffroom, and decided to move the fridge from its original position in order to create more space in the small staffroom. She placed it at the end of the entrance hallway where it opened into the staffroom. Its new position made the entrance-way much smaller and difficult to navigate. The first morning staff arrived back at the school, two women teachers approached the staffroom laughing and sharing Christmas stories and walked directly into the fridge. Annoyed and surprised at the immediate physical pain caused by the move, the teachers continued to experience increasing frustration with this change as the year progressed. The fridge was a continued annoyance for the whole staff as they daily navigated their way into the staffroom around this new obstacle. The staff never related to the new principal who, from their perspective, had unilaterally made a decision to change something that belonged to them. Any decisions she subsequently made were judged negatively by her first action of moving the fridge.

As Catherine and Ken began working together at Catherine's first school their approach to making changes was influenced directly by this story from Catherine's past experience. With each move they initiated, they stopped and asked each other, "Are we moving the fridge here?" When Catherine wanted to make a change in the staffroom she proceeded in a much different way. The staffroom cupboards, which were full of mismatched dishes, chipped cups, and bent cutlery, needed a new look, but Catherine involved the staff in even this small change. After ordering a whole new set of dishes she asked the staff to help unpack them and replace the old ones, to decide what should go and what should stay. Everyone pitched in and became physically involved in replacing old with new. The staff viewed Catherine's actions in a positive light, appreciating her concern for their space and their involvement.

The phrase "don't move the fridge" has become a private code word between Catherine and Ken for moving slowly along the uncharted roads of change. Although they now work for different school boards, the message is still shared with humor via phone or electronic mail when they attempt to introduce change in their respective schools. It cautions them to understand the traditions and culture of a school, to experience the terrain, to know the landscape well before moving in and challenging the status quo. It reminds them as administrators to understand the story of the school before attempting to dictate a new one. Although the communication between the two principals was originally private, there is a sense in which this expression "don't move the fridge" is becoming a catch phrase for gradual change among other principals who have been told the story by Catherine or Ken.

On yet another occasion Lisa, the principal, explained how the notion of "ownership" played a significant role in helping her to fit into a new environment. She told a story that focused on ownership expressed in a very physical symbolic action. As background for the story it is important to know that Lisa had felt completely in tune with her first placement as a principal at a small collaborative alternative school, so she had experienced a kind of culture shock when she arrived at Millside, where things were run quite differently. Here is Lisa's account.

The first time I came into the building by myself was on a weekend in September. No caretaker. The process seemed overwhelming because machines are not my strength. I had to phone the security company to turn off the alarm and then manage the front door, which I had not practiced. I had to use a huge key to get in, then go down the big stairs to the boiler room and "Hooray, the fire alarm was the same as at Halverston [my other school]. No problem. Turn it off." It may sound silly but it was the first time I came into my school by myself when no one else was here. And I walk in with my big key. I turn off my alarm by myself, and I take ownership. That's what it was. Ownership.

Lisa's symbolic entry to the school by herself for the first time signaled the real beginning of her principalship at Millside. Her story illustrates the powerful notion of ownership and how it relates to a sense of place on the landscape. The previous year she had not experienced ownership at Millside, feeling more like a barely tolerated guest who by her own accounts was constantly doing things wrong. Caught in the dilemma of being an outsider on the periphery of the school landscape, she was simultaneously positioned at the center as the school leader. Lisa's story was her way of making sense of experience and captures the essence of her symbolic step.

Story, poetry, and other forms of metaphorical or symbolic representation are powerful ways of representing and understanding contexts of teaching. The various depictions help us to understand why where we teach makes such a difference in our professional lives.

SCHOOL-BASED REFLEXIVE INQUIRY AND TEACHER DEVELOPMENT

Roger's and Fran's accounts elucidate the storied nature of school lives and the events that take place within contexts connected to schools. They illuminate the idiosyncrasies and nuances of those lives and contexts and the importance of understanding them, especially in relation to one's own values, goals, and practices. As Roger puts it, liking the place he works in is critically important to his practice. "I have to like the place I work in. If I don't like it, I need to change it until it is a place I like," which could mean initiating changes within a school context or moving to another more appropriate one. The point is that a teacher's (or principal's) practice is powerfully influenced by the school (and community) context in which that practice is articulated. Understanding that context is critical to understanding one's own practice. And, likewise, documenting practice is likely to illuminate issues of context worthy of inquiry.

In presenting the narrative accounts written by Roger and Fran we are upholding a particular notion of inquiry into school contexts. Such inquiry is reflexive. Above all, we are reiterating the importance of acknowledging the complex and messy, sometimes very personal, elements of practice and decision making. We are not intending to downplay other possible forms of inquiry into school contexts; rather, we are emphasizing the place of narrative in teachers' lives and professional work. It is through articulating and understanding experience—and one way we do that is through the stories we tell and retell—that we come to understand elements of our own practice. In that way, the stories told around the staffroom lunch table, for instance, are powerful examples of theory articulation, explanations of problems or issues, or statements about assumptions, ideologies, and fundamental world views. These collectively shape what teachers do in their classrooms, in the halls and corridors, and in the community, and they evidence how they view themselves in relation to others. Such stories or narratives become, on thoughtful examination, opportunities for exploration of the fundamental meanings of practice-in-context.

In Chapter 6 we briefly discussed the role of school context in supporting or constraining reflexive practice and inquiry activities. Here we elaborate the relationship between school context and teacher development with a couple of examples from research we have undertaken and reported on. In one study (Cole, 1990b) four beginning teachers, who began their careers in different settings and with their own different conceptions, expectations, and goals, each experienced the first year of teaching in dramatically different ways. Only one teacher found herself in a supportive school environment in which she was able to practice her values and beliefs about teaching and to develop her understandings with relative comfort and confidence, experienced a successful and constructive first year. The other three teachers, placed in settings that reflected varying degrees of support and incongruity with their views on teaching and professional goals, experienced difficulty, frustration, and disappointment; one seriously considered leaving teaching at the end of her first year.

In another study (Cole, 1991) the relationship between teacher development and school context was made evident by a group of thirteen new teachers who experienced their first year as part of a "caring and helping community." Their highly successful first-year experiences stood out in stark contrast to the experiences of most first-year teachers because of the norms and principles that defined the context of their work, the schools. Similarly, in other explorations of beginning teachers (e.g., Bullough & Knowles, 1990; Bullough, Knowles, & Crow, 1991; Knowles, 1992), the power of context over the experiences of teaching and conceptions of self-as-teacher or "teacher role identity" were as great as they were varied. Ultimately teachers were constrained or facilitated in their efforts to develop philosophically coherent and congruent practices by the norms and values of the school and the tone or climate that prevailed.

Explorations of "failure" among preservice teachers also evidences the power of school contexts over personal/professional experiences and practices. In examinations of prospective teachers who failed to gain teacher certification because they were pulled from their practica placements or were given "failing grades," there is considerable evidence that in some cases the school and classroom contexts contributed greatly to the demise of the teachers (Knowles & Hoefler, 1989; Sudzina & Knowles, 1993). And, as any teacher-educator knows, the experience of new, prospective teachers in schools varies greatly and is a complex interaction of the personal with the relational and the contextual. "Shattered images" was the title we gave to a study of prospective teachers' experiences as they moved into schools after being away from them for some time. Their difficulties—in a sense "culture shock"—rested mainly with the great gulf between their earlier and "later" experiences of schools as complex contexts and their negotiation of them rather than on difficulties experienced with students, parents, or teachers (Cole & Knowles, 1993). In this way the nature of a particular school context is a vitally important consideration for those whose practices are forming; it is also an equally important consideration, but for different reasons, for experienced practitioners. For all practitioners the work of teaching is made or broken, is rewarding or not, depending on the nature of the local school context in conjunction with the broader contextual elements and milieu.

The point to all of this is that it is important to understand conditions and elements that have the potential to influence practice and development in positive or negative ways. Such understanding can be gained through systematic, focused, reflexive inquiry.

ISSUES AND CONCERNS

Many of the issues raised and discussed so far also are relevant for researching schools. Two concerns that arose for Fran have particular relevance for inquiry into school contexts. As she indicates in the segments that follow, Fran's main concerns related to representation and politics. In the first segment she articulates some of her thinking about how she could meaningfully and authentically communicate the complexity of the school context. For many of the same reasons that we outlined in Chapter 5, she opted for a narrative mode of representation.

One issue that challenged me was how to convey the experience, the feeling, the life, the uniqueness of the school site. Through my writing I have come to realize that many ways of representation are possible and are dependent on the purpose of and audience for the research. It was in fact *The Velveteen Rabbit* that confirmed for me that stories, metaphor, and analogy can represent the contextual complexities of the relationships that compose the life of a particular school. Let me explain.

As a student in education courses I was used to reading research studies in which schools were depicted in terms of numbers and demographic information—if indeed they were described at all. Then I happened upon a research account on beginning teachers in which the author used an excerpt from the familiar children's story to make a point about new teachers "becoming real" with the help of the wise, old, skin horse (Cole, 1990a). As a reader I was captivated by the analogy, and I recall feeling an instant sense of resonance with the article that followed. The salient point to be made here is that not everyone would react or connect to a story example in the same way. For some readers of research, such stories might be considered irritating diversions from the factual material, but for others like myself the inclusion of metaphors, stories, and poetry as part of the research findings enhances the understanding of the whole.

In my research of schools I held this idea in mind as I experimented with diverse ways of representing the sense or meaning of a school community and teachers' understandings of such contexts. So evolved the story of the mural, the fridge story, the ownership story, and the poem "Monet to Escher." Telling stories to explain or interpret data is an act of composition similar to composing music or creating a work of art. Stories are told for a purpose and impose meaning and structure to events that exist within a social context. Stories invite the reader to connect with the events or issues of school experience in ways that are qualitatively different from figures and graphs.

Although the principal–new teacher relationship was central to my study, I understood that others within the context of the workplace and the wider system had also influenced the new teacher's professional knowledge landscape. I understood, from my many years in schools, that the school context shapes and in turn is shaped by those who dwell within its boundaries. I was particularly interested in gaining multiple perspectives of this phenomenon through participant observation in my role as a staff member. Because the school context is important and getting at "school stories" is an integral part of building the narrative database, others on staff were implicated in the emergent research design as I tried to understand the school's particular ethos and sense of community. It was through this search for understanding that I realized that for me, the mural story was a symbol for the change occurring in the school culture.

The story simmered and wrote itself in my head for weeks before it emerged on paper as my way of introducing, in an authentic voice, a particular research site. A critic might say that I was subjective in my representation; I would completely agree. That is the essential point. What about the ethical considerations about creating a story based on my interpretation of experienced events? Many teachers at the school read the story and understood it as a symbol of the process of change. Some of us saw the mural story differently within the context of two merging cultures rather than an isolated event. We saw that the mural was about all of us, not just Miss Redfern. Miss Redfern has not yet read the story.

Fran's second most pressing concern related to the politics of her inquiry.

The second issue arising from my way of researching schools was a political question. How could I conduct research and be part of the school at the same time? This highlights the political dimensions of research in schools as part of a researcher's responsiveness to context and raises questions about how participation in the study might by viewed by others in the school community. Connelly and Clandinin (1993) suggest that "everyday evidence of the political quality of school settings is seen in the negotiation that occurs between participants and others in the school, and in the interest those others show when two or more people come together in extraordinary ways" (p. 86). The intent and purpose of the research was established first with the two key participants. I had anticipated that informing the rest of the staff of my intent would demand sensitivity and care in both the initial encounter and ongoing day-to-day peer relationships. To retain credibility as a teacher I knew I must remain a staff member at all times, even though I might feel that my first priority and passion was the research inquiry. Although I felt confident about my insider role, I remained aware of the ethical and political dilemmas created by "backyard research" (Glesne & Peshkin, 1992). I anticipated that one limitation might be the acquisition of what Glesne and Peshkin call "dangerous knowledge—information that is politically risky to hold, particularly for an insider" (p. 23). I wondered whether others on staff might feel that I had special access to Lisa, the principal; however, within the context of this large, busy staff my concerns were unfounded. Although I was the central character in my own research story, anxiously balancing my role, I soon learned that the rest of the staff had little or no concern about my research endeavor. Mild interest was reflected in the occasional comment about how the research was going or whether or not I was finished yet, but basically people simply accepted my presence as a staff member and researcher.

Fran's sensitivity to the political dimensions of researching her school context reflects an important level of savvy. While Fran's concerns about how others in the school might perceive her research turned out to be unfounded, it just as easily could have turned out differently for her. Despite the happy ending for Fran, we nevertheless underscore the importance of attending to these kinds of issues and concerns.

PARTING COMMENTS

Roger and Fran offer parting comments. Roger captures the essence of our argument in this chapter:

I understand that there is very little that I can do or know until I am in it and doing it, and then I can only understand by trying to lift myself out from the everyday and looking around.

We urge you to take these words to heart and try to lift yourself out from the everyday and look around.

Fran reflects on how researching schools enhances and informs understandings of teachers and their work.

Telling and writing our stories of experience of schools informs our understanding of the broader context that shapes our work as teachers. The informal and formal research we do in schools acknowledges and celebrates the authentic voices of teachers in ways recognizable and accessible to others. Researching schools invites an alternative venue for professional learning, one that may enhance the meaning of what it means to be a teacher for researchers, teachers, and (where appropriate) readers.

RESEARCH ACTIVITIES

Schools provide an enormous range of researching possibilities, in part because of the great variation in their structures, complexity, sizes, functions, foci, students, local communities, resources, and personnel, among many other things. The key point to remember, though, is that schools are complex places in which attention to relationships should be central and that there are therefore delicate considerations to be made in carrying out inquiries. This is nothing new to the sensitive and responsive inquiring professional and it is a point we repeat. As you consider the research activities also keep in mind the needs of the greater school community and the relationship of the school to the local context. The following three activities are closely related and differ only slightly in their beginning points. The remainder are a little more specific.

• Consider some of the many books about research on and in schools that have been published. Palonsky's *900 Shows a Year* (see the Recommended Readings) is one example of a book written from a teacher's experience. There are many written from an outsider's perspective, such as Alan Peshkin's *God's Choice* (1986, about a Midwestern fundamentalist Christian school) and *The Color of Strangers, the Color of Friends* (1991, about ethnicity in school and community); Carl Grant and Christeen Sleeter's *After the School Bell Rings* (1986, about issues of race, class, gender, and "handicap" within the life of a particular school and the work of its teachers and administrators); Peter Woods' *The Happiest Days?* (1990, about how British pupils cope with school as a place of learning, socializing, and living); and Penelope Eckert's *Jocks and Burnouts* (1989, about students' social categories and identity in a Michigan high school). Explore one or several of these or similar books and draw out pertinent comparisons with your own school situation. Perhaps organize a colleagues' reading group. Use the substance of the book and your own experiences of your particular school, as well as those of your colleagues, to establish some issues worthy of individual or collaborative reflexive exploration.

• There are also a number of books written by teachers or former teachers, some of which are quite controversial in a sense and criticize the way schools are, their structures, organization, curricula, foci, and so on. There are many examples of these kinds of books. Some of them include James Nehring's *The Schools We Have, the Schools We Want* (1992, about a New York State English teacher's perspectives on "the system"); Jack Greenstein's *What the Children Taught Me* (1983, about the wisdom of students as received from a long-time teacher and principal); John Taylor Gatto's *Dumbing Us Down* (1991, about the perspectives of an award-winning teacher from the State of New York who makes stabbing criticisms of public schooling); Quincy Howe's *Under Running Laughter* (1991, which is subtitled *Notes from a Renegade Classroom*); and John Holt's classics, *The Under Achieving School* (1969), *How Children Learn* (1967), and *How Children Fail* (1964). Use one or more of these books (or others that are more pertinent, so check out the local public or university library or book stores) to help you think about the school within which you work. Conceptualize a number of issues that deserve further close attention in your context and use some of the books to help bring some focus to your reflexive inquiry interests.

• Use some formal, research- and profession-informed critiques of public schooling or reform-directed publications (there are many, so check with local schools or faculties of education, their libraries, or the administrators and curriculum specialists within your school system if you cannot readily identify some titles) as a discussion focus with a group of fellow teachers. Make sure that there is some philosophical coherence between your perspective and the publications that you access. Utilize the ideas presented as a lead in to raising questions about the context of the school. Follow up with connected and pertinent reflexive inquiries.

- Use a variety of media or communication sources to identify school issues of concern to the community at large. These may include

  - Keep a file of newspaper clippings or articles about the school to be used in class work with students as well as a vehicle for discussion with both students and fellow teachers. Identify issues that you both oppose or support. Examine these issues from a reflexive inquiry perspective and share your findings with the media or an appropriate local group.

  - Ask a local radio station or television channel or station to, on a regular basis, duplicate any conversations, commentaries, or features about local schooling and education. Use these tapes to stimulate discussion with pupils, perhaps even fellow teachers, and to generate some possibilities for inquiry projects.

  - Examine past issues/volumes of the school yearbook or other student publications (such as a regular student newspaper) to identify explicit student-identified issues worthy of investigation. Also use the publications to identify concerns that are not overtly expressed as important (in other words, examine what is not said as a way of knowing what may be addressed).

  - Examine school board, district, or principal communications with teachers as a way of identifying pressing issues or appropriate foci for changed practice and use these as springboards for individual or collaborative inquiry.

  - Analyze the staff-meeting minutes for long-standing, pervasive issues that need addressing in the school and formulate a reflexive inquiry process that explores elements of these issues.

  - Examine parent letters (either collective ones, that is, as sent to the whole staff, or individual ones) as a way to identify pressing concerns of the local community.

  - Take time to mentally note the topics of conversation in the staffroom at the school and the behind the scenes rumblings. Be methodical in your analysis and interpretations of these perspectives. Use them as discussion points with a group of colleagues and as a way to help define some possible directions of inquiry.

  - Follow processes similar to those used by Roger Field and Fran Squire in this chapter. Extend their approaches by bringing in colleagues or others to work with you.

  - Use parent-interview sessions as a venue to tap into some of the perspectives held by parents about the school. Collect perspectives over time and analyze them. Formalize your project in consideration of these issues and concerns.

- Talk to parents who have withdrawn their children from the school—or plan to do so—with the express purpose of educating the children at home. These parents have set up a "home school" and are home-educating; they are teaching their own children. They have made the ultimate criticism of public schools, and teachers and school administrators are well advised to listen to their concerns or their rationales for "exiting" their children. *Home Schooling* (Mayberry, Knowles, Ray, & Marlow, 1995, see also Knowles, Marlow, & Muchmore, 1992) provides an overview of home education in the United States and accesses the perspectives of groups of parents in several states. The perspectives presented have wider application. There are many other books on home education although most are personal perspectives and advocacy books. Check titles in local libraries. Even so, these books also provide great insights into the way these parents view schools and may greatly inform the direction of your reflexive inquiries.

• With a group of colleagues or the whole school faculty, attempt to create an institutional history of the school (this may already have been done in a superficial way, or it may have been completed in some detail by an "official" historian). Question the official history, or at least the assumptions behind it. Using the processes suggested in Chapter 3, create your individual personal histories as related to being and working in your particular school. Collectively, read and compare your individual stories with the view to analyzing them for prevalent themes, common experiences, or ongoing problems, issues, or highpoints. Make comparisons of the individual stories with the official and the institutional histories. Look for congruities and incongruities and try to explain them. Through the reflexive inquiry process develop either a group or individual project that seeks to extend the work of the teachers by examining some ongoing issue that needs attention or elaboration. Gitlin et al.'s (1992) *Teachers' Voices for School Change* is compatible with elements of what we advocate in this book and may help facilitate your work.

• Return to the Research Activities suggested at the end of Chapter 5. Choose a mode of representation that seems to lend itself to a school-based inquiry. Develop an inquiry project based on the chosen form of representation. For example, work with the notion of metaphor to explore elements of the school context or create a photographic essay that captures particular elements of the school context of interest to you.

RECOMMENDED READINGS

Dadds, M. (1995). *Passionate enquiry and school development.* London: Falmer Press.
Gitlin, A., Bringhurst, K., Burns, M., Cooley, V., Myers, B., Price, K., Russel, R., & Tiess, P. (1992). *Teachers' voices for school change: An introduction to educative research.* New York: Teachers College Press.
Jalongo, M. R., & Isenberg, J. P. (1995). *Teachers' stories: From personal narrative to professional insight.* San Francisco: Jossey-Bass.
Little, J. W., & McLaughlin, M. W. (Eds.). (1993). *Teachers' work: Individuals, colleagues, and contexts.* New York: Teachers College Press.
McLaren, P. (1980). *Cries from the corridor.* Toronto, Ontario: Methuen.
McLaren, P. (1994). *Life in schools.* New York: Longman.
Palonsky, S. B. (1986). *900 shows a year: A look at teaching from a teacher's side of the desk.* New York: McGraw-Hill Publishing.
Sawyer, D. (1979). *"Tomorrow is school and I'm sick to the heart thinking about it."* Vancouver, BC: Douglas & McIntyre.
Stuart, J. (1963). *The thread that runs so true.* New York: Charles Scribner's Sons.
Waldron, P. W., Collie, T. R., & Davies, C. M. W. (1999). *Telling stories about school: An invitation....* Upper Saddle River, NJ: Merrill.

P A R T **IV**

RESEARCHING TEACHING THROUGH COLLABORATIVE INQUIRY

Like the introduction to the previous two chapters in Part III, this introduction to researching teaching through collaborative inquiry is relatively lengthy. In Part IV we highlight the formation and nurturance of meaningful, productive, and mutual relationships as vital to authentic collaborative inquiry. The forms and methods of inquiry described in this part of the book are not much different from those already described; therefore, by way of introduction we focus not on methods but on issues associated with collaborative inquiry. This regard for issues in collaborative inquiry is a recognition of the complexities associated with collaborative work and the significance of attention to process in relational inquiry.

Teachers' work traditionally has been characterized by norms of isolation, independence, privacy, and survival. Despite the fact that schools are filled with people, teachers often describe their work as lonely. As Lieberman and Miller (1990, p. 160) put it, "With so many people engaged in so common a mission in so compact a space and time, it is perhaps the greatest irony—and the greatest tragedy of teaching—that so much is carried on in self-imposed and professionally sanctioned isolation." Increasingly, however, efforts are being made in schools to challenge the isolationist nature of teachers' work by providing opportunities for teachers to engage in collaborative or joint work. In many schools teacher-development and school-improvement initiatives are linked to notions of collegiality and collaboration. Teachers are increasingly encouraged and supported in their efforts to talk together about their work, share planning and preparation activities, observe in one another's classrooms, and facilitate one another's professional growth through collaborative arrangements such as "peer coaching."

The perceived value by teachers of the kinds of collaborative ventures encouraged varies. It is not easy for some teachers who have been long socialized to work alone "behind closed classroom doors" to readily adopt attitudes and practices of collaboration. Even many new teachers envision their work as characterized by independent, isolated activities, often perceived characteristics of teaching that attracted them to the profession in the first place. School contexts that do not operate on the principles of collegiality, openness, and mutual growth necessary for productive collaboration may not be seen by teachers as fertile or safe ground for collaborative work. Even those schools either identified or self-proclaimed as "collegial" or "collaborative" are limited in the nature and extent of mutually beneficial collaborative work that takes place within them. Such limitations are imposed by lack of time, opportunity, and resources necessary to support collaborative efforts, the organizational structure of the school, historical precedents defining teachers' work, and a lack of professional recognition and valuing of collaborative work and professional development in general.

Where collaborative work does happen (and it is still relatively rare, especially in many North American schools) it tends to be focused on issues and questions outside the realm of teachers' classroom practice. Little (1990) observes

> *Closer to the classroom is closer to the bone—closer to the day-by-day performances on which personal esteem and professional standing rest.... The closer one gets to the classroom and to central questions of curriculum and instruction, the fewer are the recorded instances of meaningful, rigorous collaboration. (p. 180)*

And yet we and many others assert that collaboration is a powerful mode for the facilitation of learning and the propelling forward of professional growth. We agree with Baum's (1971) assertion that "The important role of dialogue continues through the whole of a person's life. We come to be who we are through conversations with others. We are created through ongoing communication with others" (p. 41). Indeed, learning from peers is a basic premise of this book. As we have said before, teaching is a relational activity; relations between teachers and students, teachers and parents, teachers and fellow teachers and other educational community members, and between teachers and others are of elemental concern. "Good" teachers are "good" because of the power of the various kinds of relationships they form.

In this final section of the book we focus on methods, practices, and issues associated with inquiry into teaching through collaboration—with teacher-colleagues (Chapter 8), with students (Chapter 9), and with outside researchers (Chapter 10). Although we do not address it here, we even imagine that collaborative inquiry arrangements with particularly skilled, interested, or energetic parents who have vested interests in the well-being of the classroom may indeed be possible. We see such connections arising out of mutually defined concerns for developing and maintaining teaching environments highly conducive to students' learning. One such example springs to mind. An environmental education teacher, who worked in a geographically isolated setting at a field site some distance from other teachers and schools, sought the assistance of parents when, due to fiscal restraints, the environmental education program was in danger of being cut in the annual budget review. It was deemed not to be of great value to the pupils. Using the help of concerned parents, the teacher formed a research group whose specific aim was to garner evidence from the students about the learnings in the program, about parents' observations of their children's learning in the program, about parents' perspectives of the program, and about community members' observations and stated support for the program. These inquiry activities resulted in the development of an extensive anecdotal report through a simple survey, conversational interviews, and written accounts. The parents and teacher completed all phases of the research project and the parents presented their work to the school board, who eventually refunded the program and pledged support for an additional five years, at which time it was to be reviewed.

The methods used in collaborative and reflexive inquiry do not differ much from methods of independent inquiry. For example, personal history accounts might be written and shared for purposes of discussion and ongoing clarification; journal keeping might take the form of a dialogue wherein teachers (and perhaps others) write and exchange journals for purposes of ongoing, inquiry-focused conversation; teachers might work together to create other than traditional text-based renditions of their teaching; peer observations and discussions of elements of practice might form the basis of collaborative inquiry; teachers (and others) might work together to conduct inquiries into school and community contexts.

Central to initial and ongoing considerations of collaborative inquiry is the research relationship. Working together is a process of ongoing negotiation. It is a process of ongoing attention to relational issues. Roles, responsibilities, expectations, and goals need to be mutually decided on and a working process needs to be mutually identified and monitored. In other words, working together in meaningful and productive ways requires as much, if not more, attention to process than to the product or purpose of working together. In the remainder of this introduction to Part IV, therefore, we turn our attention to a discussion of issues associated with collaborative inquiry.

ISSUES AND QUESTIONS ASSOCIATED WITH COLLABORATIVE INQUIRY

Throughout the various activities associated with collaborative inquiry are layers of issues that require attention so that the research can be mutually developmental and truly collaborative. Collaboration is not easy. It requires ongoing recognition of and attention to inherent complexities ranging from personal characteristics and individual differences in working style, needs, professional position, purpose, and the like to contextual issues such as the political or educational implications of the work—how the work might be viewed and responded to by others. At the risk of making collaborative inquiry seem too fraught with potential problems, and therefore not worth doing, we lay out some of the key issues that we believe deserve consideration. We urge you to review and consider the issues in a general way so that you are mindful of them and then return to them as appropriate and relevant to your inquiry.

Technical Issues

Technical issues present themselves at every phase of collaborative (and independent) reflexive inquiry; they are essentially issues that revolve around the initial facilitation and ongoing continuation of the inquiry process. Although technical issues may seem mundane or superficial when compared to other issues, they can substantially influence the manner and direction in which the research proceeds. Determining logistics of time and place, working out techniques of information gathering, and management and organization of information for interpreting and reporting (if appropriate for the project at hand) are all important issues. Central to technical concerns are questions such as

- How will the planning of the project proceed?
- How much time is required for substantial and beneficial inquiry?
- How can roles and responsibilities (of self, students, colleagues) be modified to allow time for reflexive inquiry as part of professional practice?

- What arrangements need to be made for information gathering, storage, interpretation, and reporting?
- How are inquiry activities coordinated and negotiated?

Interpersonal Issues

The satisfactory resolution of interpersonal issues associated with collaborative reflexive inquiry are essential. These issues are pertinent when involving students and others as research participants as well as when engaging in collaborative research with peers, university-based researchers, and others. Researching is a dynamic process, and so too are the relationships that comprise and make possible the collaborative inquiry process. Central in our thoughts about relationships within the research process are questions such as

- Are the research relationships based on mutual respect, trust, intents, and a potential for mutual benefit?
- How are responsibilities to be appropriately assumed and/or shared throughout the inquiry? How is the research process controlled? By whom?
- How are differences in emphasis and expectations to be addressed?
- How are the (autobiographical) reflexive inquiry elements of the research project articulated in process and form? How does each participant contribute to the reflexive inquiry element of the research process?
- How are individual differences in roles and responsibilities, rhythms, and patterns of work to be accommodated?
- How are the strengths of research partners identified and considered and to what extent are they complementary?
- How are research participants such as students or parents involved in authentic and respectful ways?
- Are the research partners and/or participants comfortable with the planned process and responsibilities?
- Are others (such as secretarial, support, or technical staff) to be involved in the research process? How? Why?

Procedural Issues

Procedural issues rest in the relationship of inquiry method to context and emanate from decisions about the manner in which the research is actually carried out. Among the many issues that have arisen for us during autobiographical (and other reflexive) research are those concerning conceptualization of the work, project time frames, time and location of interviews/conversations or other information-gathering processes, and the role and use of the audio- or videotape recorders. Attention to matters related to the manner in which the research proceeds are essential for the articulation and implementation of mutually beneficial and satisfying inquiry projects. Assuming that technical and interpersonal issues are resolved, questions central to procedural issues include

- How, when, and where should the inquiry process proceed? Under what conditions?
- How do research partners coordinate their activities?

- How might the inquiry process interfere with established routines and professional responsibilities? What allowances need to be made? For example, what steps need to be taken to enable coresearchers to observe or be present during a class or classes or to participate in other school-based activities?
- What arrangements need to be made to ensure opportunities for ongoing mutual benefit?
- How will (or even, should) the reporting process proceed? How are decisions about reporting made? For example, to what extent, if at all, should reporting of the inquiry process and conclusions be made available in the local and wider contexts?

Ethical Issues

We see research focused on persons' lives as a moral act and therefore infused with ethical responsibilities. Reflexive inquiry, because of its "up close and personal" nature, is intrusive. It has great potential for benefit but also for harm (mainly of a political nature). Careful thought needs to be given to any public disclosures of elements of personal and professional lives. Concerns range from making decisions about who is to transcribe tapes to where and how information will be stored, how anonymity and confidentiality will be respected, how to respond to conflicting interpretations of data, and whose voice is heard in the reported accounts. Issues related to access to and ownership of data throughout and beyond the life of an inquiry project reflect myriad ethical as well as procedural, interpersonal, and political concerns. Some of the many ethical questions that need to be considered throughout the process are

- How will confidentiality be ensured (which is especially important when there are multiple collaborators and when students are involved)? Who will have access to the research information?
- If the research findings or conclusions are to be reported and dispersed to others, how can information be presented or reported in a way that does not place researching coresearchers at risk?
- What happens in the case of collaborative research when there are conflicting impressions and interpretations of research evidence? Whose voice is heard? How are decisions to be made about the use of the information gathered, analyses made, conclusions reached, and new or revised practices decided on?

Political Issues

Political issues, like ethical issues, are central to researching teaching, teachers' work, and classrooms. Within contexts that do not place high value on teacher inquiry, engaging in such work can be risky business. In some situations, depending on the prevailing ideology, the climate of the teachers' staffroom, or the attitudes of school administrators, it may be deemed risky at worst or questionable to even acknowledge involvement in a reflexive inquiry process. It is important to think about the implications of "going public" with one's research. Among the questions to be considered in relation to political issues are

- How will participation in this kind of inquiry be viewed by others in the school and/or school board or district, including parents?

- How is the purpose of the inquiry conceptualized?
- Who has authority over the information gathered as part of the inquiry?
- What potential impact might there be on your role and status within the classroom, school, and/or board or district?
- To what extent will peers—as well as school administrators, parents, and students—view this work as valuable?
- Are there institutional privileges associated with participation in collaborative inquiry? Are there particular disadvantages?

Educational Issues

The root purpose of inquiry into teachers' work and development, classrooms, and school contexts is, we maintain, to inform and enhance teachers' practice and pupils' learning. The central educational issue hinges on the potential for the inquiry to enhance the development of refined practice. Further, educational issues are important in that they ultimately may influence both the localized political decisions relative to the focus of any particular inquiry project and the extent to which elements of your work will be taken up by other teachers or schools beyond the immediate location of your school and practice. The latter point depends on the extent to which the work is published or dispersed, the kinds of conclusions about your practice, and the degree to which your refined notions of practice are appropriate for others. Questions that may usefully inform and guide collaborative partnership research include

- How is participation in this project likely to influence professional development in general and inform practice in the classroom, university, and beyond?
- How will students directly benefit?
- How will participation in the project inform the professional development of *all* persons involved in the work?
- To what extent is participation in the research process empowering?
- Does the research work propel others to engage in similar processes?
- How will the outcomes of the work be distributed to other interested individuals? By whom? To whom? For what purpose and under what conditions?

In spite of the complexities associated with collaborative, reflexive inquiry, we maintain that working with others provides varied and substantial professional development opportunities. Two minds are better than one; four eyes can see things two cannot; the sharing of perspectives can give rise to new ways of seeing, listening, thinking, and doing. The teacher-researchers represented in the following chapters both support these assertions and reflect on some of the process-related issues associated with researching teaching through collaborative inquiry. In Chapter 8, Danila De Sousa and Catherine Huebel reflect on their researching together and the meaning of that experience for them. Michael Prendergast separately comments on a collaborative inquiry project he was engaged in as a teacher-researcher. In Chapter 9, Jane Dalton, Marina Quattrocchi, and Michelle Lantaigne-Richard focus on their work with students as coresearchers. In Chapter 10, Jim Muchmore and Anna Henson and Dan Madigan and Vicki Koivu-Rybicki explore, from different vantage points, some issues and processes associated with collaborative inquiry with outside researchers.

8

RESEARCHING TEACHING THROUGH COLLABORATIVE INQUIRY WITH PEERS

with contributions by
DANILA DE SOUSA, CATHERINE HUEBEL,
and MICHAEL PRENDERGAST

Institutions of formal education historically have been structured, both physically and otherwise, to foster learning as an individual enterprise. Hierarchy, competition, and discrimination practices based on various kinds of privilege (intellectual, racial, class, gender) have governed formal education since its inception. And, despite substantial rhetoric aimed at challenging such traditions, schools (and other formal education institutions) continue to perpetuate these entrenched values.

Students' learning is conceptualized, designed, structured, and rewarded as a solitary endeavor. The strongest survive. (Even though, at the elementary level, values of cooperation, sharing, and helping typically are fostered among pupils, such practices have yet to find their way to the secondary level of schooling and beyond. In fact, upper elementary level teachers often report a need to discourage such practices in order to prepare pupils for the rigors of high school.) The situation is similar for teachers.

Teachers work and learn in relative isolation. The busyness of schools, crowded days and curriculum, pressures to evaluate, extracurricular demands, and a host of other chores keep teachers separated from their colleagues and tied to the exigencies of their teaching work. Conversations with peers remain mainly superficial; conversations about perplexing matters of day-to-day teaching and the intellectual rigors of being better teachers seldom happen.

Isolation is a prominent theme in teachers' discourse about teaching. Strangely, it is almost a forbidden topic in many lunchrooms, staffrooms, and faculty meetings. Being alone and feeling alone are not necessarily the same as feeling and being isolated, but they are related. To be and feel alone may be a construct of the mind; nevertheless, the end result is effectively the same. Feelings of aloneness may engender intense feelings of isolation; that isolation also may be generated by the structural and organizational elements of schools, the ways of administrators therein, and the traditions that keep teachers physically, psychologically, and intellectually separated.

Within schools prevailing norms of survival also keep teachers from working together, sharing ideas, and helping one another become better teachers. For some, this means carrying out a solo act of "performing" in front of pupils beyond the prying or critical eyes of other adults. For other teachers, keeping power and authority confined to the classroom serves to elevate and accentuate their autonomy over matters of curriculum, discipline and management, and relations with students. Still others want to guard their unique practices for fear of having them (and associated activities) absconded by other teachers. In many schools, a "rites of passage" or "survival of the fittest" mentality governs attitudes toward teaching, and, in particular, these attitudes are directed at beginning teachers. Messages that stress survival and performance over professional growth, which are conveyed to teachers in their formative years, serve to perpetuate these same patterns and traditions as experience and careers unfold. They are difficult messages to counter.

Although career-long professional learning is an explicit expectation of teachers, there is often neither time nor opportunity for such endeavors in the everyday teaching life. Despite claims of emphasis on career-long learning, when budgets are cut and priorities listed, school boards and districts typically indicate their commitment to supporting teacher learning with a stroke of the pen.

The die is cast, so to speak, for the perpetuation of physical, psychological, and intellectual isolation. But it is precisely the kinds of contexts and experiences we have described that drive the imperative to break the isolation of teaching and learning and to emancipate private fears and apprehensions associated with survival.

One of the obvious solutions to professional isolation is to develop close working relations with peers, a point of professional development that is far easier to proclaim than actually accomplish. Yet, we know that challenging traditions that value isolation, individualism, and competition is worth doing. In this chapter we focus on relational learning through collaborative reflexive inquiry with peers.

Michael Prendergast is a relatively new grade 2 teacher in eastern Ontario. He reflects on his first experience of collaborative inquiry with two other classroom teachers working at the grade 1 level and a recent graduate of a teacher preparation program who had volunteered in his classroom. The focus of their inquiry was on strategies to improve the self-confidence of children in reading and writing at the beginning developmental stages. The focus of his reflections is on the process of the research and how it influenced and changed his practices as a grade 2 classroom teacher.

Danila De Sousa and Catherine Huebel are first-year teachers who engaged in a collaborative inquiry project as part of their preservice teacher preparation program. They reflect on their experiences of working together to explore elements of young children's process of learning to spell and on the role of collaborative inquiry in the day-to-day work of teachers in schools.

DEVELOPING COLLABORATIVE RELATIONSHIPS WITH PEERS

What are the ways of coming together with like-minded teachers who are committed to the process of intellectual and professional growth? Many experienced teachers sadly announce that they would be very uncomfortable within their own schools should they actively seek to locate a peer who has similar inquiry goals. Many teachers are wary about publicizing their "private" professional development projects. There may be some resistance among peers to the notion of seriously studying elements of one's practice. To be seen as overly ambitious and to be criticized for that is an act of professional development sabotage. As with other processes and states of professional relationship that we have identified in other parts and chapters of this book, the process of finding researching collaborators needs to be entered into with great care. How?

A brief dialogue between Catherine and Danila illustrates their early thinking and actions on their collaboration.

> *Catherine:* We both wanted to know how children best learn to spell, what motivates them to spell, and why children are not spelling better than they should be. We were both working with primary classes with students of similar ages but in very different environments, in fact different schools.

> *Danila:* We picked people to work with whom we felt we would be able to work well. I wanted to work with someone I thought would be as interested in the project as I was, someone I could share ideas with.

> *Catherine:* I really wanted to work with Danila because of her enthusiasm. I knew that she would be serious about the work. I tend to want to work with people who are positive because I like to keep things positive. I really liked that about Danila. I thought she seemed really enthusiastic and gung-ho about just jumping into the inquiry. We both wanted the research to involve something more than just interviewing kids. We both wanted to do a lot of hands-on activities with the kids, and we both talked about possibly videotape recording them.

> *Danila:* And we both wanted to learn about spelling. We both were fascinated with how children learn to spell. Our specific projects were very different in nature but we shared an interest in the fundamentals of how children learn how to spell. I was interested in understanding how children are able to do better on their spelling tests based on the use of various strategies in class. Cathy was interested in looking at the role of rote memory in learning to spell.

Even though their projects were collaborative, Danila and Catherine allowed each other enough room to develop different areas of focus while sharing similar processes. They worked in different schools, designed different inquiry projects that were variations on a unifying theme, and separately gathered their information. Their collaboration took place outside of school time as they discussed their work, planned, and learned from each other.

> *Catherine:* We constantly brought together observations we made and we worked from there. Danila would tell me something. I'd tell her something. We'd say, "Oh great, that's a good idea. I'll watch for that." And at the end we brought our findings together. It was continual interaction. We continually, continually collaborated and talked about what we were doing.

> *Danila:* We talked about every aspect of the project together. No decision was ever made without the other person being somehow involved, and a lot of decisions were made together.

A central point evident in Catherine and Danila's relationship is the truly collaborative nature of their working together. "Collaboration" has become an overused and broadly interpreted term in descriptions of professional development and/or research partnerships. We want to emphasize the distinction between what we consider to be a *cooperative* research relationship and a truly *collaborative* one. Collaborative research requires substantial investments of time and energy by both parties in both the substance of the work and the process of researching together. For research to be truly collaborative it needs to be a process of ongoing negotiation that honors and respects individuals' strengths, particular expertise, interests, and time commitments and where responsibilities are mutually agreed on. It may not necessarily mean that there is an exact division of labor in every phase of the research but there is a commitment to a process of shared decision making. What distinguishes a collaborative research partnership from a cooperative one is its nonhierarchical nature and the attention given to process and the emphasis on ongoing negotiation and decision making by all involved.

COLLABORATIVE REFLEXIVE INQUIRY AND PROFESSIONAL DEVELOPMENT

Learning from and working with peers is what collaborative inquiry is all about. At its best it is a meaningful and engaging experience in relational learning. Working with one or more colleagues on a mutually defined project can be enormously satisfying on many different levels. In the following segments, Danila and Catherine comment on the satisfaction they derived from working together. They highlight one of the central elements of "successful" collaboration—mutuality. They clearly saw their relationship as one of equal commitment, engagement, and value. And this shared nature of their work was a new and rewarding experience for them.

> *Danila:* This experience of working together was different from any other experiences of working with others. In other situations in the

past I always felt as if I had to take on all the work in order to accomplish something well. This project, though, was more of a learning process. We were learning how to work together; we were learning about how kids spell; we were learning about how to implement resources in the classroom.

Catherine: The success of our collaboration had a lot to do with personality. Danila and I were also in the same mindset going into the research. We had decided that we wanted to do this inquiry and do it well and learn something from it.

Danila: The collaboration was such a sharing experience. I'd never experienced that before. It was really nice. And it taught me a lot about how to work with people—to listen to other people because other people do have wonderful ideas and that together the ideas enhance each other.

Michael also has quite a deal to say about the relational elements of working with collaborating partners. He points out an important by-product of collaborative inquiry—the development of meaningful collegial relationships that transcend the focus of the inquiry.

Two people working together change each other through the process. This can be true not only in a relationship between teacher and university researcher in creating change in the knowledge of one another, but also with teachers working in the same setting on an inquiry project. We have made progress in our personal and professional relationships because of the collaborative inquiry process. One of the positive aspects of doing research together has been the change in the relationships between colleagues with whom I have been collaborating. This type of sharing between interested professionals around a common theme seems to be benefiting not only the program and methods in our classroom but also helping us to develop our personal relationships with each other. I realize how great our research group has been at my school. It requires dedicated individuals to try to improve themselves through the process of inquiry. What began as a group of four who literally had just met in September is now a close-knit bunch who share much more than ideas around our research. Although we all contribute to the project in different ways and to varying degrees, we all have found personal understanding and respect for each other. For me this could be more important than the substantive results of the project.

Michael notes that the relational benefits led to the development of complementary perspectives.

Being relatively new to teaching causes me to question my knowledge in relation to my colleagues who have more experience and different theories and practices in use in their classroom. Because my teaching approach and methods are whole language–based and their experience also includes more "traditional" ways of teaching, we learn from each other. The ideas we discuss and our common experience of being in primary classrooms leads to our better understanding of each other as individuals. Working together has enhanced my experience in my work-place because I am with a new staff and has allowed us to feel more comfortable with each other.

Being open to other perspectives and ideas and viewing learning as an integral part of teaching and teacher development are prerequisite attitudes for engaging in collaborative inquiry. Catherine and Danila note

Danila: If I want to be a good teacher, and if I want to continue growing and learning, then I have to continue to do research on my practice. Otherwise I've sort of sold myself out and not done what I intended to do in the first place.

Catherine: There's always more to learn. I look back and think, "Gee I didn't know that three months ago." You're always learning as you go along.

ISSUES AND CONCERNS

There are many barriers to collaborative work. Time and resources are often limited. The structure of schools works against those who wish to collaborate. Timetables, rotary systems, regimented curriculum, and even the latest educational policies work against those who wish to experiment together to improve teaching. Distance between schools or conflicting demands of family, friends, and other professional activities all make collaboration difficult. Michael comments on the persistent problem of lack of time as an obstacle to collaborative work. This is followed by a poignant description by Catherine of how the rigid scheduling of teachers' time militates against collaborative work.

Michael: Teachers are among the most creative and dynamic individuals, yet often they close their doors to their peers. I have found in the past a noticeable reluctance on the part of many experienced teachers to become involved in group development activities. Many factors may cause this reaction to the sharing of theories and practice among teachers. Time is probably the single most negative influence; there simply is not enough of it to go around. Administrators typically do not give consideration to teacher research when scheduling planning time and do not allot the extra preparation time required for teachers to collaborate.

Catherine: That a lot of teachers don't talk or work together has to do with the daily schedule. A typical day for me last year was going in at eight o'clock, preparing till eight-thirty, and teaching straight through till twelve. And then we had to eat with our students in our classrooms, which I thought was too bad. If parents had been brought in for that we could have had at least twenty minutes together to sit around and talk. We all stayed in our classrooms from twelve to twelve-twenty. From twelve-twenty till one o'clock I had to supervise in the detention room. I didn't see any other teachers to talk to day in and day out. It was driving me crazy. We had no recess break because at recess time we all had to monitor different floors and make phone calls to parents. After school we also had detentions to supervise and we were all expected to tutor from half an hour to an hour after school every day. By the time we finished tutoring and supervising detention the last thing we wanted to do was sit down and say, "How are you doing?" Even if we'd wanted to collaborate we probably couldn't have unless we called each other on the phone in the evening. But by the time you go home, you need a little time to yourself.

The following anecdote, also by Catherine, speaks volumes about the isolationist nature of schools and teachers' work and the lack of encouragement and opportunity for teachers to talk with one another, discuss substantive issues related to curriculum and teaching, and to learn from and with each other.

I was really thrilled one day after school when I got about three teachers together in the hallway talking about spelling. I asked a couple of questions and then stopped and listened to them. I just stood back and observed and listened. I realized that these three primary teachers had never ever before discussed their philosophy of how they approached their teaching programs. One teacher was an adamant believer in phonics. She talked about how most of her language arts program is not really a balanced program, that it was more of a phonics-based program. Another teacher took a more balanced approach whereby phonics was only about a quarter of her program. She worked out of spellers whereas the other teacher didn't even have spellers in her classroom. And then the other teacher said, "Well, I just work a lot on writing and reading." The three teachers took very different approaches and it was interesting to hear them because they started to defend their respective programs. I just stood back and thought, "Wow, this is fascinating! They've been working together for years and nobody is really aware of what the other person is doing in her classroom!"

There probably hasn't been an opportunity for them to sit down at a workshop or over the lunch hour in staffrooms. People have other things to talk about. It's sad. It always boils down to the situation in the school and the relationships between the teachers.

Danila and Catherine comment further on teachers' tendency to not discuss their teaching or programs. Also apparent in their comments is their dramatically different attitude toward such silencing—one that they hopefully will be able to cultivate. As Catherine comments, so much depends on the context within which teachers work and the kinds of collegial relationships they are encouraged to foster.

Danila: A lot of teachers feel defensive and protective about their programs because they're always open to criticism from parents, kids, and administrators. So they take a very defensive stance. It is difficult for them to talk about their programs if they don't feel comfortable defending themselves. Talking with other teachers about their programs is something that I really enjoy. There's a lot that I have to learn and it's really nice to be able to talk to someone about it and to feel comfortable enough to say, "I'm not quite sure about what I'm doing. What do you do? Can you help me? I welcome any advice that you have to offer and if I have anything that I can help you with then we'll exchange."

Catherine: In some schools some teachers feel a little threatened by each other or a bit unwilling to share their ideas. I sat in a staffroom a few weeks ago and heard one teacher tell another teacher that somebody had "taken" her idea. I thought, "What a sad, sad situation to be in." I've also heard the opposite kind of sentiment expressed by teachers who work together and love it. It depends on the individual personalities and attitudes of people first and foremost. But second, I think it really depends on the principals—the type of community they're trying to build among the staff and within the classroom.

PARTING COMMENTS

We conclude with a short account from Michael about the role and value of collaborative reflexive inquiry in enhancing the learning of students and teachers alike.

Collaborative reflexive inquiry is self-reflective research done in a social situation to improve our practice. Is it a valid form of research in the eyes of educational researchers such as Virginia Richardson? [See Chapter 1 for an elaboration of this point.] Who cares! To me it has more than proven itself in its "validity" because my teaching has improved. My collaborators and I benefit from our discussions and sharing of ideas. Our students are exposed to new and varied practices in an attempt to help them grow as individuals.

Our project focused on how to improve the self-confidence of children who are in the beginning developmental stages of reading and writing. As we tried various strategies we were forced to examine current practices, reexamine older practices, and experiment with new methods to help our students grow. The process of inquiry causes us to ask ourselves why we teach as we do and why one method works better than another. This type of questioning helps to rationalize our practice in the classroom so that we can articulate what we are doing and justify our methods. Being able to tell a parent, an administrator, fellow teachers and, most importantly, ourselves why we do things the way we do in our classroom is critical.

Much of the time I was engaged in the inquiry I felt confused and unsure about the research process. Like any new concept or idea, doing research on your practice for the first time can be difficult to grasp. In the end I realize that my practice has improved. More importantly the attitudes of my students toward reading and writing and their confidence level in their abilities is changing. Wading through the fog in the beginning, the reflection along the way, the constant questioning of our methods, and the time and energy spent in the process have all been worthwhile.

RESEARCH ACTIVITIES

For reasons mentioned earlier in the chapter, researching with peers is perhaps one of the most difficult things to do. This is especially so if they are peers from the same department (as in a secondary school) or from the same school. Sometimes it is far easier to find researching peers who work in nearby schools or even in schools some distance away. We think, however, that the greatest inquiry possibilities may lie with working with like-minded, enthusiastic colleagues wherever they are found—individuals who envision future classrooms and schools that are different from the current ones, individuals who are enticed by the possibilities of their own different future practices. We are intentionally vague in our suggestions for research activities so that you may be more open to processes and inquiry foci that truly emanate from your own work and the school context in which you are located. Here, though, are some ways to get started:

- Make a list of immediate and nearby colleagues with whom you think you could work on a reflexive inquiry project. Develop a focal point for a small or large group meeting. Perhaps use a reading from current professional literature to focus on, or a discussion about a particular pertinent issue (although one that is not likely to divide the group). Articulate your individual and collective perspectives. Work at defining your mutual interests in researching or inquiring into your practice. One example of this might be to center your inquiry on the intersection of personal histories (yours and the other teachers') with the institutional history of the school. You could take as a topic something like school climate or tone, coping with student evaluation practices and expectations, gang and antisocial student behaviors, unintentional systemic exclusion of particular groups of students, school policies regarding the place of competitive sports or physical education in the curriculum, or the attention to the arts in the school curriculum. These are intended to be broad pervasive issues firmly grounded in the school or institutional culture. Establish some of your individual and collective assumptions about the topics of inquiry that are imbedded within teaching practices and institutional policies and practices. Use the assumptions as a way of defining appropriate foci for your inquiry work. You may wish to either question the assumptions or get a better handle on their origins and their relevance for and place in contemporary practices. The main intention of this inquiry is for you to acquire a thorough understanding of the relationship between the institutional perspective and your individual and collective personal perspectives. Gitlin et al.'s (1992) book *Teachers' Voices for School Change* may be especially helpful here.

- Use one of the many books found in the Recommended Readings (located at the end of each chapter within this book) to read about particular researching strategies. Any one of the other chapters in this book may be helpful in promoting this work although we think that Chapter 2, Teaching as Autobiographical Inquiry; Chapter 3, Personal History Inquiry; Chapter 4, Researching the Self through Journal Writing; and Chapter 5, Researching the Creative Self through Artistic Expression, may especially be suitable because they will heighten the contrast and tension among the "personal," the "collective," and the "institutional." Claudia Mitchell and Sandra Weber's book, *Beyond Nostalgia,* mentioned earlier in Chapters 2, 5, and 6, also has researching ideas appropriate for collaborative inquiry. Find a suitable venue to discuss the processes and the different foci that other teacher researchers have had in their work. You may have to work hard to bring the "personal" perspectives and means of understanding your practice (as advocated through the chapters just cited) into a collaborative context, but you can do that if you aim at defining your own issues in reference, unison, and in relation with peers. Individual work done in this way will contribute to a collective understanding. Work at defining both a focus and a process. Take, for instance, the issue of homework, or the issue of working with parents, or the needs of homosexual students, or the needs of students coping with emotional abuse at home. Each of you could define your own experiences and assumptions about these matters through "researching the self" and then bring your individual insights and articulations together to the "whole group" (however you have defined it). It is probably better to not concentrate on the big issues but rather those matters that will make a difference in classroom practices. The intention is that you will each honor the experience of your peers and that together you can establish some helpful perspectives that may either satisfy your need to establish a "new" classroom practice or will be the "informed ground" on which to begin a wholly new inquiry project. In other words, use the process of exploring the self in order to establish some common experiences, which can then lead to the development of a focus for inquiry suitable for a larger project.

• Examine again the teachers' narrative accounts within this chapter (and perhaps other chapters as well). Are there processes and foci articulated therein that will help you get started? If you are really hesitant about appropriating the processes and practices of others, insert your own assumptions and experiences and decide how they alter conceptions of inquiry.

RECOMMENDED READINGS

Daiker, D. A., & Morenberg, M. (1990). *The writing teacher as researcher: Essays in the theory and practice of class-based research.* Portsmouth, NH: Boynton/Cook.

Kemmis, S., & McTaggart, R. (Eds.). (1988). *The action research planner.* Victoria, Australia: Deakin University Press.

Mohr, M. M., & MacLean, M. S. (1987). *Working together: A guide for teacher-researchers.* Urbana, IL: National Council of Teachers of English.

Oja, S., & Smulyan, L. (1989). *Collaborative action research: A developmental approach.* London: Falmer Press.

9

RESEARCHING TEACHING THROUGH COLLABORATIVE INQUIRY WITH STUDENTS

with contributions by
JANE DALTON, MICHELLE LANTAIGNE-RICHARD,
and MARINA QUATTROCCHI

Students are the very *raison d'être* for the historical existence of schools. Even before formal schools—at least as we know them in the nineteenth and twentieth centuries— became commonplace, the informal work and roles of teachers within communities and families existed and were held in high esteem, essentially because of the close relationships formed and held with learners. Sometimes such relationships spread over a lifetime. Sometimes they were short-lived. Sometimes relationships were bound by authority and power. Sometimes they were based on love, or devotion, or adulation. Sometimes they were bound by contexts of aggression or war, or of safety and survival. Sometimes they were spawned by spiritual quests. Whatever their impetus, they hinged on the establishment of personal bonds and relationships that became the defining elements of what it means to be a pupil and what it means to be a teacher. The act of teaching and the work of teachers were defined by a body of knowledge and expertise held by an experienced person *in relationship with* students. Teachers taught people who wanted to learn survival and cultural skills, and these understandings of survival and cultural knowledge and the skills associated with them were passed down from generation to generation through intimate relationships forged of close individual, familial, or community connections.

Without pupils, and without a focus of learning, the work of informal or formal classroom teaching becomes profoundly meaningless. Although this notion about the primacy of relationships in teaching may indeed be questioned by many who have moved through modern schools as pupils, it still remains at the heart of teachers' work. Ask adults about their teachers of years earlier. Although many may not be able to recount the importance of their relationship with all of their childhood teachers, those they remember (and those who often powerfully influenced their learning) will probably be remembered *because* of their attention to developing respectful relationships. Teachers remain influential figures in peoples' lives. Teachers, too, remember the power of their relationships with pupils.

Teaching is paramountly a relational activity. It is a simultaneous and meaningful engagement of a teacher and a learner for purposes of intellectual, spiritual, emotional, social, or physical challenge and development. Without a learner there is no teaching. With a stretch we carry forward this notion to classroom inquiry: "Without a student coresearcher there is no researching." We explore this concept.

WHY INVOLVE STUDENTS?

If teaching is defined as a relational activity perhaps research also should be defined that way, especially research connected to students. Defining research in a relational manner honors the teacher-student relationship in an important way. In recent years there has been a general progression, or development and finessing, of educational research processes so that there has been a move by many educational researchers to be more collaborative in their enterprises. This is especially so of many university-based researchers working with classroom practitioners. Still, research is often conceptualized as something that the researcher does *to* the researched, a process that witnesses the implementation and maintenance of hierarchical relationships between parties. Here and throughout the book we challenge the underlying assumptions behind hierarchical relationships in the research endeavor.

Teachers who are able to facilitate productive and meaningful learning experiences for their pupils typically develop and support mutually respectful relationships with their students that transcend the particular bounds of the subject matter; "good" educational researchers, in our view, are those who are mindful of the delicate practice-inquiry link and who work to define mutually respectful relations with those whose experiences they are trying to understand. For us, just as teaching is a relational activity so, too, is researching. This notion is at the heart of the message we intend to convey through this chapter. We involve students because it is the respectful thing to do and because the actions of teaching and educating in schools or other educative settings are essentially null and void without the presence of students.

The presence of students (in a variety of ways) as active agents in teacher-induced classroom inquiries is essential if the findings or benefits of that research are to make a difference in students' and teachers' experiences of school. Involving students in researching activities is natural; it resonates with the kinds of teaching and learning processes already in place in classrooms. The idea of involving students as collaborators in classroom inquiry is an extension of the relatively recent shift in educational research in which external researchers research *with* teachers, not *on* teachers. Continuing the analogy, teacher research in classrooms needs to be *with* students, not *on* them. Recall Lydia's reflections in Chapter 6 on her involvement of grade 2 students in an inquiry into their school experiences. Her comments are apt here as well.

In this chapter, like the pattern we have established in other chapters, we draw on the work of teacher-researchers. Jane Dalton, Marina Quattrocchi, and Michelle Lantaigne-Richard reveal elements of their processes of involving students as coresearchers in their respective classroom inquiries. Jane is a community college teacher and situates her inquiry in the classroom in which she has worked for the past twelve years. She teaches adults who are in college in order to acquire skills and knowledge that they did not learn during their high school years. In the program in which she teaches, adults study mathematical, English language, job search, and computer skills they need in order to be successful in either work or further education. Marina is a former elementary school teacher who currently teaches high school English to all grades and levels of students. Michelle teaches grade 8 in a multicultural, middle-class area near Toronto, Ontario.

Jane sums up this section with a brief comment in which she reasons through the question, "Why involve the students?"

My main reason for adopting a reflexive, self-checking approach through involving students as coresearchers was my belief that one cannot truly be an observer in a situation without being implicated in the activities and actions of the whole. When one is observing, the vision that is generated is always filtered through the lens of the observer. In addition, I could not be sure if suspicions about aspects of learning that I observed were "real" without checking them with the student-learners.

Since students are most astute observers of teaching practice they have important contributions to make. This position is underscored and elaborated throughout the chapter by Jane, Marina, and Michelle.

WAYS OF INVOLVING STUDENTS
AS CORESEARCHERS

On a spectrum of research connected to classrooms and students there is a rainbow of inquiry approaches from traditional quantitative, experimental research to quantitative survey or questionnaire research, to quasi-qualitative observational and interview research, to participant observation and ethnographiclike research, to interview-based research, to participatory action research, to life history research, to phenomenological (lived experience) work. Our point here is that within the range of research perspectives available to teacher-researchers, there is a need to thoughtfully involve students in the work of researching. Some of these forms of inquiry are more open than others to student involvement. Moreover, the form of students' involvement will be shaped by the research perspective that drives the inquiry of the teacher-researcher. In the many shapes of reflexive inquiry the experiences and perspectives of the teacher-researcher are laid alongside the experiences and perspectives of students. With an intention of mutual engagement and mutual benefit and a belief in what Dave Hunt calls "the equity of expertise" (Hunt, 1987), teachers and students become coresearchers.

Jane involved students in a classroom inquiry because she wanted to understand more about her teaching, their learning, and her evaluation of them. Rather than conducting several short-term investigations, Jane carried out an inquiry that spanned three years. This time frame was possible because the students with whom she works remain with her for the duration of their program.

I decided to research my own teaching situation because I wanted to learn more about the ways of knowing involved in teaching, learning, and evaluating. The time span for this inquiry was three years. For the first year I made audiotape recordings of class sessions for a period of six months, held interviews with volunteer student coresearchers who wanted to facilitate my understanding of their learning within our classroom, and kept a daily journal of my reflections on practice and the process. During the second and third years I infused my developing analysis into the classroom both in text form as well as in discussions. A lot of student feedback was collected—too much to deal with. Even now, after the completion of that inquiry, learners continue to question the differences between their previous learning experiences and the ones in which they are currently involved. In a way, the research continues.

Michelle began formal classroom inquiry five years into her teaching career. The project she reflects on here was developed within the context of the media literacy curriculum and was a collaborative venture with her grade 8 students. Over the course of a six-month period the project, completed in two phases, took shape with the help of her students.

During the first phase of the project I familiarized the students with gender issues in the mass media. Introductory lessons and discussions were followed by deliberations on the issues within small group settings. The focus of these discussions was the students' impressions of gender issues in the various media samples they had collected (e.g., an episode of a popular television show, teen magazines, a radio broadcast, television commercials, and current popular and rock music videos). Approximately six or seven students, along with one adult facilitator, made up each of five discussion groups. (I was able to acquire the assistance of another teacher for this work.) Conversations were audiotape recorded for subsequent analysis.

Phase two of the project gave the students an occasion to privately and independently voice their concerns, issues, and perceptions with regard to gender issues in the media. In privacy students recorded their feelings about the topic on audiotape. This medley of voices, my journals detailing experiences researching with the students, and the students' reflections were then studied. With the students' assistance I developed new understandings of my teaching that had definite, ongoing implications for my practice.

Marina is an avid proponent of dreamwork. Like Michelle, she conceptualized a research project that was also, primarily in her case, a curriculum development venture.

I have a strong belief that dreams are the inner screens of our psyche. The scenes they project guide and direct us in our daily lives, increase self-awareness, and challenge us toward self-actualization. They are projected in a language that seeks to balance the dreamer. It is a metaphorical language rich in symbolism, imagery, and often playful humor. As Fromm (1951) states, it is a "forgotten language" although, like music, it is a language that is truly universal. Andrews (1991) says that although dreams may mystify and perplex us, more importantly they unite us. Whether we are rich or poor, mighty or weak, male or female, dreaming is one experience we all share. "If for no other reason than its universality, dream work should be a part of our overall educational process" (p. 5).

My own "Canadian dream" for education is that one day dreamwork would be universally accepted for students of all ages. This work would be considered both valuable and meaningful in directing students toward their greatest potential. Dreamwork would find a place in language arts, secondary-level English literature, art, drama, music, and religious studies. I look forward to a day when dreams are considered an important method of holistic education nourishing the mental, physical, emotional, and spiritual needs of students. I envision a time when inner work such as dreams, guided imagery, contemplation, and active imagination are not considered unique, mystical, or mysterious. Teachers would not only feel comfortable engaging in this work but would experience the satisfaction and purpose it brings to students' lives.

I decided to begin to realize my dream in my own grade 11 English literature classroom, where I involved students as cocurriculum developers and coresearchers in a collaborative inquiry into the prospects and possibilities of dreamwork as part of the educational process and curriculum. It was my hope that by reflecting back on dream experiences, students would transform ordinary dreams into extraordinary messages. Our existing curriculum contained a science fiction novel, *The Lathe of Heaven,* by Ursula LeGuin, which focused on the potential power of dreams. This was a meaningful coincidence and I took the opportunity to "seize the moment."

The greatest challenge to involving students as coresearchers in inquiries into teaching or classroom and school projects is connected to defining the nature of their involvement. The culture of school boards or districts and the climate of parental responses to their children being involved in formal research mean that there are some delicate paths to tread in the forest of legal and procedural requirements established by these agencies and the public's demands. Behind our urgings to work closely with students is our belief that the researching process ultimately must be for the improvement of classroom practice. In this regard the focus is not to inquire about the students' experiences simply for the sake of knowing about them; the purpose is to improve practice and change the status quo. Our view is that since the foregrounding within the inquiry is on teachers' actions or classroom activities or curriculum and the importance of professional practice, and the middle and backgrounds are probably the students' experiences, then the same formal approval channels set up for formal researching activities in schools are not appropriate. It is the purpose of the research that makes a difference between formal researching activities and more reflexive, informal, improved practice motives of the kind of work we are advocating. All of the discussion that may result from a comparison of these two very different purposes underscores the importance of a sensitive, responsive, relational stance. There are several options for how to proceed in coresearching with students.

An obvious way to involve students—and this could be possible within a range of ability and age groups—is to conceptualize a project with them. Perhaps the focus of the inquiry is entirely generated by students, say, as arising from their explicit experiences in or out of the classroom. Perhaps they see the issue as imperative to understand or resolve. It is their "political" action, then, that precipitates the research process. Perhaps the focus is something that both the teacher and the students recognize together. Or, perhaps the focus begins with the teacher who is able to persuade the students of its value and relevance. Whatever the impetus, in conceptualizing inquiry with students the projects and goals of teaching likely become the vehicles for inquiry. In such collaborative work the goals of teaching and the goals of inquiry are often intermeshed. Inquiries that are conceptualized largely by students are taken up by the teacher as a "curriculum project" or as a vehicle for essentially underwriting mandated learnings within the curriculum.

Many teachers do this kind of inquiry work with students naturally or intuitively but they may not instantly recognize it as such. They see an issue that needs resolve, define it within the arena of classroom action, set a project for students, support the students through the inquiry work, foster the examination of information, and facilitate group or whole-class analyses and representations of the work. Perhaps the findings are pinned up on bulletin boards; perhaps they are simply discussed, but the teacher moves on to rethink the nature and form of practice. Alternative actions emerge from the inquiry. The students in this model are not necessarily actively involved in the implementation of new practice arising from the research. Depending on the teacher-student relationship, though, students are engaged throughout all phases of the research process from conceptualization to design of information-gathering details, analyses of information, articulation of findings, representation and writing up, and sharing the findings with others. Such processes are, of course, represented and replicated in many areas of the formal, mandated school curriculum, and this makes this inquiry work possible in virtually all subject areas (we cannot think of exceptions). In addition, even though this process may be analogous to the scientific method in that the processes are connected in a loose kind of way, we are not intending to foster the use of the formal scientific method, which focuses particularly on hypothesis generation, hypothesis testing, data gathering, theory generation, and so on. Such applications of the scientific method are appropriately more relevant in sciences and mathematics, or perhaps in contexts that focus on other than explorations of human experience and the delicate teaching-learning process and relationship.

Another way to work with students is to selectively involve them in various phases of the research process. In this scenario, for example, students may be only involved in information gathering. Say you were trying to understand aspects of students' school or curricular experiences. You could do something similar to what Lydia did with her grade 2 students (see Chapter 6) except that you could ask the students themselves to record their experiences over several days of classes or to write or talk about (perhaps audiotape record) their school days. (The nature of student involvement would naturally depend on their age and maturity and on your relationship with them.) Alternatively, you could involve students as informal interviewers to solicit accounts of experience from other students. In this kind of work attention needs to be paid to student-student relational issues and the ethical responsibility among students. Sharing information-gathering responsibilities with different class members over the course of a period of time and in different inquiry projects can help to cultivate a classroom culture of inquiry and learning. The manner in which we envision this happening can only occur within a context where everyone knows that the teacher, or inquirer, is utterly mindful and respectful of individuals and the values connected with fostering mutually caring relationships.

Another alternative level of student involvement may be to invite students at opportune times throughout the inquiry process—one that you as teacher have devised—to provide ongoing commentary on either the process as you inform them of it or the findings that you develop. Either way, and there are many ways to conceptualize this kind of consultative relationship, the teacher and the students engage in exchanges about the work. An essential feature of this kind of working relationship rests in defining the focus and the goals of the work and the underlying assumptions as they affect the quality and level of students' input, so that the exchange is rooted in some common understandings and leads to the potential for valuable insights to be revealed. This is the least-intense level of student-teacher collaboration, but nevertheless it provides valuable opportunities for the growth of both parties. More than anything it places value on the potential contributions of students to the refinement of professional practice.

Although we have already mentioned the place of student-initiated projects that are facilitated by teachers in substantial ways, there may be opportunities for students to initiate and direct inquiries with only very minimal guidance and facilitation by teachers. We see this kind of activity as having a feel that is distinctly different from something that is largely facilitated by a teacher. The impetus for this action may also be political, social, academic, and rest entirely in students' experiences or reactions to events or circumstances, but the teacher's role is perhaps relegated to that of an occasional resource person, one who is an "expert" in process. The teacher may lay out fundamental procedures at the onset of the work, for example, but nevertheless takes a backseat role. We acknowledge that this kind of involvement may be incredibly emancipating for students but we also know that only cohesive groups of students with ample meaningful time under the tutelage of relationally strong teachers will be able to pull off this kind of work. Given that the inquiry work, from conception to conclusion, rests in the hands of students, the benefits to teachers will only become apparent as knowledge is acquired through the process and made explicit from the representation of the findings by students. In this way teachers' practices can be influenced by student work. This is the loosest form of collaborative enterprise.

FOSTERING COLLABORATIVE RELATIONSHIPS—CHALLENGING TRADITIONAL ROLES

Involving students as coresearchers presents numerous challenges to both teachers and students, at the heart of which is the challenge to alter traditional, hierarchically defined roles and relationships. Students have certain expectations of teachers and of their own roles in the classroom and school and in relation to teachers. Likewise for teachers. In order for teachers and students to engage as coresearchers, both parties must examine and likely reframe conceptions and expectations associated with their respective roles, relationships, and responsibilities in the teaching-learning enterprise. Jane comments.

The way in which I researched my work environment was to place myself as a participant/learner. This positioning was difficult not only for the student-learners, who were studying with me, but also for me. Such a positioning opens up a hall of mirrors that is complex to both research and live. What most of us know is that learners expect their instructors to know. By placing myself in a position of learner/inquirer, I also acknowledged that I may not know and that I was desirous to learn that which I did not know. I told the students that I wanted to find out how they learned *with* me, not *from* me. Philosophically, I believe that knowledge is neither a fixed entity nor something that can be owned. I see knowledge as a progression of thoughts, ideas, and experimentations.

Michelle ventured into collaborating with students in a cautious manner, as her account evidences.

Working in collaboration with students was a new experience for me. I had always valued the opinions and thoughts of students with regard to procedural matters in the classroom, but I felt hesitant about giving them ownership in the development of a curriculum unit and in establishing a direction for my inquiry. I realized, however, that collaboration with the students was important if this project was to be productive. Hesitatingly at first, I allowed the students the opportunity to assist in the development of the research and curriculum development project.

In fact, the project took on a new life when I let go of my doubts and allowed the students more participation. I then realized that I could capitalize on the collaboration, and the project became a chance for students to have a voice with regard to gender issues in the media.

I introduced the project to the class by explaining that I wanted to work with them as coresearchers. We discussed the framework for the project. Students offered suggestions about which media samples they would like to discuss, how the discussion groups would be determined and organized, the amount of time needed for the project, and ideas about followup work.

COLLABORATIVE INQUIRY—
FOR WHOM AND WHAT?

In defense of teachers and in support of their equal involvement in educational research conducted by university-based researchers, we often ask the question, "Who is the research for?" Our purpose in doing so is to point out that educational research must be perceived by teachers as meaningful and relevant to their work and professional lives. It must be grounded in and return to practice (broadly construed). We extend this notion to students and the overall classroom, curricular, and school context. Who is research for? For teachers and students for purposes of improving practice; developing curriculum; enhancing educational experiences; and informing understandings about teaching-learning processes, relationships, and contexts. In this section we underscore the importance of inquiry being mutually beneficial for everyone involved and for the overall educational experience of teachers and students. The days of research benefiting only the researcher are long gone—in schools, at least.

For Jane, the benefits of inquiry with students rested in the opportunity for the generation of reciprocity.

The student-coresearchers were extremely gracious with their time and steadfast commitments to help me analyze my hunches. One of the most serious realizations I experienced during this period of "re-reflection" was that even though the coresearchers were willing to give time and energy toward my goal, reciprocity occurred when we spent time discussing their personal issues. Each time we talked, the interviews with the coresearchers concluded with discussions about their personal lives. It was almost as if the questions about the research prompted considerations about life outside of the school context. At the time I was impressed by both the consistency of this shift in conversation from school to the personal and the importance of reciprocity in inquiry. Today I consider this shift an important consideration for educators. It is possible that, even though education may be the main focus for the "teacher" it is only one part of the focus for the "learners." Perhaps the question becomes, "How can educators be involved in reciprocal educational ventures?"

Similarly, Michelle comments on the reciprocal nature of the collaborative inquiry and the beneficial effects it had for the students, herself, and the whole classroom milieu.

I realized that I was learning and growing so much because I was detailing experiences of my practice through a professional journal. I felt the students would also benefit by reflecting and analyzing (at their own level). Thus the second phase of the project was created: students were given an opportunity to speak frankly and genuinely about issues discussed in class and recorded their comments on audiotape. This was a very powerful exercise for them. They seemed to have a sense of accomplishment when they had finished their session and were eager for me to listen to their well-thought-out comments.

During the taperecording activity students were unable to influence one another's answers. Many students expressed their gratitude for sharing in this project and for their strides in learning. This exercise made me realize that students have much on their minds but do not have sufficient opportunity to express themselves (or voice) in a constructive manner. It reinforced the need for journals or other forms of reflection in the classroom milieu.

Collaborative classroom inquiry has been a very powerful and valuable tool for me and my students. I have taken many risks in collaborating with the students and listening to their unadulterated voices with regard to various aspects of our focus of inquiry. I had to leave myself open to new ways of understanding and knowing both myself and my thirteen- and fourteen-year-old students.

Listening to the voices of the students was a great opportunity for me to hear many of them from a different perspective. This way of working has opened up new ways of knowing my pupils. Prior to the project I had not had or taken the chance to fully acquaint myself with the students' particular ideas on gender issues in the media. The taped conversations and personal narratives gave me many insights into the class as a group, the small group culture, and individuals.

I believe one reason for the success of the project was the level of collaboration between me and the grade 8 students. They had a feeling of ownership from the outset and as a result were genuinely curious and eager to work on the project. My classroom seemed to transform into a bustling, energetic venue in which real learning began to happen both for the students and myself.

For Michelle, engaging in research on her teaching has had a renewing effect. She comments both on how reflexive inquiry, particularly when conducted in collaboration with students, has informed her ongoing professional development and how indirectly and unexpectedly her inquiry work has strengthened relationships with colleagues.

Five years into my teaching career I had a gnawing feeling that something intangible was lacking. On the surface I was successful as I worked diligently planning and preparing daily lessons. I developed many exciting curriculum units and I fulfilled all my professional duties. Yet I still felt that something was missing. I yearned to deepen my personal and professional growth but I was unsure how to proceed with this on my own. Then I was introduced to the idea of teacher-research. The notion of investigating and reflecting on my teaching experiences gave me the freedom to develop my implicit theories. More importantly, it was an opportunity to inform and direct my practice and to fill the void I had experienced in my professional life.

I was encouraged when I felt that my practice became more intimate and immediate through the inquiry process. It became obvious that reflexive inquiry was a wonderful experience and that analyzing, learning, and understanding the complexities of my classroom would be a lifelong process.

Not only has research on my teaching assisted me in connecting with students but it has also connected me with colleagues. In the busyness of my professional life I sometimes feel alone among the masses. Although I am with people all day I still feel lonely. With this project I had an interesting way to connect with my class and with other educators. I was able to include other staff members as group facilitators but I also discussed many facets of this project with colleagues in the staffroom. One day I engrossed the staff in a very lively and somewhat heated conversation about sexist language in the classroom. As a result of this discussion the principal was invited to my classroom to give an impromptu lesson about her views on nonsexist language in the classroom.

Michelle's and Marina's inquiries were directly related to curricular issues. According to Michelle,

Listening to the voices of students through collaboration is essential for effective planning and work as a classroom teacher-researcher. I discovered that when I include students in the process of curriculum development, the learning that results is profound and has long-lasting effects.

In the following and final account, Marina describes her curriculum development/research with students and comments on the understanding and encouragement she gained from the work.

I began by conducting an informal survey of thirty questions regarding dreams. The two most important questions were "Would you feel uncomfortable discussing your dreams in class?" and "Would you feel uncomfortable if I asked you to keep a dream journal as a writing assignment?" Almost every student answered that he or she had no reservations.

In mid-March we began studying *The Lathe of Heaven.* Around the same time each student was given a sixteen-page information booklet on dreams. The booklet dealt with dream research, brain waves, dream theorists, the Senoi, keeping a journal of dreams, tips for dream recall, guidelines for interpretation, and symbolism. To begin each class we read and discussed a page of the booklet. Students were fascinated and intrigued by the material.

Once students had acquired some skills in retrieving their dreams and understanding the symbolism, I encouraged them to also begin sharing their dreams in class. We had several dream dictionaries in the classroom that students could consult. Initially only one or two students would share their dreams. This increased steadily as students became more adept at remembering their dreams and their comfort level with classmates increased. Within a few weeks their enthusiasm was staggering. We never had enough time to discuss everyone's dreams. On a few occasions we devoted the entire eighty-minute period to discussing individual dreams. After a student related a dream, classmates would offer feelings and insights as to what the dream could mean. Our goal was never to reach one definitive meaning. We focused on dream appreciation, honoring and valuing our dream messages, rather than dream interpretation. Listening to their dreams, their ideas, and insights was truly remarkable. Many students seemed to possess an instinctive innate ability at cutting through to the core of their dreams. Reliance on the dream dictionaries varied. Many students found they needed the dictionaries initially to generate possible ideas, but their final meaning was often completely intrinsic.

I urged each student to keep a written journal of their dreams. Students were given approximately two months to journal their dreams. At the end of this time they were asked to select three dreams that they felt were significant and to write approximately one page for each dream, discussing or analyzing the symbolic significance. They could also include any creative aspect of their choice—a poem, drawing, painting, collage, or song—that illustrated their dream themes. The final part of the assignment was a one-page summary in which students described what they had learned overall from keeping a journal of their dreams.

The outcomes were tremendous. It was the first time ever as an English teacher that all students handed in their assignments. Their insights contained more remarkable wisdom and depth. I found myself experiencing the same awe, fascination, and excitement over each of their dreams as I did with my own. Overall their dreams facilitated greater awareness, directions, and personal insights. They used their dreams to problem solve, particularly in regard to troubling relationships. For many students their connection to all of humanity and to spiritual realms became apparent. Many of their dreams were "prophetic"—preparing them psychologically for future events. As a class we were definitely closer owing to our dream discussions. Instead of operating on a level of "surface knowing" we knew and respected each other on a much deeper personal level.

A year later I selected six of these students, three males and three females, and interviewed them in depth regarding our dreamwork together. Every student was extremely positive about our class experiment. Three of the six students have continued to keep dream journals. They all felt that keeping a journal of their dreams was a skill they would continue to use, particularly when they were going through a difficult period in their lives. As a teacher this was a unique opportunity to evaluate our work together—a rare opportunity to receive honest feedback in a situation where students were not being "graded."

I concluded the interviews feeling that this was perhaps the most meaningful work I had done as a teacher. No exercise had ever elicited such innate wisdom from my students. I felt we had truly traveled on a "class trip" to tremendous new heights. I was energized by these interviews to begin a similar dream journey with future students.

Jane, Michelle, and Marina each engaged in collaborative inquiry with their students in ways that made sense to them, and they monitored the students' involvement on an ongoing basis. Throughout the inquiries they reflected on the inquiry process, their progress in relation to the project goals, the students' responses, and their own learning. As such, their reflexive inquiries substantially informed how they thought about the role of students in the educative process.

ISSUES AND CONCERNS

Earlier in this part of the book we mentioned the importance of attending to a whole range of issues in partnership research. We invite you to return to those pages as you consider some of the issues associated with collaborative inquiry with students. Working with students is perhaps more dependent on sound relationships and partnerships than working with any other group of people. We reiterate the importance of the researching relationship being collaborative and in partnership above all else. Indeed, working with students in the researching process may be the ultimate test of true partnership research.

For Jane and Michelle three issues in particular stood out. Jane's reference to the power differential inherent in traditionally defined student-teacher relationships, especially as it is understood and perhaps manifested in evaluative ways, is an abiding issue. Ironically, this fear of reprisal is also reflected in teachers' expressed concerns about engaging in reflexive inquiry. (Recall how Todd, in Chapter 6, expressed the initial difficulty he had observing his own teaching because of his long-held association of observation with evaluation.) Unfortunately, education, like many other institutions, has become hierarchically defined and evaluation based. As Jane remarks, perhaps the only way to deal with this kind of issue is "to accept this as a given and try to work around it."

To examine oneself, with the desire to be true to oneself, is problematic. The road to fooling oneself is easily built. In order to try to deal with an avoidance of deception, I laid many safeguards in place. Involving the students as coresearchers was my main safeguard; however, the history of relationships between "teacher" and "student," as based on power differences and hierarchy, was difficult to overcome. Fear of the teacher's opinion, which I believe is related to fear of judgment or retaliation in the form of grades or recommendations, is always present somewhere in the background of students' thinking. I had to accept this as a given and try to work around it.

One of Michelle's main concerns pervades all forms of inquiry and professional development; indeed, it is teachers' biggest enemy—lack of time.

While completing my inquiry project many issues and concerns surfaced. When I look back over my journal entries written over the course of the inquiry I am reminded of the frustration and impatience I felt over not being able to devote as much time as I wanted to my research. I made many references to the other demands on my time such as [athletic] coaching, parent information evenings, fund-raising activities, staff meetings, and discipline difficulties. I began to realize that if I wanted to effectively participate in inquiry into my teaching, it needed to be an integral part of my curriculum. I could not fathom having to add on the research to all of the other things I was doing with my grade 8 students. Using existing curriculum units such as media literacy as the foundation for my inquiry project was the most convenient and effective way to ensure success.

Michelle's strategy for addressing the issue of lack of time was helpful not only from a time-management perspective but also, and we think more importantly, from a professional development standpoint. When Michelle makes the point that linking reflexive inquiry to curriculum development ensured success, she is also underscoring the main theme of this book—teaching is inquiry. Formal and informal investigations of classroom and teaching practice must be perceived and conceptualized as an integral part of that practice. To suggest that teachers add something else to their already overflowing platter of responsibilities is not only insulting and ludicrous, it also misses the point of reflexive inquiry as professional development.

The other main issue that arose for Michelle during her work with students relates to a point we discussed earlier—the challenge of determining the nature of student involvement.

At times, students are not always cooperative and mature coresearchers. Just prior to the initial lessons for phase one of the project (which I could not wait to share) an unfortunate and unpleasant incident arose between two students. Both students engaged in racial slurs and proceeded to become very physical with one another. I was so disappointed with their behavior that I lost my earlier enthusiasm for the introductory lesson. This incident reminded me that as a classroom teacher-researcher I need to be very flexible and able to teach and research under any circumstance.

As a result of this occurrence I had a concern about the maturity level of the coresearchers and wondered if they would be able to handle the content of the project and work in a productive manner. I chiefly found that the students could easily be responsible for the content of their discussions. During the first phase of the project one group had difficulty maintaining an acceptable maturity level. Generally, their discussion was fruitful but not always audible on the tape as they tried to outspeak and frequently interrupt one another. In the future I will review the standards for coresearchers more carefully with the students.

In spite of some of the inherent difficulties of involving students as coresearchers, teachers who have done so consistently insist that the benefits far outweigh the problems.

PARTING COMMENTS

We give the last words to Michelle and Jane.

> *Michelle:* Classroom inquiry has made my learning more meaningful. I have been inspired by this risk-taking experience. Individuals who do not take risks in their teaching limit their chances to peer through the kaleidoscope of life and behold different perspectives. This is the essence of collaborative inquiry with students; it is the opportunity that facilitates growth for teachers and students.

> *Jane:* I see the enterprise of assuming the position of "researcher as researched" as a vehicle for educators to learn more about themselves and those whom they have the opportunity to "teach." It is like an addictive drug—once such a vision of oneself is enacted, it cannot be forgotten even when any one research project reaches its long-awaited conclusion.

RESEARCH ACTIVITIES

Because most inquiries related to curriculum, school experiences, or teaching practice can be enhanced through involvement of students as coresearchers, the research activities we suggest here are mainly examples of different ways of working with students. The first two research activities are suggestions for ways of helping students become familiar with the inquiry process. The third is more related to the relationship between teacher and pupils.

• Develop a "curriculum unit" around the process of reflexive inquiry so as to familiarize pupils with the various elements of the inquiry process. Use the occasion to play out their learnings about inquiry, that is, teach about inquiry through inquiry. Explorations of school community topics of interest and concern may be an appropriate way to prepare students to engage in more extensive inquiry work in the community or local area. A school-based focus may be on some aspect of their school lives, for example, with the express purpose of changing the quality of their experiences of school. Taking the findings and conclusions of their inquiry activities to, say, the school council, school administrators, or parent groups may be ways to bring their concerns and action plans into reality. (This process may prepare them for more extensive inquiries within the community, such as ones pertaining to environmental issues, for example, including matters of ecology or recycling, urban planning, community health, leisure or recreation activities, transportation, and social issues.) While the pupils are engaged in developing their study, you also might fashion a parallel project so that you and the students are simultaneously engaged in inquiries on the same topic. Your findings, taken together but from very different vantage points, have potential to yield considerable insight.

• Develop a "unit of inquiry" around, for example, economic, social, environmental, or political change in the local area or community. Use the process of inquiry into the community as a way to familiarize the students with the reflexive inquiry process. The students derive their focus of inquiry from an issue that is directly connected to their lives. Encourage the students to take their findings to a local political or other body or agency. Then bring the inquiry process into the school. Facilitate students to bring about change within their social and educational groups by studying the issues and contexts that concern them through the same reflexive inquiry process. In both cases facilitate their development of a focus, information gathering, interpretation of information, representation, and dispersion of their conclusions and suggestions for action.

• Earlier in the chapter we mentioned a number of different ways to accomplish inquiry work in relation with students. The spectrum of relationships include

  • students as conceptualizers and investigators (where they are totally responsible for developing the focus of inquiry and you as teacher are merely a facilitator)

  • students as coconceptualizers, coinvestigators, or collaborators (where pupils and teacher develop a focus out of some shared concern or issue)

  • students as cooperating collaborators (where you take the lead in developing a focus of inquiry but solicit the aid of the students to help you because there are clear benefits to them at each point in the process either because of the topic or the potential outcomes)

  • students as cooperators (where you solicit students to gather information, perhaps from other students, or assist in analysis of information that is pertinent to their interests)

  • students as informants (where you merely solicit information from the students)

  • students as evaluators (where you play out your analyses of information gathered—perhaps from students—with the students who help you evaluate the interpretation of information or the findings of your work)

  • students as policy makers (where you obtain the help of students to develop "policies" for the implementation of your findings)

  • students as action planners and implementors (where students help in translating the research findings into action-in-practice).

Develop an inquiry project that reflects any one of the above relationships.

RECOMMENDED READINGS

Cullingford, C. (1991). *The inner world of the school: Children's ideas about schools.* London: Cassell Educational.

Paley, V. G. (1981). *Wally's stories.* Cambridge, MA: Harvard University Press.

Paley, V. G. (1986). *Mollie is three: Growing up in school.* Chicago: University of Chicago Press.

Paley, V. G. (1990). *The boy who would be a helicopter.* Cambridge, MA: Harvard University Press.

Paley, V. G. (1992). *You can't say you can't play.* Cambridge, MA: Harvard University Press.

Woods, P. (1990). *The happiest days?: How pupils cope with school.* London: Falmer Press.

10

RESEARCHING TEACHING THROUGH COLLABORATIVE INQUIRY WITH OUTSIDE RESEARCHERS

with contributions by
ANNA HENSON,[1] VICKI KOIVU-RYBICKI,
DAN MADIGAN, and JAMES A. MUCHMORE

After a long history and tradition of passive involvement in educational research, teachers have finally begun to assume their rightful place at the head and heart of classroom inquiry. Many teachers have exerted pressure on researchers to modify the foci and modes of inquiry in classroom and school research projects. Traditional approaches to research into teaching and classroom life do not take into account the exigencies and complexities of classrooms, do not honor practice as a starting point for research and theory development, and do not involve teachers as partners in inquiry and theory building. These traditional approaches have more or less been pushed aside in many contexts. In the place of this kind of research are approaches that respect the importance of mutuality in conception, purpose, involvement, processes, and benefit. Teachers, as holders and makers of "insider" and "craft" knowledge, are increasingly being involved as bona fide coresearchers in partnership inquiry with those outside classrooms and schools—typically, with university-based researchers for whom formal research and publication are an important part of their professional roles and responsibilities.

---

[1]"Anna Henson" is a pseudonym. For reasons discussed later in the chapter, "Anna" chose to remain anonymous in published accounts of her research with Jim.

A fundamental shift from research *on* teachers and students to research *with* teachers and students has placed new importance on the centrality of the research relationship and has prompted heightened awareness of the need for sensitivity and responsiveness to issues associated with the research process. Indeed, this shift honors and is consistent with the relational nature of teaching. (We could even make the argument that one of the ways in which we judge the authority, authenticity, and value of most classroom and teaching research is by the extent to which it mirrors or reflects the fundamental qualities of "good" teaching. Further, we might insist that it reflects, in process and conclusions, the complexity of teaching and learning.) In the introduction to this part of the book, Part IV, we raised a number of questions related to technical, procedural, interpersonal, ethical, and political issues associated with collaborative research. We invite you to revisit those questions as you give further thought to the prospects and possibilities of engaging in collaborative research with "outside" researchers, that is, researchers who are not fully embedded in the context in which the research is focused.

In this chapter we hear voices from both sides. Coresearchers Jim Muchmore and Anna Henson and Vicki Koivu-Rybicki and Dan Madigan reflect on their experiences of researching from their respective vantage points of classroom-based researcher and university-based researcher. Anna is a long-experienced public high school English teacher in Detroit, Michigan. Jim has just completed his doctoral studies at the University of Michigan. They have been working together for about six years in a collaborative research project focused on the history and evolution of Anna's beliefs about literacy and how those beliefs find expression in Anna's practice. Their research is the basis of Jim's doctoral dissertation, which reflects many of the same qualities and principles that we advocate in this book. It is reflexive, also, in the manner in which Jim has explored his own experiences as a literacy or language arts teacher. Vicki and Dan have worked together for even longer. Dan is a former high school teacher and currently a professor of English at Bowling Green State University in Bowling Green, Ohio. Vicki is a long-experienced classroom teacher in an inner-city Detroit public elementary school. Her innovative and highly successful ways of working with minority students and their communities to promote literacy was the basis for their collaborative work focused on understanding issues and processes of literacy education teaching. Throughout this chapter we draw on the work of these coresearchers.

To honor the dialogic nature of their collaboration Anna and Jim reflect through the medium of dialogue on elements of their research relationship and joint work. They speak of their different vantage points of observation, how they learned from one another, and how they developed a sound, respectful, and trusting relationship. Similarly, reflecting one of the primary modes of their collaboration, Dan highlights the role of electronic mail exchanges with Vicki as a forum for them to learn through the exchange of stories about teaching and learning. Vicki comments mainly on the development of their researching relationship over time and the many benefits and spin-offs resulting from their collaborative work.

WHY ENGAGE IN COLLABORATIVE INQUIRY
WITH OUTSIDE RESEARCHERS?

Deciding to collaborate in matters of researching is no easy matter. There are a number of very good reasons, however, why teachers and other educators might want to consider working with an outside researcher. Some of the reasons relate to personal and professional energy (including enhanced interpersonal or synergetic energy), different levels and kinds of reciprocal exchange, resources, perspectives, technical expertise, dispersion of findings or conclusions, access to available literature, and theories or insights from previous or other collaborative work.

There is value in collaborating with persons who have, through their professional interests and affiliations, considerable knowledge in an area you are interested in exploring. Imagine, for instance, that you and some teacher-colleagues are interested in exploring the value and place of homework for pupils within your school and for parents' understandings of their children's academic work and development. There is a university relatively close by. On inquiry you find that there are some professors who may be interested in helping you think through issues associated with assigning homework. One is interested in homework and home-based learning, another in parental involvement in the educational process. Both professors are interested in working with teachers either through preservice teacher-education programs or through inservice activities. You also discover that there are graduate students who may be interested in locating their research work in schools. Perhaps you then locate some of the professors' publications to get a sense of their work. You might ask around about the viability of working with these university-based people. Then you arrange to talk with them about your issues, concerns, and ideas for exploring the topic of homework. After some discussion, you and your colleagues decide to invite the researchers to work with you. You feel that you and your colleagues can potentially benefit from the outside researchers' involvement because of the ways in which their knowledge about the scholarship related to the topic of homework might enrich your practice-based knowledge and experiences (especially given your extensive time commitments to teaching and curriculum development).

The establishment of a collaborative team with broad expertise is likely to facilitate the conception and development of the inquiry project. During initial precommitment meetings discussion is likely to be organized around determining a focus of inquiry, individuals' reasons for wanting to explore that particular topic, some of the issues associated with homework in the schools, and who would benefit from such a study and how. The power of multiple yet related perspectives will no doubt play out in the clarity of focus eventually established in your inquiry. Given that the most difficult and crucial element of collaborative inquiry—actually, of all forms of inquiry—is the conceptualization of the work in the broadest sense, it is appropriate to involve a number of people. This is especially true for uncovering perspectives on a topic that may prove to be thorny and complicated.

The professional and personal energy available to the project can multiply as more committed people become involved. Members of the inquiry team can then find their niches in the process through negotiation and make visible their contributions. The potential for productive work is magnified by the inclusion of outside researchers simply because of their potential to contribute on a broad front. Often outside researchers will have time for the project because such activities are considered a legitimate part of their institutional workload or reward structure. Accordingly, there may be flexibility associated with time and role (and resource) commitments of university-based personnel.

Provided that considerable attention is given to forming a collaborative team whose members are connected in spirit, intent, and philosophy, the hope is that enhanced interpersonal or synergetic energy will become available to the inquiry. Our experience is that this is a delicate matter but that it can and does happen. Our advice is simply to look to establish inquiry connections with people who either already work well together or who have great potential to closely and collegially work "in relation"—whatever that means in *your* context and according to your experience. Mutuality in philosophy, purpose and goals, processes, and expectations, as well as a commitment to negotiating through the difficult spots in the complex relationship, will ensure that the chances of synergy within your work are heightened. Synergy develops through attention to the relational issues of researching and working together in close proximity. In Vicki's and Dan's case undergraduate students from the university visited Vicki's classroom to learn, and parents, uncles, aunts, and other extended family members and friends of the children often visited to learn and teach.

Working with outside researchers may open the doors to greater resources being brought to bear on your inquiry project. (Of course, their commitment to "your" project has already, in itself, brought greater personnel resources to bear. Yet, as they and you work together the project becomes jointly owned and guided.) Available resources may also be increased through

- library and media assistance, say, for accessing printed or published findings and accounts of similar kinds of studies
- financial assistance, for instance, with gathering information through conversational interviews; for audiotape recording and transcribing audiotapes; for videotape recording (and possibly editing); for assisting with information analyses of various kinds; or for writing, reporting or printing, and distributing the outcomes of collaborative work
- possible connections that might come about because of the different networks with which university personnel may be associated, for example, and which might lead to contact with practitioners and researchers across the country, throughout North America and beyond, and to exchanges of perspectives, joint conference or workshop participation, and writing and publishing opportunities
- infusions of "new blood" into schools by way of new and prospective teachers and the establishment of collaborative arrangements connected to teacher development, say, when universities are explicitly looking for practicum sites for preservice teacher education fieldwork
- special situations that might be possible, for instance, when universities are seeking sites for more extensive locations of intellectual and practical activities connected to teacher education and development (such as the establishment of

"professional development schools" where the university expects to make financial and resource commitments in the service of teacher education and development and school improvement)

None of these resource benefits is likely to occur—and indeed probably should not be
expected—unless solid relational activities around a highly relevant and meaningful
project are initiated. Mutuality of purpose is probably the key condition for these extended benefits to occur. Having said this, we acknowledge that a solid relationship often leads to new and unexpected ideas and topics for inquiry. In other words, research
purposes often emerge from strong relationships developed in the spirit of inquiry.

Although university resources may be able to fund a variety of pursuits related
to the inquiry process, the additional involvement of undergraduate and graduate students (especially those working on theses or dissertations) will augment that of
teaching colleagues. Even though it is important for you, and perhaps other centrally
involved coresearchers, to maintain conceptual or literal leadership of the project,
others may be able to contribute to the project work in significant ways. They may,
for example, provide assistance with observing and making field notes, talking with
people, or doing some library or archival research.

In the following segment, Vicki reflects on her process of becoming a coresearcher. She comments on her initial misgivings, fears, and perceptions of herself as
a teacher but *not* a researcher. Apparent in her writing are the development of her
self-confidence over time as well as the increasing significance of the role of collaborative inquiry in her teaching. Vicki's chronicle of her relationship with Dan (and
other researchers) highlights some of the numerous ways in which Vicki felt that she
and her students were enriched by their coresearching experiences.

In the late 1980s I returned to university studies to explore my practice as a
teacher. At the time I questioned the validity of my elementary classroom work.
Written reflections on my practice were of particular interest to one of my university professors and to a university colleague. They were inspired by the depth of
my reflections in response to course assignments. They admired my knowledge
of the urban African American community as well as my relationships with the
families of my neighborhood students. It was not long before both of them asked
to visit my classroom and for me to consider collaborating with them on a writing
project.

At the time I was confident with my knowledge of the lives of my students. I
cared for them while remaining a firm disciplinarian. I considered myself a well-
prepared practitioner and I managed an organized classroom. I was spiritual (in
the traditional sense) and focused often on conflict resolution and values clarification with my students—an asset that I viewed critical to my practice as a
teacher. I had fears, however, about the thoroughness of my reading and writing
instruction. I did not view myself as a writer or a reader and therefore I did not
believe in myself as a thinker. I had researched and experimented with alternative English language arts projects but considered my work "incomplete."

The two colleagues and I agreed to work together and for them to visit
weekly with me and my fourth-grade students in our classroom. I introduced

them to the students as my research "friends" (though I didn't know either of them very well at all) and "teachers." I requested that their research directly benefit the children—that it be instructional, experiential, and collaborative among the three of us. All other visitors to our classroom had a history of sharing their expertise and experiences. I hoped for the same with this initiative.

My colleagues' "academic knowledge," I assumed, would serve to inform and support my classroom practice and certainly benefit the students. I was timid and reserved about the process and asked no questions about the project after our initial meeting. I listened carefully for a plan of work from them, trusting the "experts'" suggestions.

Four months into our work together, a university student on an independent study, whom the researchers invited to observe and interact with the young students, privately shared her observations of our research group's collaboration. She challenged my relationship with the study team and our relationships with each other. The university student was concerned that I was not asserting leadership with the group—not valuing my own expertise—and that one of the visiting researchers seemed more interested in collecting specific kinds of data, an unaddressed conflict that continued for over a year.[2]

Our research group arranged for frequent conversations. We discussed our observations and writing project during lunch and after school. We also met during my teacher-preparation periods. I continued to feel inadequate and hesitant to speak during our conferencing times.

My colleagues encouraged me to write on electronic mail (long before the popular e-mail communications we share today), daily, from home or school. They suggested alternatives to writing in a journal, anything to make it easier for me to communicate my stories of experience with students, parents, and administrators. We agreed that my written journal account would be a partial requirement for an independent study course that I would complete under the direction of one of the researchers. It was suggested that I periodically examine my reflections and comment in the margins. For a long time, writing my responses in a journal was difficult for me because I experienced a deep fear of writing and because I did not consider my thoughts to be "scholarly."

Our meetings focused on our written observations of the students' interactions with each other during their peer-writing process. I became more comfortable as the group offered positive responses to my teaching practice: my interactions with the students, my caring, and my invitations for life narratives. We planned the curriculum informed by our journal observations of the students' reflections on their life experiences, parent and community interaction, and the support of multiperspective literature that informed these issues.

Writing life narratives, our neighborhood-tour stories, journal reflections on children's literature, and a few intense case studies of my students became the focus of our literacy curriculum and the foundation for my subsequent autobiographical writing. The young third- and fourth-grade students became accountable for their learning and responsible writers in response to our collaborative

---

[2]During our second year together as a study team, the researcher who seemed to visit solely for student interviews and data collection assumed commitments elsewhere.

initiatives. The students presented both their writings and writing instruction to adult audiences—and so did I. Over four years, the young writers' classroom published two paperback books of their life stories. Dan and I have coauthored articles and a book about our collaborative research with the children and their families.[3] Dan provided several forums so that I and my students could teach others about what it means to be a young writer. My confidence in my own researching skills has grown considerably.

Dan Madigan (as well as interested university students and colleagues from another institution) and I have coresearched within our classroom community over the subsequent years. At some point after our research relationship was well established, Dan suggested that we invite graduate and undergraduate students as well as professors into our classroom to work with the children-writers. Several served as "extensions of me" (and us) as they monitored and supported the students' peer editing, conversations, storying, reading, and presentations. The "alternative" researchers served as teachers and students and modeled as equals with the young students.

An undergraduate preservice teacher began a peer-teacher mentoring program in which a small group of former students, from the fifth-grade class, conversed about their observations of good teachers before monitoring the fourth-grade students that day. Their work in the classroom involved individual or small-group support. The peer-teachers were accountable to write their own stories in order to more fully participate in the writing and editing experience. After the work with the younger students, the peer-teachers returned to their small mentoring group (with the preservice teacher) to reflect on their practice as peer-teachers.

The peer-teacher mentoring program has served as a connection for former students, now attending middle school and high school, to revisit classes and groups as young guest authors. We have arranged for cross-aged young student writers to share their peer-editing expertise with preservice teachers and other university students. The experiences of these students has influenced my participation at academic conferences. My own life-story writing for our fourth-grade audience and our student-teacher editing is reflective of the interactive forums in which I have presented my work at English language arts teachers' conferences.

Researchers of song and drama have taught the students to dramatize grammar usage. The interplay of these lessons was the inspiration for the ways in which we reviewed our "culturally appropriate" classroom presentations of Sharon Bell Mathis's *The Hundred Penny Box* with broader audiences. A liberated African American woman's poetry workshop influenced our young students' radio recordings of their own poetry written and narrated to the rhythm of their choice of rap music and popular recordings. These poetic expressions have been an alternative genre for the young writers' revitalized interest in poetic expression.

Last night, a former student telephoned to request sources for the female African American poetry she remembered from her third-grade readings and recitations. Taria has called repeatedly over the past five years to share her writing experiences and to discuss her readings and literacy interests. Entertaining these conversations are a teacher's "thank-you" and a reminder of the multiple

---

[3]Madigan, D., & Koivu-Rybicki, V. T. (1997). *The writing lives of children.* York, ME: Stenhouse.

voices that have serviced the transformative nature of teaching and learning in our classroom.

COLLABORATION OR COOPERATION? ENSURING MUTUALLY PRODUCTIVE RESEARCH RELATIONSHIPS

We make the distinction between "collaboration in name only" and "collaboration in practice," as we might make the distinction between cooperation and collaboration. Over the years we have seen a good number of research projects initiated under the guise of collaboration. Unfortunately, we even have been members of such arrangements that, in the end, while fruitful for one party have had relatively little influence on the development of enhanced classroom practice.

The scientific-inquiry model typically does not allow space for the kind of reflexive and mutually beneficial roles and processes that we envision in collaborative, partnership inquiry. Researchers often work closely with a second party for the achievement of a common goal but the matter of mutuality and the importance of relational elements are largely ignored either for ideological reasons, convenience, or through just plain oversight. We also are aware of a great deal of research-generated literature in the field of education that points to the value of the collaborative enterprise. On perusal and from our perspective, however, much of this literature falls short. A great deal of that written is in practice merely evidence of cooperation, not collaboration, between two or more parties. For us, though, and given our interest in refining practice at all levels, cooperation is simply not good enough since it reduces the possibility that all members of a research collaborative may in the end be truly benefited. When we talk of benefit we infer that the consequences of the inquiry must enhance the individual and collective professional conditions, thinking, or practice of the collaborative members, be regenerative in spirit, and offer possibilities for more and fruitful joint work if that is appropriate. And, not to forget, benefits ultimately are assumed to mean benefits to the students for whom teachers have educational responsibility.

In the introduction to Part IV (which includes this chapter) we referred readers to a set of key issues that we feel are important considerations in collaborative, partnership research. We encourage you to revisit those issues, issues of technical, interpersonal, procedural, political, and educational importance. Note that we have intentionally included the idea of partnership, a term we have used from time to time throughout the book. For us, "partnership" connotes a number of notions about relationships in the research endeavor:

- equality of influence in the relationship
- nonhierarchical lines of influence, responsibility, and power within the relationship
- care of individual and collective needs within the relationship
- mutuality of purpose and benefit within the relationship
- thoughtfulness toward people and process, and about "product" in the relationship

- purposefulness about the roles within the relationship
- mindfulness about the ongoing quality of the collaborative relationship

All this suggests that a great deal of effort be given to establishing, supporting, and maintaining the integrity, authority, and spirit of the collaborative inquiry partnership as expressed in the personal and professional relationships. These nurturing actions will render the partnership—in all its complexity and intertwined purposes and processes—robust and secure rather than fragile and tentative. Such a partnership is likely to lead to professional fulfillment for all involved.

In the following segment Vicki describes how she, Dan, and the students introduced themselves to one another and negotiated their research relationship. Of particular significance in Vicki's description is her (and their) attention to the students' and her own authority, which honors and respects their classroom and neighborhood contexts as well as their individual and collective needs, interests, and goals.

When our "friends" first arrived in the classroom, we formed a circle. This idea was based on a Native American model that we deeply respected. We introduced ourselves to each other with ideas of what was important to us: our favorite sports, playtime activities, and family events. Eventually, we generated stories that revealed much more about who we are.

The researchers didn't know the children or their culture, customs, or neighborhood; the young students were also very curious about their new "friends." They expressed an initial mistrust of the researchers, whom they addressed as "White folks." They asked, "Why did you White folks come to our school anyway?" Both students and researchers had questions about each other's cultural and life experience and differences. The conversation led to the fourth graders' idea of a neighborhood walking tour, which they designed and guided the following week.

While guiding the tour, the young students shared feelings about their neighborhood and their daily lives. They presented their less than desirable surroundings with some apologies for us, as Whites, and bravely communicated a deep love of their "home." Later they wrote stories asking outside audiences to trust that they are good persons—in spite of how folks in the media may view them.

Jim and Anna agreed to work together after Jim expressed an interest in exploring the history and evolution of Anna's beliefs about literacy and how those beliefs have been related to her teaching practices throughout her career. Jim was interested both in understanding Anna's teaching and in learning about ways of researching that honored its many dimensions and complexities. He explains the ways in which they worked together to gather information about Anna's practice and about the importance they placed on developing a trusting and respectful relationship:

My methods included numerous audiorecorded interviews and conversations with Anna, as well as frequent visits to her classroom in the role of a participant observer. Under Anna's direction, I also spoke with several of her friends, relatives, colleagues, and past and present students—all of whom are familiar, to varying degrees, with her teaching practices and her thinking about literacy. In addition, Anna provided me with a collection of academic papers that she has written in which she has discussed various issues related to literacy and teaching throughout her career. Finally, she provided me with copies of various professional documents—including newspaper clippings about her, past and present evaluations of her teaching conducted by various school administrators, and other professional documents.

In many ways, such a project can be an incredibly intrusive undertaking—one that requires the building of a great deal of trust. For Anna and me, this trust was initially based on our preexisting friendship; we already knew each other and already had a working relationship before we began this collaboration. Over time, however, this trust would no doubt have waned if we had not worked hard to maintain it. For example, I have always tried to share my thinking with Anna, and I have provided her with copies of everything that I have written—including my fieldnotes, my interview transcripts, and my analyses. My work in turn has benefited considerably from her insights and feedback. I also have made a special effort not to delve into areas that Anna and I have agreed are off the record, and I have encouraged her to largely define the nature and scope of her participation.

For her part Anna has always been honest and forthright with me in making suggestions and offering opinions about my work. And she has been incredibly patient with me as a beginning qualitative researcher, having provided me with a great deal of latitude to figure out what I was doing and supporting me when I stumbled. Anna has always been much more of a colleague to me—or even a mentor—rather than simply a "research subject," and we have spent a great deal of time talking about how we both have been influenced by our work together.

LEARNING WITH AND FROM EACH OTHER

One of the fundamental assumptions (and goals) we have for reflexive modes of inquiry in collaboration with outside researchers is that the mutuality that we advocate actually plays out in the learning each achieves. Mutuality of purpose throughout the inquiry process is transcended by mutuality of learning. It bears repeating, although here in a different way, that each partner in the inquiry process contributes particular and important expertise, and that the relationship between outsider and insider is multifaceted, nonhierarchical, and mutually beneficial. Learning that occurs in and from this relationship is not linear but complex, reflexive, and multidimensional.

The outsider is often able to recast wider contextual circumstances, close observations, commentary, and details of process or practice in ways that illuminate the insights, thinking, and practice of the insider, and vice versa. Events, circumstances, practices and, say, students' or parents' responses to practice, which may appear clouded by routine activities and responsibilities, might be clarified by the new, fresh eyes of another sympathetic, compatible observer or practitioner. Moreover, an outsider, especially one grounded in university-based scholarship, may bring to bear on an observation of the insider's practice the conceptual perspectives, lenses, and frameworks of other philosophically compatible positions, which in the end may result in substantial insight. Likewise, the outsider, who may be more grounded in notions of abstracted or general theory than in concepts of practice, may well be able to make theory-practice links that both inform outsider-generated theories and honor the practice-based theories and knowledge of the insider. Reciprocal learning occurs in the process of making such connections. Thus in the process of collaborative reflexive inquiry each coresearcher will learn from the other; each will learn differently and in ways that honor the intersection created by different personal histories and the assumptions about practice and inquiry that arise from those personal histories.

Through dialogue Anna and Jim reflect on their collaborative inquiry. Their text highlights the inadequacies of one-sided, short-sighted interpretations of classroom practice, which are often based on superficial outsider observations; they point to the importance of the insider's perspective to complement and inform. At the same time, it is clear from their comments that they learned from and with each other and were positively influenced by each other's perspective. Anna was inspired to think differently about her practice and classroom because of Jim's presence and their ongoing negotiated interpretation of her practice. Jim learned about "appropriate" ways of observing, recording, and representing Anna's practice. Jim learned about himself as researcher and helped Anna to learn about herself as teacher. The conversations represented here took place while their research was still in progress.

> *Anna:* I've given quite a bit of thought to how my classroom is different as a result of our work. I'm not reluctant to say that my classroom will never be the same as a result of the work that we've done. Our collaboration has transformed the space in the room. The analogy that I keep using to myself is that it's like a home that's been prepared for a guest. There's sort of a state of readiness. In your writing, you've characterized some of my actions in the classroom as being like those of a hostess, and I think that there is some sense of hospitality that I'm not afraid to talk about now. I think of my classroom as a place that is hospitable to a certain kind of thinking and action and interaction, just as a room that's prepared for a guest is a transformed space. It's not a private, closed, excluding space, but one that invites a lot of different possibilities. And what I'm trying to think about now is exactly how that transformation took place. What is the consequence of thinking about a classroom as an inviting place, one that is prepared for guests? It's not just open to outsiders, but it welcomes outsiders. It's a place where students have that sense as well—that not only are they welcome, but their friends and their family are welcome too. It's a place where they can make those kinds of choices and invitations too.

> *Jim:* Yes, I'm very interested in that too. What impact did I have on the setting in which I spent so much time? And, how did I change throughout this collaboration?

> *Anna:* This idea of a transformed space came to me when I thought back to your early visits and the way in which you characterized my classroom that I found humbling. I saw so much more happening than what you described. You made the classroom sound like a

place where not much could happen because of the size of the school, the age of the building, and so on. And I had always envisioned the space as being very different from that. You even did computer-assisted drawings of my classroom that made it seem like such a static, cold, and uninviting place. My vision of my cozy little room was so much livelier.

Jim: I remember that. It shows where I was in how I was thinking of the research. At that time, I was trying to get a sense of what your classroom was all about, and I was trying to grasp it in a way that I now realize was not really productive. I remember that I felt as if I had to record everything I saw and that everything was equally important. But that was simply an impossible task. It was somewhat like trying to grasp a handful of sand and trying not to let any escape through my fingers. It's just impossible. I had to learn that it was more important to pay attention to the sand that was still in the palm of my hand than to worry about the grains that were slipping through my fingers.

Anna: Contrast that with the way that you write now and the things that catch your attention now. Physical space was really important as a way of really bringing me into your vision of what was going on in the room.

Jim: I even drew little dotted lines to show how you moved around the room!

Anna: Yeah! And you can imagine how it felt to be researched as a stick figure (laughing). There seemed to be this split between what I imagined you were doing and what I saw you doing, and I started having all kinds of questions about what the research looked like.

Jim: I did too. I was coming from a much more traditional research background based on a scientific-inquiry model, and I had a lot to learn.

Anna: There were also what I felt were implicit judgments about me and my teaching in those kinds of representations. But fortunately all of that gradually peeled away until you were eventually looking at very different kinds of things. And I'm glad that change did occur because I think I would have had real doubts about contributing to that kind of research and subjecting myself and my students to that kind of looking into our classroom.

Vicki and Dan learned and continue to learn with and from each other through their collaborative inquiry. Because of the physical distance between Vicki's and Dan's place of work (Detroit, Michigan, and Bowling Green, Ohio, respectively) they have had to find creative ways of keeping their collaboration alive. Between Dan's visits to Vicki's classroom they continue to explore literacy education through the medium of e-mail. Dan explains.

Vicki and I use e-mail to describe our observations and ideas and how those stories shape our thoughts in many ways. E-mail offers not only the space to write important stories, but it served as a dialogic journal: story in answer to story. E-mail provides space for our stories—a place where characters emerge, evolve, and dialogue with one another—and cyberspace serves as a bound volume of those stories. I can't imagine technology as having such a profound influence on teacher-researchers that they abandon more familiar and convenient places in which they typically share important stories that shape their thinking; however, technology does seem to offer some interesting possibilities for the creation of alternative and new spaces in which important stories might emerge.

Vicki comments on how she has learned from their continuous narrative engagement.

From the beginning of our work together, Dan and I journaled daily via e-mail. Dan appreciates what I consider a "casual conversation of the day." He often responds with an academic response, which I do not always acknowledge. The daily written messages communicate my reflections and responses to my daily life and practice as a teacher. I had never thought of myself as a storyteller, yet as I explore the value of story, I recognize that I teach through stories and that I journal in stories as well.

I remain faithful to a "daily" journal in which I review my responses to the events of the day. Story highlights of this journal record are written in the e-mail messages to Dan. Although my daily journal conversations are more in accord with the "conscience" of my responses to students, parents, and administrators, my e-mail dialogue chronicles my teaching process and observations of myself in relationship, the underpinning for real teaching. For me, both the personal and the interactive dialogue are necessary.

Occasionally, another specifically "personal" journal entry addresses the issues of crises in my personal life. The personal journal serves as a place to share where I am hesitant to speak without meditation and more organized thought. The personal journal was inspired by my satisfaction with participation in daily journal writing and e-mail letters.

Dan, too, realizes the significance of their research in his ongoing understanding of literacy education and teaching. In the narrative account that follows Dan reflects on their processes of inquiry and how and what he has learned from and with Vicki. He begins by quoting from their e-mail correspondence.

E-mail: An Alternative Site for the Construction of Story
To: d56f@bsu.edu
Subj: Trying out e-mail
Date: November 5, 1989
Well, this thing (e-mail) can get to be very time consuming but it will be worth it in the long run. I can't wait to get this thing hooked up in the classroom. I'm at the terminal right now and can see, feel it in my bones, the value of such a system to our program.

To: vc2r@cc.edu
subj: We are on our way
Date: November 5, 1989
I hope you will find the e-mail useful. It will be my lifeline to you and the students in Detroit! –d

The many e-mail notes and stories that were generated by Vicki and me began soon after we had embarked on a collaborative literacy program involving her students. At the time, we were searching for ways to broaden and extend our conversations and descriptions about literacy—to produce narratives that we felt were critical for our own development as teacher-researchers, and for the development of our elementary language arts program. We reasoned that e-mail would provide us with an alternative site and the space in which to construct those extended narratives/stories. In looking back over the past several years since we began our e-mail conversations, we now see that e-mail has not only provided us with an additional space in which to write our descriptive narratives in a convenient and timely manner, but also a means to capture our stories in juxtaposition, freeze-frame stories, thus allowing for a unique way in which to reflect on our experiences. In all, we have written hundreds of pages, and hundreds of stories that represent our constructed lives and thinking as teacher-researchers. Each story is significant and informative as a separate text, yet when combined they form an even more informative and meaningful text that we can reflect upon for the purpose of ethical action and the responsible teaching of literacy.

Since 1989, Vicki and I have been engaged in descriptive study that has been represented as research about adults and children from an urban setting who see writing as transformative. And, although we have never taken ourselves out of the picture while representing our research, we also have never focused on ourselves either, that is, as teacher-researchers whose voices and lives intersect with the voices of those we choose to learn with. We still believe that the children and adults from the community in which we work and live are most important in our research and teaching. Yet we also have come to believe that we must describe a more complete picture of our relationships with those individuals, to thicken the description of the story.

Vicki has been teaching in several urban elementary schools in the same city for thirty years. Her e-mail stories are refreshingly poignant. The following e-mail vignette describes a glimpse of her teaching environment, in which we both worked:

To: d56f@bsu.edu
Subj: You won't believe it!
Date: November 18, 1993
While we tested on Friday, the men came with a cherrypicker truck to repair two of my upper windows. They busted them out, and pounded in the new windows. It was terrible. Even if it hadn't been a testing time I could have cried! Our children are abused in every sense of the word. Tell me, do you think they will clean up the glass that spattered all over the windowsill, desks, floor, books, and bookshelves? I don't.

Although this vignette doesn't capture the whole environment in which Vicki works daily, it nevertheless is representative of an environment in which she struggles daily to teach amid interruptions (including those that result from the dynamics of an overcrowded classroom of thirty-five children) that significantly threaten to disrupt the learning of her children. I taught in high school for fifteen years and have recently become a teacher at a university. I've chosen to spend time as a guest teacher in Vicki's classroom. E-mail is an important tool used in our inquiry. For example, e-mail not only holds our stories momentarily so that they can be viewed in juxtaposition (a feature that we believe facilitates and prompts the writing of new stories), it serves as a repository for our stories. This allows for a kind of reflection that significantly informs our thinking about teaching, research, and community involvement.

Within our more personal e-mail stories, a definite story pattern emerged in which Vicki and I purposefully constructed images of ourselves as teachers, family members, researchers, and community activists. It is these stories that give a better understanding of the self-image we construct over e-mail and not only how those images reinforce previously held beliefs, but also how our beliefs are constantly changing. After six years of working closely together, we find it increasingly difficult to hold back our deepest feelings about what it means to be a teacher.

In the broader context of our initial descriptive study, we were better able to understand why we represented our actions as we did and how our actions affected us in myriad complicated ways. We had, for example, written about ourselves as political activists when we were pressured by an uncompromising school district. We told of our families and how they affected our thinking. In all, the many autobiographical stories we have shared with each other have contributed to our thinking about our identities and the many roles that describe our lives.

Even so, other kinds of stories were just as powerful and informative. Stories about the children in our class helped us to understand the lives of those children and our own thinking about how we might work with them in a responsible manner. During the last seven years, we have shared as many as a hundred or more e-mail stories about the eight- and nine-year-old children who were students in Vicki's language arts class. Such stories describe a rainbow of children's feelings, their thinking about important issues, and their ways of seeing and acting upon the world.

The dynamics of our e-mail stories are complex. At times and on one level, Vicki's stories beg for an immediate response, perhaps a reinforcement of her observations about a particular student. Vicki's one story about a troubled yet creative student motivated me to inquire further about the student's reasons for writing. And when I did, I too noticed the student's unique understanding of language, her control and power of it. I was also impressed with how the student thought to influence others with her writing. The student confided in me that she wanted others to understand her feelings. At the time, she reminded me of other writers in the class who believed that they could change how others think with the stories that they wrote. Both Vicki and I wanted to learn more about that student (and the others). As a consequence, our e-mail stories about the student continued throughout the year.

Many of the children in our class were risk takers, and they wrote as part of their risk taking. We learned from these children that in their writing they were willing to expose their feelings and thoughts if they thought there might be a chance that others would listen—and perhaps be influenced to think differently as a result. Such a notion about risk taking had a profound impact on how Vicki and I began to understand the value of literacy for the children we taught. We believe that we would have recognized these risk takers without our e-mail stories; however, our stories about others seemed to impact us more when we wrote them down and discussed them. Perhaps it was because we had more time to think about the stories as they unfolded on the computer screen and could be reread in time. Sharing stories on the run—stories we told about children after class, in the hallway, or on the phone—just never seemed to offer the staying power of our e-mail stories. But perhaps in retrospect it was a combination of our verbal and written stories about children that had the most effect on us, not just the e-mail story versions.

The stories Vicki and I wrote and shared over e-mail had a significant impact on how we conceptualized notions of literacy and how we eventually conceptualized our language arts curriculum. In one instance (in 1992), Vicki wrote a series of e-mail stories about Michael. His poem "Why me" explored how others came to think about him. In one line he wrote, "Why me do people hate me?" Vicki's e-mail story about Michael described his anxieties and the children's tauntings and then concluded that "Michael's questions are every person's questions.... Just as they have said adult books can be for children, I say children's writings can be for adults. This could lead to new kinds of collaborative work."

Vicki, the storymaker, used Michael's experiences as a way in which she might teach others, and as a storyteller she intended to shape others' ideas about collaborative work as well.

ISSUES AND CONCERNS

Relationships such as Vicki's and Dan's and Jim's and Anna's are developed over time and with careful and ongoing attention to matters of trust, respect, and sensitivity. Even so, issues arise that demand careful and negotiated consideration. As we outlined earlier, there are numerous issues to be attended to when engaging in collaborative research. One of the central concerns for Anna was maintaining her anonymity in any publications related to her and Jim's work. The issue of anonymity in teacher-research is a thorny one fraught with contradiction. On the one hand, it is important for teachers to be "seen" researching and writing about their work; on the other hand, there are potentially serious political pitfalls associated with such visibility.

In an article entitled, "Now You See Them, Now You Don't: Anonymity Versus Visibility in Case Studies of Teachers," Judith Shulman (1990) discusses the issue of anonymity in teacher research. The discussion is based on a highly complex set of problems and dilemmas that arose when a group of teachers with whom she worked on a collaborative research project objected to modifications of controversial data text requested by school district officials. They felt that such requests censored and diluted the messages they wanted to convey through the publication of their work. Shulman summarizes the ethical dilemma in this way:

> *When teachers forego the protection of anonymity, they become vulnerable to the disapproval and recrimination of peers and administrators. Unlike…researchers who leave the scene when their work is over, teachers rarely leave the scene. They must bear the burden of their written words, for they remain participants long after they complete their roles as formal observers and writers. Ironically, the school district also becomes vulnerable under these circumstances. We [as researchers] are justifiably committed to providing opportunities for the expression of the teacher's voice. Yet as teachers cast off their cloaks of anonymity, they place their institutions at some risk as well. We as a research community must learn to consider the rights of all individuals and institutions who collaborate with us. (p. 14)*

Here are Jim's and Anna's thoughts on the issue.

Jim: I struggled for a long time partly because I was really unclear as to the kind of research I was doing and what it should look like in writing. I was very reluctant to share any of it with you because I knew that it probably wasn't going to measure up to your expectations either. I needed a lot of time to work that out.

Anna: But even in your reluctance—and this is a tribute to your ethical responsibility—you did share everything with me. That was important to me. I think trust was built through those uncomfortable moments.

Jim: I did take my ethical responsibility to you very seriously, and I have always tried to share things with you—my writing as well as my concerns about the potential risks you might face. For example, your anonymity in my writing, or possibly your lack thereof, has long been an issue that we've struggled with, and it has again become an issue right here as we've prepared this dialogue.

Anna: And I'm still a bit confused. You've given me the option of anonymity, which I welcome, because I still don't feel as if I know all of the potential risks.

Jim: The way I see it, if you're anonymous, then that greatly lowers the risk that outside readers, whom you don't know, may contact you against your wishes or unfairly criticize you in their own writing. Depending on how I craft my dissertation, I would probably be making myself more vulnerable to this kind of criticism than you, but the risk remains nonetheless. When I interpret your teaching practices and interpret your career, I may be doing so with great respect and responsibility and with your whole-hearted support, but once I publish something, I will be throwing it to the wind in a manner of speaking. Except through my careful choice of words, I have little control over how someone else might interpret my work. And as we both know, people come to texts with all kinds of previous conceptions, and they might read something that is very contextual, take it out of context, and then inappropriately incorporate it into their own pieces of writing. Or you could be lauded in such a way that you could be held up by someone as an exemplar. You're concerned about my work possibly doing that. Once my work is published, all of that will be out of our control. So I think that it is very important for you to use a pseudonym, because it can discourage a level of personal scrutiny that you don't want. Just by having a pseudonym—even if it's a transparent one—we're sending an implicit message to anyone who may read my work that you're not seeking attention.

Anna: That's fine; however, my primary concern has always been not putting kids at risk, not putting the school at risk, or any of my colleagues, or administrators for that matter.

Jim: I think we can read that risk a little better, because you know those individuals so well. As you read my work and give me suggestions for revisions, you can put yourself in the position of various people in the school and read from their point of view. Then you can decide whether or not something might be harmful or offensive to them. I'll also be going out of my way to try to avoid known "land mines."

Anna: And you've done that skillfully and artfully, to date.

Jim: Well, I'm prepared to stand up to anyone who might press me to be more informative or more revealing about issues that we have agreed are out-of-bounds. I just have to remind myself that I'm not an investigative journalist. My job isn't to uncover the "truth" so to speak, to get to the bottom of things in an abrasive sort of way. My job is to understand the answers to my questions as we have negotiated them. There may be a lot of other things going on in your school that would be interesting to explore, but that interest is definitely outweighed by the ethical considerations. That is my answer to anyone who would press me to get into issues related to teacher gossip or underlying school politics. I haven't gone in with that as my goal, and for me to start uncovering things like that and making them central to my research at this stage would be unfair to a lot of people on so many different levels. There are certainly enough interesting things going on in your classroom to merit my attention and concentration.

Another issue that appeared central in Anna's and Jim's collaboration had to do with Jim's representation or portrayal of Anna's practice. They took care in their research relationship to be honest and open with each other and to present their observations and understandings in a nonjudgmental way. It was critical to maintain a commitment to these principles through to the representation of Anna's practice. In the following conversation, Jim and Anna talk about this issue.

Anna: Even though we're talking about me, in a way I don't feel like the object of a study because I keep seeing this as a chance to look back on classroom practices of a lifetime. Even though they're mine, it's not like—How can I say it? It's not like my story.

Jim: Are you saying that you can look back very objectively?

Anna: Yeah, you've helped me to do that. Even when we're looking at something that's ongoing in the classroom together, it feels...

Jim: ...It feels as if I bring a perspective that pulls you away from the closeness with which you normally experience things and enable you to see things from another point of view?

Anna: No, you bring that other point of view—but it's not like mirroring. That's not the right image either. I simply feel that we're looking at a public practice. That, I guess, is what I'm thinking. This isn't like looking at something that shouldn't be exposed. It seems to me that teachers' work is very much a public act, and that these are things that people should know more about rather than less. In that sense, I don't feel guarded. You didn't construct this as an "exemplary practice" kind of thing. Instead, we're looking at somebody who's kind of fumbled her way through things and eventually found some ways to make things work.

...It's such a peculiar thing, but I do feel a distance from your work in a peculiar kind of way. And I think it's the quality of your writing. You've attended so carefully to, I think, a mode of fictionalizing. I really think your writing has grown so much since you began, and it sounds so much less researchy than it did. It has a very artful style. But I feel as if I'm reading about somebody else. I'm kind of a private person, and I'm much less self-conscious about our work than I was initially. I used to think that I couldn't read anything with my name in it or even that was talking about my students. I felt very awkward about that.

Jim's "nonresearchy" style and "fictionalizing" mode was important to Anna. It seemed to Anna like a more honest way of representing her work—one that she could relate to, feel comfortable with, and learn from.

PARTING COMMENTS

We conclude with some parting thoughts from Vicki on how her collaboration with Dan has been, according to her, "a conduit for literacy change." Vicki's words attest to the potential power and impact of reflexive collaborative inquiry relationships. Collaborative relationships based on a mutually negotiated investment of the self have transformative power that goes well beyond the initially determined purpose of an inquiry. Embedded in Vicki's comments is the essence of reflexivity and reflexive teaching.

Attending to our collaborative research has influenced my teaching pedagogy and developed my practice as a teacher in the following ways:

- I assume responsibility for the unique knowledge of and relationship with the African American neighborhood community where I teach.
- It is vital to me and for my practice as a teacher that I am in touch with my own culture.
- Our students' academic curriculum and personal empowerment grow out of their own life stories.
- My most effective educational strategies involve adults and children sharing the teaching and learning process together.
- We embrace the expertise of significant others—parents, community members, colleagues, and former students—within and outside the classroom environment who serve to extend our educational experience.
- Reflection on literature is a significant informant for us as teachers and students.
- Former students have an impact on the adult and student community by assuming responsibility to return and share, both publicly and privately, the growth of experience from their integrated knowledge.
- I need an ongoing relationship with individual neighborhood students and their families in order to make evident "living the life."
- My students and I value and publish our life stories and classroom practice narratives informed by journals and sharing.
- Dan Madigan models behaviors with students that influence my practice with our students (e.g., suggesting that students edit teachers' work, advocating positive comments, accepting students' efforts).

RESEARCH ACTIVITIES

The Research Activities are geared to helping you make contacts with outside researchers and develop working relationships. The key to working with outside researchers is to find a way or ways in which your separate interests and energies can come together in a mutually beneficial way. This will not be easy but we know from our own experience and from watching and listening to the experiences of others that it can and does happen with considerable frequency.

- Attendance at professional or educational research conferences will alert you to some individuals with whom you can work. Although we know that the preferable position would be to work with local researchers, it is not altogether unheard of or unfeasible to collaborate with a researcher from a distance.

- Taking course work at a local or distant university may also promote professional connections and collaboration possibilities both with institutional researchers and professors, for example.

- Linking up with (other) graduate students, especially Master's and doctoral degree candidates, may lead to fruitful opportunities for collaborative work. They may come with particular notions of their inquiries or they may be completely open to suggestion. Make a particular point of talking with graduate students about their researching interests.

• School boards may sometimes have researchers who might see your particular project as a worthy investment of energies although we typically expect such personnel to be fully occupied with the mandates of their school board or district superintendent.

The establishment of a sound and philosophically synergetic relationship may be the major facilitator of this collaboration. Because of these reasons we urge you to find ways to explore perspectives in depth.

Earlier in the chapter we talked about the various ways in which the resources of your inquiry focus or project may be enhanced. Explore some of the possibilities we outlined and use them for both contacting and developing a working relationship with outside researchers. More specifically,

• Develop a statement about your researching ideas and pass it by local professors and educational researchers. Use it as a discussion point to explore ways of working together. Perhaps do the same with local graduate students. Do not hesitate to visit several institutions in your vicinity.

• Seek out research reports that connect and resonate with your ideas and are written by local authors. Invite them to visit with you and some colleagues or to visit your classroom to talk about their ideas in relation to your teaching. Offer your classroom as a context in which you might explore, together, some of their ideas or processes.

• Explore and obtain through citation indexes or though the internet articles, chapters, or books that present research reports on topics connected to your interests or which may inform your work. Contact the authors and invite them to talk to you about their research work and its potential connections to your own interests. Perhaps develop an ongoing correspondence with the view to inviting them to join researching with you in some way.

• Make it known what it is that you stand for, both in your classroom teaching and in your broader practice of being a teacher. Work at being very articulate about this. Also work at sharing your perspectives with people known for their research work and interests in inquiry, and do this in a variety of venues, including professional meetings, conferences, and workshops. You may well find that researchers come to you because they find your work compelling or of interest in some way. Such relationships may in time become collaborative researching ones. The book by Dan Madigan and Vicki Koivu-Rybicki, *The Writing Lives of Children,* is both about a teacher's work and about a long-term collaborative researching relationship (and you have already read about their collaborative relationship earlier in the chapter).

RECOMMENDED READINGS

Clandinin, D. J., Davies, A., Hogan, P., & Kennard, B. (Eds.). (1993). *Learning to teach teaching to learn: Stories of collaboration in teacher education.* New York: Teachers College Press.

Dadds, M. (1995). *Passionate enquiry and school development: A story about teacher action research.* London: Falmer Press.

Gitlin, A., Bringhurst, K., Burns, M., Cooley, V., Myers, B., Price, K., Russell, R., & Tiess, P. (1992). *Teachers' voices for school change: An introduction to educative research.* New York: Teachers College Press.

Kagan, D. M., with Chestnut, J. R., Hunter, L. B., Burch, C. B., & Wilson, E. K. (1993). *Laura and Jim and what they taught me about the gap between educational theory and practice.* Albany, NY: State University of New York Press.

Madigan, D., & Koivu-Rybicki, V. T. (1997). *The writing lives of children.* York, ME: Stenhouse.

Miller, J. L. (1990). *Creating spaces and finding voices: Teachers collaborating for empowerment.* Albany, NY: State University of New York Press.

POSTSCRIPT: EXTENDING NOTIONS OF RESEARCHING TEACHING: A REFLEXIVE CONCLUSION

with contributions by
CATHERINE EBBS

As teachers, teacher-inquirers, teacher educators, educational researchers, and professors of education we continue to develop and articulate ourselves and our practice according to an ethic of authenticity. We endeavor as much as possible to practice what we preach, to do what we espouse, to enact the beliefs, values, and principles we hold, to listen to and follow our own exhortations. We teach, research, and otherwise practice what we know and feel. In short, we teach (research, supervise, and so on) who we are.

Throughout this book we have strongly and consistently advocated the notion of reflexive inquiry. In Chapter 2 in particular we attempted, through excerpts from some of our own reflexive inquiries, to lead by example. We expect that by now you have a sense of who we are as teachers and researchers. In thinking about how to conclude this book we were mindful that we wanted to underscore the importance we place on authenticity. We wanted to emphasize that what we are advocating for teachers is what we believe in and apply to and in our own professional situations. Accordingly, we conclude with an example of collaborative reflexive inquiry from our own ongoing reflexive inquiry agenda. In our account we explore a particular pedagogical issue of mutual interest—the place of questioning in our classroom practice. In addition, we include the voice of another university-based teacher educator and educational researcher who also extends the notion of reflexive inquiry into her own practice. Catherine, a former school teacher, reflects on some of her experiences of engaging in collaborative inquiry with preservice teachers and the transformative nature of those experiences on her practice. In her inquiry work she wanted to know, from a life history and personal narrative perspective, the place of personal history–based literacy experiences in the professional thinking of relatively young elementary preservice teachers.

We begin with our account[1] and conclude the Postscript with Catherine's.

QUESTIONING OUR PRACTICE

In our "program" of reflexive inquiry we seek to understand the multiple roles, contexts, and relationships that comprise our practices. For example, in an attempt to understand the many facets of our work and how they relate to one another, we focus on our professional roles as learners, teachers, researchers, writers, supervisors, colleagues, and faculty members. We reflect on teacher education in general and what it means to be a teacher educator within the respective institutions with which we are affiliated and in the broader teacher education and education communities.

Here we focus on one element of our practice—teaching—and illustrate some of what we have learned about ourselves as teachers and teacher educators. The use of questioning is central in our respective pedagogies and, because it illustrates our ongoing authentic engagement with problematic elements of our teaching work, it also serves as a useful tool for illustrating the reflexive inquiry process.

Although we both use questioning as a primary pedagogical tool, our focus on questioning in our pedagogical practice began as a concern for Gary. In trying to facilitate preservice teachers in their development of critical, reflexive pedagogies, Gary, like many teacher-educators, consistently challenges individuals to substantiate their thinking and practice. He embeds his practice within a pedagogy that expressly makes opportunities for preservice teachers to explore their prior experiences, and he is particularly concerned about facilitating internal consistency between the assumptions and arguments that new teachers make. Questioning is central to this pedagogical stance. As the following excerpts from Gary's journal indicate, such questioning presents problems for some preservice teachers.

> In the context of the [alternative, graduate teacher preparation] program we rely on the holistic, integrative nature of subject matter and acknowledge the "personal" as being central in becoming a teacher. Each prospective teacher in the program brings a lot to the table. Because I am

---

[1]A version of this writing appeared as part of an article entitled, "Researching the 'good life': Reflections on professorial practice," published in the *Professional Educator,* 1994, Volume 17, Number 1. We thank the editor for permission to reprint segments of that article. At the time of this writing Gary was a professor at the University of Michigan. Currently, we are both at the Ontario Institute for Studies in Education of the University of Toronto.

not "presenting material" I use questioning more frequently in class than others might do. My questions are intended to encourage clarification and inquiry into the underlying frameworks of preservice teachers' thinking, but they initially see little connection between their values and beliefs, their arguments or discussions about practice, their experiences, and their actual practice. They complain about being questioned, usually quietly, but sometimes vocally. They appear uncomfortable even with peers asking questions. (Gary's journal, March 2, 1993)

They often interpret my questions as being "intimidating." Sometimes I ask, "Why do you believe that?" and "What are the assumptions behind your thinking?" Many of these highly able preservice teachers deem such questions as almost impertinent. As [one preservice teacher] stated, "Why do you have to ask questions all the time? I know what I think. I know what I want to do as a teacher. Why do I need to make public my private thinking about practice? I may not have all the answers, but your questions are not useful. We want to be *given* insights into practice, not asked questions about our thinking." (Gary's journal, December 12, 1992)

The excerpts from Gary's journal reveal a level of dissonance between the intentions and pedagogical beliefs underlying Gary's questioning practice and the preservice teachers' perceptions (and perhaps prior experiences) of such questioning practice. Considered at another level, such dissonance is indicative of the existing tension between traditional and progressive orientations to teacher education. Preservice teachers enter teacher-education programs with preconceptions and expectations of how they will learn to be teachers. For the most part they expect, as the preservice teacher in Gary's class said, "to be given insights into practice, not asked questions about [their] thinking"—a view in fundamental opposition to the inquiry-oriented perspective on which Gary's (and other educators') practice is based. Leaving incongruencies unexamined does little to ameliorate such dissonance. Hence the importance of exploring assumptions underlying one's pedagogical practices.

The preservice teachers in Gary's cohort responded negatively to his questioning stance and had difficulty broadening their perspective to incorporate an alternative view of pedagogy. They continued to feel frustrated and intimidated by his persistent practice of asking questions until they had an opportunity to observe Gary adopt his familiar questioning practice in an interaction with a high school student. That event, described in Gary's journal, helped some of them to understand, and even appreciate, his pedagogy:

I saw a breakthrough. On visiting [an alternative school], a mature, articulate, knowledgeable, and self-confident grade 10 student led us in a discussion about the school's curriculum. I asked him a number of searching, clarification questions, and he ably responded. Afterward, [one of the preservice teachers] commented: "[The grade 10 student] handled you far better than we ever have. He easily answered your questions. Being able to sit back and watch you work—ask questions of someone else—gave me a different view on your practice. Your questions really pushed the student to make clear his thinking. I guess that's what [your questions] have done for us." Another said: "I'm finally beginning to appreciate your pedagogy. I always thought your questions were so intimidating." (Gary's journal, March 2, 1993)

In spite of the "breakthrough," Gary continued to be troubled by the preservice teachers' perceptions of his practice as "intimidating." He struggled for an explanation. "What does it mean to be intimidating? Does the 'intimidation' come from the question or the questioner? What do preservice teachers expect of university professors? What are their conceptions about the process of becoming a teacher? What place do they see for discussions about fundamental and personal 'whys' and 'wherefores' of teaching?" These were some of the many questions Gary asked himself during private reflections and posed to others in conversation. In one e-mail exchange with Ardra, he explored the role of context in his teaching practice.

> *Gary:* Why do you think that some preservice teachers see my questions as intimidating? ... Is it something that has to do with the classroom climate—I think you would call it "the setting"—that I create? Do I not pay enough attention to that?

> *Ardra:* Making underlying assumptions explicit is at one level always threatening to people, no matter how hard you work at creating an appropriate setting. Sometimes group dynamics make it difficult for everyone to feel sufficiently at ease to engage in the kind of discussion you like to engender. One of the more readily identifiable sources of discomfort is the teacher, whether the teacher *is* or *is not* directly responsible.... Your directness and openness may be difficult for some as well. Perhaps you don't pay enough attention to preparing the context for your students, taking too much for granted in believing that they can be open.

> *Gary:* Perhaps I'm less concerned now than in the past with developing the context for my questioning. Perhaps I have come to expect everyone to be as direct as I am. (e-mail messages, March 3–5, 1993)

In a subsequent discussion with Stella, a faculty colleague with whom Gary team teaches, he further explored the preservice teachers' responses to his questioning. Stella had only relatively recently come to the United States of America.

Stella shed some light on my concern about the preservice teachers' aversion to being asked questions. She, too, was struck by it. She said something like, "This is a graduate course...after all. What do they expect? Graduate school is a place where ideas are thrashed out intellectually—supposedly. Why is it that students do not want to be asked to back up their positions? Is there a cultural basis for these very prevalent attitudes? Asking questions is the hallmark of professorial work. Why is it that 'caring' teachers are placed ahead of intellectually rigorous ones?

To what extent is this matter a cultural artifact of 'being American'? In South Africa the academic climate is much more confrontive. Students expect to be challenged!" (Gary's journal, March 22, 1993)

Because Gary and Stella had very similar perspectives on and responses to the preservice teachers' resistance, the conversation with Stella provided Gary much needed affirmation of his pedagogical stance but not an adequate explanation for the dissonance.

To better understand both the students' responses and his questioning practice, Gary explored the roots of his use of questioning in his own experience of school as a student. A journal entry in which he wrote about the origins of his questioning practice illuminates the link between his experiences of school as a learner and his teaching practice. His tendency to ask searching questions is a pedagogical practice embedded in his personal history and lifelong approach to learning.

As a child growing up in a small rural community I wasn't a verbally inquisitive child. I was observant and intrigued by things mechanical, but I didn't ask questions in class. A shy, reserved, awkward youngster, I came out of my shell when placed in a classroom in which the teacher, Mr. Gee, gave me permission to ask difficult questions. I was about eleven years old at the time. Then, in high school, the geography classes in which I did well academically were taught by teachers who encouraged my questioning. I asked questions, it seems, to clarify my thinking, check my understandings, and to find out more. I was genuinely interested, my curiosity was sparked, and my attention riveted by these teachers. They were patient with me and willing to be interrupted. A high school physics teacher, recognizing my struggle with the subject matter, actively encouraged me to ask questions when I did not understand. And ask I did. For the first time I recognized the power of questions as a learning technique. I passed college physics simply because I asked questions. (Gary's journal, March 8, 1993)

By tracing the roots of his questioning practice to his experiences of school as a student, Gary gained a clearer understanding of the basis on which his questioning practice was founded. What he did not have, however, was similar insights into the preservice teachers' responses. What experiences with questioning did they bring to the preservice program? What links could be made between their experiences as school learners and their responses to certain pedagogical practices? Although Gary's practice encouraged them to explore their prior experiences and the meanings attached to those experiences, they did not focus on articulating their understandings about the use of questioning in the classroom.

An exploration of the use of questioning as a pedagogical tool in Ardra's teaching shed additional light on the issue with which Gary was grappling. It also illuminated the broader issue of the role of personal histories in teaching practices. The use of questioning arose in a postobservation discussion with Madeleine, a doctoral candidate coresearcher who had spent considerable time observing Ardra's teaching; however, the context in which it was identified as a significant part of her pedagogy was quite different from the context in which the issue arose for Gary. For instance, Ardra's use of questioning, also central in her pedagogy, was not presented as problematic. In contrast to Gary's situation, the students in Ardra's class responded favorably to her use of questioning. A summary comment from Madeleine illustrates.

> I am beginning to see a pattern in the way you teach. I don't think you are conscious of the techniques you use. They are part of who you are.... You do not answer questions.... You throw [a question that was asked] back out to the group and allow them to talk about things. You draw threads from the various conversations and pull them together, and then provide an answer that is better than any one person could have done, and that provides time for people to be creative and to have input. Then you make connections or you ask the class to make them, "What connections do you see?" is an example from today's class. (Interview with Ardra, November 2, 1993)

In an attempt to determine why students in Ardra's class responded differently than those in Gary's class to what we understood to be a very similar pedagogical practice, we looked again to prior experiences. Like Gary, Ardra explored the roots of her questioning practice in her experiences as a learner; however, unlike Gary, Ardra was not encouraged to ask questions and did not experience success doing so. The following excerpt from a life-history interview illuminates the personal history–professional practice link.

> I have a very high regard for questioning and a high regard for curiosity. Perhaps I am not as spontaneous in my expression of curiosity and question asking as I would like to be because it does not come naturally.... I feel differently about question asking when I am the teacher and when I am the learner. I think questioning is really important and as a teacher I have developed an ability to encourage people to ask questions and to value different perspectives. I try to encourage learners to find and want to find answers to questions.
>
> In the role of learner I don't ask questions. I have great difficulty asking questions [outside of my role as teacher or researcher]. If I have a question I think it is unimportant, so I stop myself. When questions come to mind, I feel I should not ask if I don't already know the answer. I can encourage others to ask questions but I cannot ask questions in a way that I would like to be able to....
>
> At home [growing up] we were never encouraged to ask questions. Curiosity was not a value that was instilled in us, which is really unfortunate. I also had a very bad experience at school where I was blatantly discouraged from asking questions, and that had a major impact on me. I had an English literature teacher who was a very humiliating, intimidating, sarcastic person. I remember one incident where I happened to be in class and to be actually enjoying what was going on [both of which were unusual occurrences at that point in my adolescent life]. I asked a question and he ridiculed me saying, in effect, "Unless you know the answer,

don't ask the question." I remember his response so vividly. I think that has had a very, very significant impact on me. (Interview with Ardra, May 27, 1993)

Given the strong similarities in our pedagogical beliefs and practices we were (and continue to be) interested in how differently our beliefs are played out and practices interpreted. There are myriad reasons why we and our students respond differently at different times, and we continue to try to uncover and make sense of these reasons. We sense that these differences are explained in large part by the kinds of personal history experiences on which our professional practices are based. As a learner Gary was encouraged to ask questions, and he experienced repeated success by doing so. For him questioning clarified understanding, promoted curiosity, and opened his mind to new ways of thinking and viewing the world. Thus he developed a firm belief in the value of questioning as a learning tool. He carried this belief with him to his teaching practice, expecting that students would value questioning as he had as a learner.

Ardra, on the other hand, was discouraged from asking questions both at home and in school, and she had some very deflating experiences with question asking. She came to teaching with little confidence in her own ability to ask questions but with a sense of the value of questioning in teaching and learning. As a result of her own experiences as a learner, she did not have the same high expectations as Gary that students would favorably respond to question asking. Because of her own experiences of being ridiculed, she perhaps focuses more than Gary on preparing the context in which questions are asked and on students' level of comfort with her questioning practice.

The following e-mail message to Gary following a visit to Ardra's advanced qualitative research methods class, when he asked the doctoral students questions about their research, is illustrative of some of these differences.

Your visit to my class last week created more disequilibrium than we had initially thought. The exchange between you and Kate caught most people off guard. I understand that you were simply looking for clarification of Kate's ideas but I guess [the students] were not used to your manner of questioning.

I knew Kate was upset, so I made a point of seeking her out before the next class. We had a long talk. She felt both intimidated by your questioning and surprised at her response. She is probably one of the most reflexive, self-aware, and articulate students with whom I have worked. She knows her passions and is not afraid to tackle critical issues head on, yet after your interaction with her she began to question herself and her abilities. She apparently spent considerable time reliving your conversation both on her own and with her peers. You sure threw her for a loop.

In class today we spent time talking about what had happened last week. Interestingly enough the conversation was not directly focused on your interaction with Kate. It was more about what the class has come to mean to the students and how, in some way, they felt that their privacy had been violated by your presence. Both overtly and covertly we have worked to create what one student called "a safe place where we feel supported in our thinking in whatever state it's in." I had no idea until today just how insular and insulated they had become.... You were an outsider and I did not see the "No Trespassing" sign.

Most of what we do in class challenges our own and each other's assumptions as well as the various assumptions underlying what we read. It's not as if the substance of your questions was unfamiliar. I guess it had more to do with the context in which they were asked and by whom. It looks like "trespassers" have to earn certain privileges. (e-mail message from Ardra, March 25, 1993)

The complexity of teaching and learning and the need for a holistic analysis of practice is repeatedly evidenced in our reflections. We could not (and cannot) make sense of our pedagogical use of questioning in isolation. For example, the issue of questioning is integrally connected to another important theme characterizing our practice: the learning context. Our ongoing reflexive inquiry and reflective conversations help us to identify and make sense of these and other patterns in our teaching, and to become aware of incongruencies between what we *think* we do and what students *perceive* us to be doing, so that we might better understand who we are and what we do as teachers and teacher educators.

Clearly we cannot make sense of our teaching by merely analyzing its constituent elements or by considering instances out of the contexts in which they take place; teaching is far too complex and contextual for such an activity to be of much use. The examples we cite are but snapshots of teaching experiences bounded by time and context. The meanings we derive from the examples are but part of our ongoing sense making. With different students under different circumstances, the same pedagogical approaches might be differently interpreted and have different meanings for us and them. But since much of teaching work is context specific, so too is this work. Having said this, we are all products of the personal experiences that influence the ways we each conceptualize and carry out our roles as teachers and teacher educators, and although the complex and context-specific nature of teaching defies generalization, we believe that exploring teaching practices within the context of personal histories articulates foundational understandings.

We conclude with Catherine's reflexive account of her experience of researching with preservice teachers. Embedded in Catherine's writing and research are many of the same values and principles foundational to and communicated throughout this book. As such it is a most appropriate way to end.

INQUIRY INTO INQUIRY

Of phenomenological engagement Van Manen claims that "it is an appeal to each one of us, to how we understand things, how we stand in life, how we understand ourselves as educators" (1990, p. 156) and that human science research is a way of being and of becoming. My research journey exemplifies these claims. What occurred was not only deep learning about the nature of inquiry but also how it can be a pedagogic form of life (Van Manen, 1990). I began to articulate more carefully and challenge more often my own positions on the ethics of research, my sense of who I was as a teacher educator and my positions on issues in my field of research, namely, the development of literacy. It was a process of becoming validated, renewed, challenged, and transformed.

Contrary to Van Manen's claim, the process went beyond a mere appeal to having a transformative effect. I simply was not the same coming out of the research as I had been going into it. I believe the deep engagement and relational nature required in the research provided a natural context for heightened awareness of both ethics and self-inquiry and as such contributed to its transformative nature.

This form of professional inquiry was very powerful as a tool for personal and professional development. First, as the teachers' stories unfolded and I learned more and more about their lives I began, unintentionally at first, to use these as frames for reflecting on my own life. Second, because relationships were central to my research efforts, the ethics of procedures, methods, analysis, and writing were foremost in my mind. I struggled to safeguard the trust of, dignity for, and open and honest negotiation with the preservice teachers. I engaged in an ongoing inquiry into the ethics of my research methods, which in turn transferred to the ethics inherent in my classroom teaching. I developed a greater understanding of the "sacredness" of research (Lincoln, 1993), teaching, and learning. I not only engaged in ongoing discourse about the ethics and procedures of research in order to safeguard the teachers and the authenticity of the research but I also engaged in self-reflections. I inquired into who I was as a researcher and teacher educator and my positions on issues relating to my field of research, literacy education. I believe the self-reflections and discourse were the agents of transformation.

Reflections on the Process

Throughout the research I centered on the ethics of collaborative partnership research. I realize that the deep relationship of trust and respect I built with the preservice teachers induced me to safeguard their interests and to critique and reflect on my actions. I constantly questioned procedures and my role as a researcher. This act of inquiry was critical to my own development and learning.

From the beginning of the interview process I adopted an inquiry stance concerning such issues as the potential invasive nature of life history interviewing; my roles in the research efforts; reciprocity; autonomy, control of the research agenda; the contribution the research played in the teachers' lives; the psychological consequences of the research, and the authenticity of text. Furthermore, the stance of critique and reflection heightened my self-awareness and informed my ongoing practices. The following sections detail how the process influenced my development as a researcher and teacher educator.

The Personal History Interview

My sense of what an interview consisted of changed over time. Previously an "interview," to me, was a "question-answer" process of knowledge dissemination and challenge. Now I do not believe that a question-answer process represents at all the nature of personal history interviews. Our interviews were much more multidimensional. They were conversational. They were a negotiated search for meaning. They were interpretive. Not only did they involve a back and forth of information but the teachers also meandered through seemingly unrelated territory. At times the teachers provided me with insights and I them. I grew to understand that the meanderings, feedback, and interpretations were what contributed to a rich understanding of experience.

The potentially invasive nature of interviewing became evident in the first round of the conversational interviews I had with the preservice teachers. Over time, as our relationships grew and as they reconstructed their literacy histories, the preservice teachers journeyed into private family lives as well as private thoughts about diverse and complex experiences. I grew to understand, respect, and keep sacred the very privileged position they had entrusted to me. Decisions about research procedures had to be jointly negotiated to ensure their comfort.

I developed a heightened sensitivity to my intrusion into their privacy. I began to understand that there were appropriate moments to probe further for information, appropriate moments to intervene thinking with an insight, and appropriate moments to say nothing but to be a good listener. For example, when an insight led to clearer interpretation or added a challenge to a thought, I added one. When the preservice teachers needed time to think or articulate, I remained silent.

I was continually learning about myself as a teacher throughout the interviews. I had to stop myself from adopting a question-and-answer approach. I learned how ingrained that method had become throughout my teaching career as I engaged in the interviews. Fortunately and early on in the process the question-answer mentality that had been part of my schooling and training as a teacher was eventually replaced by a new respect for listening, conversation, feedback, reflection, meanderings, and joint questioning. Thus the interviews not only informed my research but informed and challenged me to rethink past and current teaching practices.

A Researcher's Many Roles

I had to adopt many roles in the inquiry process. I was a supporter, storyteller, participant, interpreter, facilitator, questioner, observer, listener, writer, articulator, and teacher, to name a few.

Throughout the interviews, reading of the interview transcripts, and writing up the narrative accounts, I was a supporter. For example, when the preservice teachers saw their transcripts for the first time and commented on the inconsistencies and incoherencies of their speech patterns I reminded them that oral language was not speech written down. I reminded them that written language goes through many revisions before it is ready for a public audience. As they grew to understand the differences between oral and written language they became more comfortable reading their own transcripts.

During the course of the interviews, when the teachers reconstructed painful experiences I offered my support as a compassionate listener willing to journey through the pain with them. I developed a heightened sensitivity to the consequences of the research process.

I was also a storyteller of my literacy experiences. I reconstructed my own literacy accounts within family, school, work, and community contexts and often shared the experiences with the teachers. I wanted the preservice teachers to know I was exploring *my* literacy history as *they* explored theirs.

I was a cointerpreter throughout the process. I learned to offer my interpretations as a researcher who came to the process with alternative perspectives based on wide reading of a relevant body of literature. I learned to watch for themes but to recognize, as new information became available, that an initial explanation or interpretation may fall short, and this recognition allowed the research question and focus to remain open to modification. I learned that a conversational partnership revealed the limits and possibilities of interpretive achievements (Van Manen, 1990).

The flexibility required made me appreciate the complexity of inquiry and helped me to understand that arriving at interpretive insights is not necessarily a rule-bound process but a relational one. This understanding also has helped me rethink teacher education course work. I frequently reflect on the variety of roles that classroom teaching requires of me and adopt a similar stance of flexibility when I am in classrooms.

Reciprocity

A frequent issue that arose over the course of the research was that of reciprocity. Because of the relational nature of research I continually questioned how reciprocal the research agenda was. Throughout the process I needed to know that the research was not just to satisfy my own agenda but contributed to the teachers' understanding, self-determination, and autonomy as well.

The original intent of the inquiry was to describe the literacy histories of four preservice teachers and explore how their experiences across multiple contexts contributed to their understanding of what literacy was. It became evident, however, that the research was much more than what I had at first anticipated. It became evident that the process was more than a mere description or gathering of information. It was interpretive, an exploration into the meaning of experiences. During the interviews I asked the preservice teachers to think about the meanings of their experiences. This interpretive description brought "the range of meanings of life's phenomena to our reflective awareness" (Van Manen, 1990, p. 18). The teachers constructed an understanding of who they had been and become through their literacy experiences, of how, as literate people or literacy users, they had been perceived by individuals in school systems, families, and work places. By locating their narratives within wider social, cultural, and political contexts they reflected on their experiences in ways they told me were new to them. As I observed the process of interpretation I began to understand more deeply the connections between researching and theorizing. I began to see them as "interchangeable concepts" (Van Manen, 1990) necessary for reflexive understanding.

I felt satisfied that for the preservice teachers and for myself the research was contributing to a deep personal and professional understanding and on many occasions received just such reassurance from the teachers. By negotiating control of the process, autonomy in procedural decisions and ultimately more authority over the data with the teachers, reciprocity was ensured.

I developed a respect for equity issues as the inquiry process continued. As we negotiated control and narration of each preservice teachers' story, its representation and interpretation, I reflected on my past thinking about research and the politics of power. I began to theorize about democratic approaches to research and believed that the more democratic the research effort the more self-dignity the teachers gained as coresearchers. I believe that the research was enriched with this democratic stance and now see research as a social process.

As I theorized about issues of equity and reciprocity during the process, I developed a heightened sensitivity to first the hierarchical structures within the universities with which I was associated and second the politics of power in everyday conversations, meetings, and social relationships. For example, I more often noticed social discourse that silenced others. I reflected on my reactions to such discourse and theorized about ways I might begin to dismantle oppressive structures beginning first of all in my own classroom. I felt convinced I had engaged in action-sensitive research when this began to happen.

What frequently struck me throughout the research process was how unquestioning I had been in the past about the capacity of hierarchical models to silence others. I knew more about these preservice teachers than any others I had known and I questioned why that was so. What resulted from this knowledge was a respect for their ability to teach me about teaching, about learning, and about myself. This learning created a greater sense of equity for me because it meant we were learners together. Although I have tried to break apart some power barriers in my own university classroom by using alternative assessment strategies and communication styles, I have come to realize how systemic these notions of power are in myself and the preservice teachers at large. When I present alternative forms of assessment that require their opinions and ideas they ask for more familiar multiple choice test options. More than once this year I heard preservice teachers in the classroom say, "Just ask the questions and I'll give you the answers you are looking for" and, "You mean you actually want my opinion?" What has the education system said to me and to these learners?

This research therefore made me question traditional hierarchical models of power in my own thinking and in education at large, and I will, as a result, continue to strive for more equitable curricula in which all voices are valued for their capacity to teach.

A Pedagogical Orientation

Out of respect for the teachers and throughout the process I knew I had to document my place in the process. As the research relationships intensified I had to be true to the teachers, and this meant clarifying for myself, the teachers, and eventually a wider, more public, audience, my place in the research. Through this process I articulated my positions on the subject of the inquiry work research, on my role in the interpretation and representation of experiences and in the writing of the narrative accounts. I wanted to maintain authenticity of text.

A clarity of thought and position occurred as a result of this documentation. I developed richer understandings of the role past research had played in my current understandings, of myself as a writer, an interviewer, and a researcher. I understood that this form of research had a pedagogical orientation. It taught me about myself as it taught me to research.

The research process forced me to rethink many of my own assumptions and perspectives. I explored theoretical perspectives I held on such issues as power and the act of thinking. What surprised me was the extent to which I reconsidered many perspectives on concepts sometimes seemingly removed from the topic at hand.

I have reconsidered what thinking means to me. Throughout the inquiry process, as I observed the flexible, dynamic, and very creative, "seamless" thinking of the teachers, I began to apply it to my own thinking and have been much more conscious of knowledge compartmentalization, a concept endemic in literacy curriculum (Heath, 1990). I have also developed a heightened sensitivity to my own language. For example, I reflect frequently on specific words and the assumptions behind them. I have replaced the word "student" with the words "preservice teacher" in my discourse with others. I have learned to follow reflection with action.

This research was also a joint construction, not transmission of knowledge, and was characterized by negotiation, feedback, and respect for each other. This constructivist perspective has added a further dimension to my thinking on teaching and learning. I seek activities and opportunities in my own classrooms that maximize constructivist principles.

To conclude, this research was a meaning-making process. Experiences were interpreted from different perspectives. Such fresh perspectives can open the door to alternative interpretations. The preservice teachers unintentionally, but as part of the research process, provided me with alternative insights for interpreting my own experiences. The process taught me to look more closely at connections among experiences, at how relationships I had with literate others changed my ways of viewing myself and the world, and to entertain alternative interpretive frames. I discovered the limitations of my own thinking throughout the process.

Although at times I felt very excited, somewhat anxious about treading into unfamiliar research methodology, and was overwhelmed by the sheer volume and breadth of the data, the inquiry process felt very comfortable. The direction of the research, shared discovery of experiences, had a good feeling about it. As any good research should do, I am left with new questions. How can this kind of shared discovery be established in a university classroom setting so that a greater sense of community results is one such question. I return to my beginnings and reiterate that more than anything, this inquiry process has been exciting and invigorating and ultimately a pedagogic form of life.

REFERENCES

Andrews, T. (1991). *Dream alchemy.* St. Paul, MN: Llewellyn Publications.

Ashton-Warner, S. (1963). *Teacher.* New York: Simon & Schuster.

Ayers, W. (1988). *Teaching and being: Connecting teachers' accounts of their lives with classroom practice.* Paper presented at the Annual meeting of the American Educational Research Association, New Orleans.

Ayers, W. (1989). *The good preschool teacher.* New York: Teachers College Press.

Baldwin, C. (1990). *Life's companion: Journal writing as a spiritual quest.* New York: Bantam Books.

Ball, S., & Goodson, I. F. (Eds.). (1985). *Teachers' lives and careers.* London: Falmer Press.

Barone, T. (1983). Education as aesthetic experience: "Art in germ." *Educational Leadership, 40*(4), 21–26.

Bateson, M. C. (1994). *Peripheral visions: Learning along the way.* New York: HarperCollins.

Baum, G. (1971). *Man becoming.* New York: Herder & Herder.

Belenky, M., Clinchy, B., Goldberger, N., & Tarule, J. (1986). *Women's ways of knowing.* New York: Basic Books.

Bissex, G. L., & Bullock, R. H. (1987). *Seeing for ourselves.* Portsmouth, NH: Heinemann.

Bruner, J. (1988). Life as narrative. *Language Arts, 65*(6), 574–583.

Bullough, R. V., Jr., & Gitlin, A. (1995). *Becoming a student of teaching: Methodologies for exploring the self and school context.* New York: Garland.

Bullough, R. V., Jr., & Knowles, J. G. (1990). Becoming a teacher: Struggles of a second career beginning teacher. *International Journal of Qualitative Studies in Education, 3*(2), 101–112.

Bullough, R. V., Jr., Knowles, J. G., & Crow, N. A. (1991). *Emerging as a teacher.* London: Routledge & Kegan Paul.

Burnaford, G., Fischer, J., & Hobson, D. (Eds.). (1996). *Teachers doing research.* Mahwah, NJ: Lawrence Erlbaum Associates.

Carr, W., & Kemmis, S. (1986). *Becoming critical: Education, knowledge, and action research.* London: Falmer Press.

Carter, K, & Doyle, W. (1987). Teacher' knowledge structures and comprehension processes. In J. Calderhead (Ed.), *Exploring teachers' thinking* (pp. 147–160). London: Cassell.

Clandinin, D. J. (1986). *Classroom practice: Teacher images in action.* London: Falmer Press.

Clandinin, D. J., & Connelly, F. M. (1994). Personal experience methods. In N. K. Denzin & Y. S. Lincoln (Eds.), *Handbook of qualitative research.* Thousand Oaks, CA: Sage.

Clandinin, D. J., & Connelly, F. M. (1995). *Teachers' professional knowledge landscapes.* New York: Teachers College Press.

Clark, C. M. (1986). Ten years of conceptual development in research on teacher thinking. In M. Ben-Peretz, R. Bromme, & R. Halkes (Eds.), *Advances of research on teacher thinking* (pp. 7–20). Lisse: Swets & Zeitlinger.

Cochran-Smith, M., & Lytle, S. L. (1993). *Inside/outside: Teacher research and knowledge.* New York: Teachers College Press.

Cole, A. L. (1988). Personal signals in spontaneous teaching practice. *International Journal of Qualitative Studies in Education, 2*(1), 25–39.

Cole, A. L. (1990a). Helping teachers become REAL: Opportunities in teacher induction. *Journal of Staff Development, 11*(4), 6–10.

Cole, A. L. (1990b). Personal theories of teaching: Development in the formative years. *Alberta Journal of Educational Research, 36*(3), 203–222.

Cole, A. L. (1991). Relationships in the workplace: Doing what comes naturally? *International Journal of Teaching and Teacher Education, 7*(5/6), 415–426.

Cole, A. L., & Knowles, J. G. (1993). Shattered images: Understanding expectations and realities of field experiences. *Teaching and Teacher Education, 9*(5/6), 457–471.

Connelly, F. M., & Clandinin, D. J. (1985). Personal practical knowledge and the modes of knowing: Relevance for teaching and learning. In E. Eisner (Ed.), *Learning and teaching the ways of knowing: Eighty-fourth yearbook for the National Society for the Study of Education* (pp. 174–198). Chicago: National Society for the Study of Education.

Connelly, F. M., & Clandinin, D. J. (1988). *Teachers as curriculum planners: Narratives of experience.* New York/Toronto: Teachers College Press/OISE Press.

Connelly, F. M., & Clandinin, D. J. (1990). Stories of experience and narrative inquiry, *Educational Researcher, 19*(5), 2–14.

Connelly, M. & Clandinin, J. (1993). The promise of collaborative research in the political context. In S. Hollingsworth & H. Sochett (Eds.), *Teacher research and educational reform* (pp. 86–102). Chicago: University of Chicago Press.

Cooper. J. E. (1991). Telling our own stories: The reading and writing of journals or diaries. In C. Witherell & N. Noddings (Eds.), *Stories lives tell: Narrative and dialogue in education* (pp. 96–112). New York: Teachers College Press.

Cullingford, C. (1987). Children's attitudes to teaching styles. *Oxford Review of Education, 13*(3), 331–338.

Cullingford, C. (1991). *The inner world of the school: Children's ideas about schools.* London: Cassell Educational Limited.

Dadds, M. (1995). *Passionate enquiry and school development: A story about teacher action research.* London: Falmer Press.

Daiker, D. A., & Morenberg, M. (1990). *The writing teacher as researcher: Essays in the theory and practice of class-based research.* Portsmouth, NH: Boynton Cook.

Diamond, C. T. P. (1991). *Teacher education as transformation.* Buckingham, England: Open University Press.

Diamond, C. T. P. (1993). Writing to reclaim self: The use of narrative in teacher education. *Teaching and Teacher Education, 9*(5/6), 511–517.

Diamond, C. T. P. (1995). Personal communication.

Doyle, W. (1986). Classroom organization and management. In M. C. Wittrock (Ed.), *Handbook of research on teaching* (3rd ed., pp. 392–431). New York: Macmillan.

Eckert, P. (1989). *Jocks and burnouts: Social categories and identity in the high school.* New York: Teachers College.

Eisner, E. W. (1979). *The educational imagination: On the design and education of school programs.* New York: Macmillan.

Eisner, E. W. (1983). The art and craft of teaching. *Educational Leadership, 40*(4), 4–13.

Eisner, E. W. (1993). Forms of understanding and the future of educational research. *Educational Researcher, 22*(7), 5–11.

Elliott, J. (1991). *Action research for educational change.* Buckingham, England: Open University Press.

Eraut, M. (1987). Inservice teacher education. In M. Dunkin (Ed.), *The international encyclopedia of teaching and teacher education.* New York: Pergamon Press.

Erickson, F. (1992). Students' experiences of the curriculum. In P. W. Jackson (Ed.), *Handbook of research on curriculum.* New York: Macmillan.

Fromm, E. (1951). *The forgotten language: An introduction to the understanding of dreams, fairy tales and myths.* New York: Grove Weidenfeld.

Gatto, J. T. (1991). *Dumbing us down: The hidden curriculum of compulsory schooling.* Gabriola Island, BC: New Society.

Gitlin, A., Bringhurst, K., Burns, M., Cooley, V., Myers, B., Price, K., Russell, R., & Tiess, P. (1992). *Teachers' voices for school change: An introduction to educative research.* New York: Teachers College Press.

Glesne, C., & Peshkin, A. (1992). *Becoming qualitative researchers: An introduction.* White Plains, NY: Longman.

Goodson, I. F. (Ed.). (1992). *Studying teachers' lives.* London: Routledge.

Goswami, D., & Stillman, P. R. (1987). *Reclaiming the classroom.* Upper Montclair, NJ: Boynton Cook.

Grant, C. A., & Sleeter, C. E. (1986). *After the school bell rings.* London: Falmer Press.

Greene, M. (1978). *Landscapes of learning.* New York: Teachers College Press.

Greenstein, J. (1983). *What the children taught me.* Chicago: University of Chicago Press.

Grossman, P. (1987). *A tale of two teachers: The role of subject matter orientation in teaching.* Paper presented at the Annual Meeting of the American Educational Research Association, Washington, DC.

Grossman, P. (1990). *The making of a teacher: Teacher knowledge and teacher education.* New York: Teachers College Press.

Grumet, M. (1983). The line is drawn. *Educational Leadership, 40*(4), 28–38.

Grumet, M. H. (1981). Restitution and reconstruction of educational experience: An autobiographical method for curriculum theory. In M. Lawn & L. Barton (Eds.), *Rethinking curriculum studies: A radical approach.* New York: John Wiley & Sons.

Gudmundsdöttir, S. (1990). Values in pedagogical context knowledge. *Journal of Teacher Education, 41*(3), 44–52.

Gudmundsdöttir, S. (1993). Pedagogical models of subject matter. In J. Brophy (Ed.), *Advances in Research on Teaching.* Greenwich, CT: JAI Press.

Hargreaves, A. (1993). Individualism and individuality: Reinterpreting the teacher culture. In J. W. Little & M. W. McLaughlin (Eds.), *Teachers' work: Individuals, colleagues, and contexts* (pp. 51–76). New York: Teachers College Press.

Heath, S. B. (1990). The fourth vision: Literate language at work. In A. A. Lunsford, H. Mogle, & J. Slevin (Eds.), *The right to literacy* (pp. 288–306). New York: Modern Language Association of America.

Hollingsworth, S., Dybdahl, M., & Minarik, L. T. (1993). By chart and chance and passion: The importance of relational knowing in learning to teach. *Curriculum Inquiry, 23*(1), 5–35.

Holly, M. L. (1989). *Writing to grow: Keeping a personal-professional journal.* Portsmouth, NH: Heinemann.

Holt, J. (1964). *How children fail.* New York: Dell Publishing.

Holt, J. (1967). *How children learn.* New York: Dell Publishing.

Holt, J. (1969). *The underachieving school.* New York: Dell Publishing.

Howe, Q., Jr. (1991). *Under running laughter: Notes from a renegade classroom.* New York/Toronto, ON: Free Press/Collier Macmillan.

Hunt, D. E. (1987). *Beginning with ourselves: In practice, theory, and human affairs.* Cambridge, MA and Toronto, ON: Brookline Books & OISE Press.

Hunt, D. E. (1991). *The renewal of personal energy.* Toronto, ON: OISE Press.

Jackson, P. W. (1992). Helping teachers develop. In A. Hargreaves & M. G. Fullan (Eds.), *Understanding teacher development.* New York: Teachers College Press.

Jalongo, M. (1992). Teachers' stories: Our ways of knowing. *Educational Leadership, 49*(7), 68–72.

Jalongo, M. R., & Isenberg, J. P. (1995). *Teachers' stories: From personal narrative to professional insight.* San Francisco: Jossey-Bass.

Jersild, A. T. (1955). *When teachers face themselves.* New York: Teachers College Press.

Johnson, S. M. (1990). *Teachers at work: Achieving success in our schools .* New York: Basic Books/HarperCollins.

Joseph, P. B., & Burnaford, G. E. (Eds.). (1994). *Images of schoolteachers in twentieth-century America: Paragons, polarities, complexities.* New York: St. Martin's Press.

Kincheloe, J. L. (1991). *Teachers as researchers: Qualitative inquiry as a path to empowerment.* London: Falmer Press.

Knowles, J. G. (1992). Models for understanding preservice and beginning teachers' biographies: Illustrations from case studies. In I. F. Goodson (Ed.), *Studying teachers' lives* (pp. 99–152). London: Falmer Press.

Knowles, J. G. (1993). Life-history accounts as mirrors: A practical avenue for the conceptualization of reflection in teacher education. In J. Calderhead & P. Gates (Eds.), *Conceptualizing reflection in teacher development* (pp. 70–92). London: Falmer Press.

Knowles, J. G., & Cole, A. L. (1994). Researching the "good life": Reflections on professorial practice. *The Professional Educator, 17*(1), 49–60.

Knowles, J. G., & Cole, A. L., with Presswood, C. S. (1994). *Through preservice teachers' eyes: Exploring field experiences through narrative and inquiry.* New York: Merlin.

Knowles, J. G., & Hoefler, V. B. (1989). The student teacher who wouldn't go away: Learning from failure. *Journal of Experiential Education, 12* (2), 14–21.

Knowles, J. G., & Holt-Reynolds, D. (Eds.; Special Issue). (1994). Personal histories in teacher education. *Teacher Education Quarterly, 21*(1).

Knowles, J. G., Marlow, S. E., & Muchmore, J. A. (1992). From pedagogy to ideology: Origins and phases of home education in the United States, 1970–1990. *American Journal of Education, 100*(2), 195–235.

Lamott, A. (1994). *Bird by bird: Some instructions on writing and life.* New York: Pantheon Books.

Langer, E. (1989). *Mindfulness.* Reading, MA: Addison-Wesley.

Ledoux, D. (1993). *Turning memories into memoirs: A handbook for writing lifestories.* Lisbon Falls, ME: Soleil.

LeGuin, U. K. (1971). *The lathe of heaven.* New York: Avon Books.

Levin, B. (1997, November 1). High hopes for our schools spring eternal. *The Globe and Mail,* D3.

Lieberman, A., & Miller, L. (1990). The social realities of teaching. In A. Lieberman (Ed.), *Schools as collaborative cultures: Creating the future now* (pp. 153–163). London: Falmer Press.

Little, J. W. (1990). Teachers as colleagues. In A. Lieberman (Ed.), *Schools as collaborative cultures: Creating the future now* (pp. 165–193). London: Falmer Press.

Madigan, D., & Koivu-Rybicki, V. T. (1997). *The writing lives of children.* York, ME: Stenhouse.

May, R. (1974). *The courage to create.* New York: W. W. Norton.

Mayberry, M., Knowles, J. G., Ray, B., & Marlow, S. (1995). *Home schooling: Parents as educators.* Thousand Oaks, CA: Corwin Press.

McLaren, P. (1986). *Schooling as a ritual performance: Towards a political economy of educational symbols and gestures.* London: Routledge & Kagan Paul.

McLaren, P. (1994). *Life in schools.* New York: Longman.

Miller, J. P. (1994). *The contemplative practitioner: Meditation in education and the professions.* Toronto, ON: OISE Press.

Mitchell, C., & Weber, S. (1998). *Beyond nostalgia: Reinventing ourselves as teachers.* London: Falmer Press.

Muchmore, J. A. (1999). *Knowing Anna, knowing myself.* Unpublished doctoral dissertation, University of Michigan.

Munby, H. (1986). Metaphor in the thinking of teachers: An exploratory study. *Journal of Curriculum Studies, 18*(2), 197–209.

Munby, H. (1987). Metaphor and teachers' knowledge. *Research in the Teaching of English, 21,* 377–397.

Munby, H., & Russell, T. (1994). The authority of experience in learning to teach. *Journal of Teacher Education, 45*(2), 86–95.

Murray, F. B. (1996). (Ed.). *The teacher educator's handbook: Building a knowledge base for the preparation of teachers.* San Francisco: Jossey-Bass.

Nehring, J. (1992). *The schools we have, the schools we want: An American teacher on the front line.* San Francisco: Jossey-Bass.

Neilsen, L. (1994). *A stone in my shoe: Teaching literacy in times of change.* Winnipeg, MB: Peguis.

Newman, J. M. (1989). *Finding our own way: Teachers exploring their assumptions.* Portsmouth, NH: Heinemann.

Nias, J., Southworth, G., & Yeomans, R. (1989). *Staff relationships in the primary school: A study of organizational culture.* London: Cassell.

Noddings, N. (1984). *Caring: A feminine approach to ethics and moral education.* Berkeley, CA: University of California Press.

Olney, J. (Ed.). (1980). *Autobiography: Essays theoretical and critical.* Princeton, NJ: Princeton University Press.

Paley, V. G. (1989). Foreword. In W. Ayers (Ed.), *The good preschool teacher.* New York: Teachers College Press.

Palonsky, S. B. (1986). *900 shows a year: A look at teaching from a teacher's side of the desk.* New York: McGraw-Hill Publishing.

Peshkin, A. (1986). *God's choice: The total world of a fundamentalist Christian school.* Chicago: University of Chicago Press.

Peshkin, A. (1991). *The color of strangers, the color of friends: The play of ethnicity in school and community.* Chicago: University of Chicago Press.

Pinar, W. F. (1981). "Whole, bright, deep with understanding": Issues in qualitative research and autobiographical method. *Journal of Curriculum Studies, 13*(3), 173–188.

Pinar, W. F. (1994). *Autobiography, politics and sexuality.* New York: Peter Lang.

Pinnegar, S. (1988). *Throwing a hardball into a stack of cotton: An examination of the term "with me."* Paper presented at the Annual Meeting of the American Educational Research Association, New Orleans.

Pinnegar, S. (1989). Teachers' knowledge of students and classrooms. (Unpublished doctoral dissertation, University of Arizona, Tucson).

Polanyi, M. (1967). *The tacit dimension.* Garden City, NY: Doubleday.

Richardson, V. (1996). The case for formal research and practical inquiry in teacher education. In F. B. Murray (Ed.), *The teacher educator's handbook.* San Francisco: Jossey-Bass.

Richert, A. E. (1990). Teaching teachers to reflect: A consideration of programme structure. *Journal of Curriculum Studies, 22*(6), 509–527.

Richert, A. E. (1992). The content of student teachers' reflections within different structures for facilitating the reflective process. In T. Russell & H. Munby (Eds.), *Teachers and teaching: From classroom to reflection* (pp. 171–191). London: Falmer Press.

Rosenholtz, S. (1989). *Teachers' workplace.* New York: Teachers College Press.

Rubin, L. J. (1985). *Artistry and teaching.* New York: Harper & Row.

Russell, H. (1995). Personal communication.

Russell, T., & Munby, H. (1991). Reframing: The role of experience in developing teachers' professional knowledge. In D. A. Schön (Ed.), *The reflective turn: Case studies in and on educational practice* (pp. 164–187). New York: Teachers College Press.

Russell, T., Munby, H., Spafford, C., & Johnston, P. (1988). Learning the professional knowledge of teaching: Metaphors, puzzles, and the theory-practice relationship. In P. Grimmett & G. L. Erickson (Eds.), *Reflection in teacher education* (pp. 67–90). New York: Teachers College Press.

Ryle, G. (1949). *The concept of mind.* Harmondsworth, England: Penguin Books.

Schön, D. A. (1983). *The reflective practitioner: How professionals think in action.* New York: Basic Books.

Shulman, J. H. (1990). Now you see them, now you don't: Anonymity versus visibility in case studies of teachers. *Educational Researcher, 19*(6), 11–15.

Shulman, L. S. (1987). Knowledge and teaching: Foundations of the new reform. *Harvard Educational Review, 57*(2), 4–14

Stenhouse, L. (1984). Artistry and teaching: The teacher as focus of research and development. In D. Hopkins & M. Wideen (Eds.), *Alternative perspectives on school improvement* (pp. 67–76). London: Falmer Press.

Sudzina, M., & Knowles, J. G. (1993). Personal, professional and contextual circumstances of student teachers who "fail": Setting a course for understanding failure in teacher education. *Journal of Teacher Education, 44*(4), 254–262.

Tama, C. M., & Peterson, K. (1991). Achieving reflectivity through literature. *Educational Leadership, 22*–24.

Van Manen, M. (1990). *Researching lived experience: Human science for an action-sensitive pedagogy.* Albany, NY/London, Ontario: State University of New York Press/Althouse Press.

Walker, A. (1982). *The color purple.* New York: Washington Square Press.

Weber, S., & Mitchell, C. (1995). *That's funny, you don't look like a teacher! Interrogating images and identity in popular culture.* London: Falmer Press.

Woods, P. (1990). *The happiest days? How pupils cope with school.* London: Falmer Press.

Zeichner, K. (1987). Preparing reflective teachers. *International Journal of Educational Research, 11*(5), 565–575.

Zeichner, K. (1993). Connecting genuine teacher development to the struggle for social justice. *Journal of Education for Teaching, 19*(1), 5–20.

BIBLIOGRAPHY

Ashton-Warner, S. (1963). *Teacher.* New York: Simon & Schuster.

Ayers, W. (1989). *The good preschool teacher.* New York: Teachers College Press.

Ben-Peretz, M., Broome, R., & Halkes, R. (Eds.). (1986). *Advances of research on teacher thinking.* Lisse: Swets & Zeitlinger.

Bissex, G. L., & Bullock, R. H. (1987). *Seeing for ourselves.* Portsmouth, NH: Heinemann.

Burnaford, G., Fischer, J., & Hobson, D. (Eds.). (1996). *Teachers doing research.* Mahwah, NJ: Lawrence Erlbaum Associates.

Carlgren, I., Handel, G., & Vaage, S. (Eds.). (1994). *Teachers' minds and actions: Research on teacher's thinking and practice.* London: Falmer Press.

Clandinin, D. J., Davies, A., Hogan, P., & Kennard, B. (Eds.). (1993). *Learning to teach teaching to learn: Stories of collaboration in teacher education.* New York: Teachers College Press.

Cochran-Smith, M., & Lytle, S. L. (1993). *Inside/outside: Teacher research and knowledge.* New York: Teachers College Press.

Connelly, F. M., & Clandinin, D. J. (1988). *Teachers as curriculum planners: Narratives of experience.* New York/Toronto: Teachers College Press/OISE Press.

Cullingford, C. (1991). *The inner world of the school: Children's ideas about schools.* London: Cassell Educational Limited.

Dadds, M. (1995). *Passionate enquiry and school development: A story about teacher action research.* London: Falmer Press.

Daiker, D. A., & Morenberg, M. (1990). *The writing teacher as researcher: Essays in the theory and practice of class-based research.* Portsmouth, NH: Boynton Cook.

Diamond, C. T. P. (1991). *Teacher education as transformation.* Buckingham, England: Open University Press.

Diaz, A. (1992). *Freeing the creative spirit: Drawing on the power of art to tap the magic and wisdom within.* San Francisco: HarperCollins.

Egan, K. (1986). *Teaching as story telling.* London, ON: Althouse Press.

Fontana, D. (1993). *The secret language of symbols: A visual key to symbols and their meanings.* San Francisco: Chronicle Books.

Fulwiler, T. (1987). *The journal book.* Portsmouth, NH: Boynton/Cook.

Gish, S. C. (1994). *"Mr. Gish, may I go to the bathroom?": My first year as a high school teacher.* Seattle: Peanut Butter Publishing.

Gitlin, A., Bringhurst, K., Burns, M., Cooley, V., Myers, B., Price, K., Russell, R., & Tiess, P. (1992). *Teachers' voices for school change: An introduction to educative research.* New York: Teachers College Press.

Goldberg, N. (1986). *Writing down the bones.* Boston: Shambhala Press.

Goldberger, P. (1983). *The intuitive edge: Understanding intuition and applying it in everyday life.* New York: Jeremy P. Tarcher/Perigree.

Goswami, D., & Stillman, P. R. (1987). *Reclaiming the classroom.* Upper Montclair, NJ: Boynton Cook.

Graham, R. (1991). *Reading and writing the self: Autobiography in education and the curriculum.* New York: Teachers College Press.

Halsall, N. D., & Hossack, L. A. (Eds.). (1996). *Act reflect revise...revitalize.* Mississauga, ON: Ontario Public School Teachers' Federation.

Holly, M. L. (1989). *Writing to grow: Keeping a personal-professional journal.* Portsmouth, NH: Heinemann.

Hubbard, R., & Power, B. M. (1993). *The art of classroom inquiry: A handbook for teacher researchers.* Portsmouth, NH: Heinemann.

Hunt, D. E. (1987). *Beginning with ourselves: In practice, theory, and human affairs.* Cambridge, MA/Toronto: Brookline Books/OISE Press.

Jagla, V. M. (1994). *Teachers' everyday use of imagination and intuition: In pursuit of the elusive image.* Albany, NY: State University of New York Press.

Jalongo, M. R., & Isenberg, J. P. (1995). *Teachers' stories: From personal narrative to professional insight.* San Francisco: Jossey-Bass.

Jones, G. (1991). *Crocus Hill notebook.* London, ON: Althouse Press.

Joseph, P. B., & Burnaford, G. E. (Eds.). (1994). *Images of schoolteachers in twentieth-century America: Paragons, polarities, complexities.* New York: St. Martin's Press.

Kagan, D. M., with Chestnut, J. R., Hunter, L. B., Burch, C. B., & Wilson, E. K. (1993). *Laura and Jim and what they taught me about the gap between educational theory and practice.* Albany, NY: State University of New York Press.

Kemmis, S., & McTaggart, R. (Eds.). (1988). *The action research planner.* Victoria, Australia: Deakin University Press.

Knowles, J. G., Cole, A. L., with Presswood, C. S. (1994). *Through preservice teachers' eyes: Exploring field experiences through narrative and inquiry.* New York: Merrill.

Lakoff, G., & Johnson, M. (1980). *Metaphors we live by.* Chicago: University of Chicago Press.

Ledoux, D. (1993). *Turning memories into memoirs: A handbook for writing lifestories.* Lisbon Falls, ME: Soleil.

Lee, J. (1994). *Writing from the body.* New York: St. Martin's Press.

Little, J. W., & McLaughlin, M. W. (Eds.). (1993). *Teachers' work: Individuals, colleagues, and contexts.* New York: Teachers College Press.

Madigan, D., & Koivu-Rybicki, V. T. (1997). *The writing lives of children.* York, ME: Stenhouse.

McEwan, H., & Egan, K. (Eds.). (1995). *Narrative in teaching, learning, and research.* New York: Teachers College Press.

McLaren, P. (1980). *Cries from the corridor.* Toronto, ON: Methuen.

McLaren P. (1994). *Life in schools.* New York: Longman.

Miller, J. L. (1990). *Creating spaces and finding voices: Teachers collaborating for empowerment.* Albany, NY: State University of New York Press.

Mitchell, C., & Weber, S. (1998). *Beyond nostalgia: Reinventing ourselves as teachers.* London: Falmer Press.

Mohr, M. M., & MacLean, M. S. (1987). *Working together: A guide for teacher-researchers.* Urbana, IL: National Council of Teachers of English.

Murray, F. B. (Ed.). (1996). *The teacher educator's handbook:* Building a knowledge base for the preparation of teachers. San Francisco, CA: Jossey-Bass.

Newman, J. M. (Ed.). (1993). *In our own words: Poems by teachers.* Halifax, NS: Braesido Books.

Oja, S., & Smulyan, L. (1989). *Collaborative action research: A developmental approach.* London: Falmer Press.

Oliver, M. (1994). *A poetry handbook: A prose guide to understanding and writing poetry.* New York: Harcourt Brace.

Olsen, J. (1992). *Understanding teaching.* Buckingham, England: Open University Press.

Paley, V. G. (1981). *Wally's stories.* Cambridge, MA: Harvard University Press.

Paley, V. G. (1986). *Mollie is three: Growing up in school.* Chicago: University of Chicago Press.

Paley, V. G. (1990). *The boy who would be a helicopter.* Cambridge, MA: Harvard University Press.

Paley, V. G. (1992). *You can't say you can't play.* Cambridge, MA: Harvard University Press.

Palonsky, S. B. (1986). *900 shows a year: A look at teaching from a teacher's side of the desk.* New York: McGraw-Hill Publishing.

Pinar, W. F. (1994). *Autobiography, politics and sexuality.* New York: Peter Lang.

Pinar, W. F., and Reynolds, W. M. (Eds.). (1992). *Understanding curriculum as phenomenological and deconstructed text.* New York: Teachers College Press.

Progoff, I. (1975). *At a journal workshop: The basic text and guide for using the Intensive Journal® process.* New York: Dialogue House Library.

Ross, E. W., Cornett, J. W., & McCutcheon, G. (Eds). (1992). *Teacher personal theorizing: Connecting curriculum practice, theory, and research.* Albany, NY: State University of New York Press.

Sawyer, D. (1979). *"Tomorrow is school and I'm sick to the heart thinking about it."* Vancouver, BC: Douglas & McIntyre.

Schubert, W. H., & Ayers, W. C. (Eds.). (1992). *Teacher lore: Learning from our own experience.* New York: Longman.

Solnicki, J. (1992). *The real me is gonna be a shock: A year in the life of a front-line teacher.* Toronto, ON: Lester Publishing.

Staton, J., Shuy, R. W., Peyton, J. K., & Reed, L. (1988). *Dialogue journal communication: Classroom, linguistic, social and cognitive views.* Norwood, NJ: Ablex Publishing.

Stuart, J. (1963). *The thread that runs so true.* New York: Charles Scribner's Sons.

Thomas, D. (Ed.). (1995). *Teachers' stories.* Buckingham, England: Open University Press.

Waldron, P. W., Collie, T. R., & Davies, C. M. W. (1999). Telling stories about school: An invitation.... Upper Saddle River, NJ: Merrill.

Winsey, V. R. (1992). *Your self as history: Family history and its effects on your personality: A research guide.* New York: Pace University Press.

Winter, R. (1989). *Learning from experience: Principles and practices in action research.* London: Falmer Press.

Witherell, C., & Noddings, N. (Eds.). (1991). *Stories lives tell: Narrative and dialogue in education.* New York: Teachers College Press.

Woods, P. (1990). *The happiest days? How pupils cope with school.* London: Falmer Press.

AUTHOR INDEX

SUBJECT INDEX